Radio Amateurs of Canada

Amateur Radio Emergency Service

Operations Training Manual

Document RAC-ARES-OPS

Release 2:01

Sept 2015

This training material has been prepared by volunteers on a not-
for-profit basis in order to serve the public good. To the greatest
degree practical, externally sourced information has been attributed and authorization sought for use, where required. Proprietary
information and copyrighted material has not been intentionally
included.

Contact:

Chief Field Services Officer, Radio Amateurs of Canada Inc.,
Suite 217, 720 Belfast Road, Ottawa, Ontario, Canada K1G 0Z5.

Contributors to this manual included the National Training
Resource Group: Bob Boyd VE3SV, Bob Cooke VE3BDB, David
Drinnan VE9FK, Don Mackinnon VE4DJ, Eric Jacksch VA3DSP,
Forbes Purcell VE6FMP, Glenn Killam VE3GNA, Ian Snow VA3QT,
John P. Cunningham W1AI, Jeff Dovyak VE4MBQ, Lance Peterson
VA3LP, Monte L. Simpson K2MLS, Pierre Mainville VA3PM, and
Tim Smith VE3HCB. Please see "Acknowledgements" on page 1-2.

This manual was created using Adobe FrameMaker™.

2008-10-01

The task of creating a new manual to facilitate training for the Amateur Radio Emergency Service (ARES) is daunting to say the least.

Times change, as do the needs associated with ARES and the methods used to meet ARES goals.

However, I believe this document has risen to the challenge of providing information and training support for use in the field by ARES, and by those Radio Amateur groups that have chosen not to be part of the ARES organization.

This manual affords the opportunity to operate in a consistent manner that will facilitate common Emcomm methods from Section to Section and between ARES in Canada and the USA.

It is the result of extensive deliberation by RAC's National Training Resource Group (NTRG), members of which are named on a subsequent page herein.

One of those members, David Drinnan, VE9FK, who is RAC's appointed National Training Coordinator (NTC), edited this manual and oversaw its creation.

A graduate of Carleton University, Dave possesses degrees in Physics and Psychology and is a professional technical writer with a broad background in training and human performance factors. He has been a licenced Radio Amateur for some 30 years. We are very fortunate to have him leading the new training initiative for ARES and the related National Traffic System (NTS).

Dave's involvement in emergency communications began with his participation in the Emergency Measures Radio Group (EMRG) in Ottawa in the 1980s. He has also served as the ARES Emergency Coordinator in Saint John, New Brunswick.

I extend sincere thanks to Dave and indeed to all who played a part in bringing this project to fruition. Many years of pertinent experience are represented among those volunteers.

To satisfy the access capabilities and operational needs of all, this publication is being made available for download, at no charge, on the Radio Amateurs of Canada website at www.rac.ca, and in hard copy from RAC headquarters for a nominal fee.

Every ARES member is encouraged to embrace the new manual, to use it in training and operations, and to provide constructive feedback for improvement.

There can be no doubt that, with the roll out of this document, ARES and other Emcomm operators have a vital and broadly focused standard guide to add to their existing resources.

73,

Bob Cooke VE3BDB
Vice President Field Services
Radio Amateurs of Canada Inc.

www.rac.ca/fieldorg/

TABLE OF CONTENTS

Section 15: Station configuration

Section 16: Frequently asked questions

Section 17: Digital communications

Section 18: After your deployment is over   18-1

Volume 2 - Support component

Section 19: Station management   19-1

Section 20: Managing communications operations   20-1

Section 21: Scheduling and selecting net controllers   21-1

Volume 3 - Emergency Coordinator component

Volume 4 - Reference information

Section 35: Safety issues for ARES personnel   35-1

Section 36: First aid techniques   36-1

Section 37: Using this manual in your training   37-1

SECTION 1: USING THIS TRAINING MANUAL

This training manual provides information needed by ARES operators participating in ARES operations within Canada.

PURPOSE OF ARES TRAINING

Formal ARES training serves the following purposes:

- Ensures that all ARES participants have the skills and knowledge needed to deliver basic ARES services

- Gives ARES participants a greater understanding of emergency management operations, the roles they will perform, and the organizations with which they will interact.

WHO SHOULD USE THIS TRAINING MANUAL

ARES operators

This training manual is intended to be used by new ARES members who want self-paced training, as a way of familiarizing themselves with ARES. It can also be used as the basis for leader-led in-classroom training.

ARES support personnel

This training manual is also intended to be used by personnel who are going to serve supporting roles within an ARES organization and during ARES activations. These roles include communications supervisors, station managers, and technical support primes.

The second volume contains information intended specifically for support personnel.

ARES emergency coordinators

This training manual is also useful to current and prospective ARES emergency coordinators (EC).

Both operators and ECs should familiarize themselves with the first volume of this manual. ECs should also become familiar with the information provided in the second volume.

The third volume contains information intended specifically for ECs.

1-1

BEFORE YOU BEGIN

Before beginning this training, ensure that you:

- Clearly understand basic technical concepts such as simplex and repeater radio systems, data communications, and propagation

- Are comfortable with station setup and basic radio operation

- Are able to troubleshoot basic equipment, power and antenna problems

- Are familiar with the concept of the use of amateur radio for emergency communications.

WHY WAS A NEW TRAINING MANUAL NEEDED?

RAC is committed to ensuring that ARES is available to radio amateurs and served agencies across Canada. In response to that commitment, RAC has taken a number of steps to improve its support of ARES and emergency communications. A national emergency coordinator (NEC) and national training coordinator (NTC) have been appointed, and a number of training resources are being made available to help individual ARES groups develop and deliver effective, consistent training to ARES participants.

This training manual is a part of that effort to improve ARES training and support. The manual is intended to serve as a common reference for all ARES groups in Canada. The manual updates information provided in earlier references, bringing together new standards with currently available best practices.

ACKNOWLEDGEMENTS

This manual builds on the work of Doug Leach VE3XK/VE1CH/VA3PM/VE6AFO, who edited and contributed to the original RAC Emergency Coordinator's Manual, of Kathy Kerr Davidson VA3KKD, Richard Sargent VE3OYU, Vic Henderson VE3FOX, David Friesen VE3WTJ, and Bob Spencer VE3DHP, who developed the original ARES Instructor's Manual, and of Joe MacPherson VE1CH, Pierre Mainville VA3PM, and Ken Oelke VE6AFO.

This manual also includes content from other public-domain sources, and a range of contributions by Forbes Purcell VE6FMP, Monte L. Simpson K2MLS, David Drinnan VE9FK, and the Saint John regional ARES group. Thanks goes to Ian Snow VA3QT for the section on digital communications.

Special thanks go to all the members of RAC's National Training Resource Group (NTRG), who contributed time and effort to review this manual: Bob Boyd VE3SV, Bob Cooke VE3BDB, David Drinnan VE9FK, Don Mackinnon VE4DJ, Eric Jacksch VA3DSP, Forbes Purcell VE6FMP, Glenn Killam VE3GNA, Ian Snow VA3QT, John P. Cunningham W1AI, Jeff Dovyak VE4MBQ, Lance Peterson VA3LP, Monte L. Simpson K2MLS, Pierre Mainville VA3PM, and Tim Smith VE3HCB.

1-2

HOW TO USE THIS MANUAL

If you are an ARES operator, or interested in becoming one, read through Volume 1 (Sections 1 to 18). Volume 1 contains all the training required to certify you as an ARES Operator.

If you are an ARES EC, or interested in becoming one, read through Volumes 1 and 2 (Sections 1 to 21). Volume 3 contains all the training required to certify you as an ARES EC.

For additional information about emergency communications, read through Volume 4 (Sections 30 to 38).

If you are preparing a training program based on this manual, see "Using this manual in your training" on page 37.1.

Ensuring you have the most recent version

This training manual is designed to allow periodic updates of content. To ensure that you have the most recent version, visit the RAC website at http://www.wp.rac.ca, or contact the RAC National Training Coordinator.

Using content from this manual in your regional ARES documentation and training

Content from this manual can be used in documentation you prepare for your regional ARES group, and in training material you create for your team.

To extract content from this document:

• Select the text copy tool in Acrobat, and copy the desired text, or

• Select Save As from the File menu in Acrobat.

Online features

This manual is designed to be printed or used online. Blue text is hyperlinked, letting you jump to related topics or web pages in the online version.

DOCUMENTATION STANDARDS

This manual was authored in Adobe FrameMaker® using a template provided free of charge by Nocturne Communications Inc. This document uses standard Canadian spelling and conventions for technical communications.

AMENDING THIS MANUAL

You can help keep this manual current and appropriate. Forward your recommendations for changes and additions using the form provided at the end of the manual.

1-3

SECTION 2: ABOUT ARES

This section provides an introduction to the Amateur Radio Emergency Service (ARES).

Once you complete this section, you will be able to:

- Explain ARES

- Describe the history of ARES

- Discuss the value of amateur communications

- Understand the value of participation in ARES.

WHAT IS ARES

ARES is a public service organization that delivers communications services during emergencies. ARES (pronounced *AIR-EEZ*) provides qualified communications personnel who establish ad-hoc radio communications links where and when they are needed.

> *Note: Any and all use of the RAC AMATEUR RADIO EMERGENCY SERVICE and the associated design trademark requires a written licence or permission from Radio Amateurs of Canada Incorporated.*

ARES may be defined as the emergency public service arm of Radio Amateurs of Canada (RAC), and in the US, the Amateur Radio Relay League (ARRL). Its purpose is to advance the public interest and the interests of amateur radio by providing a volunteer emergency telecommunications service to federal, provincial, municipal or other local government departments and agencies, designated non-government organizations (NGO) and critical public utilities during an emergency or disaster, including necessary training and incidental activities.

The major roles played by ARES typically include:

- Mitigation of telecommunications failures

- Supplementary telecommunications support or augmentation

- Command and control level interoperability (for example, communications from a command post to an EOC and between EOCs)

- Special assignments such as observation and reporting.

ARES does not typically replace the communications infrastructure used by police or other emergency responders, or the systems in place to support agencies and recovery organizations. Instead, it augments existing communications infrastructure, providing added flexibility and capacity that is often needed during emergencies (for example, between emergency operations centers, community shelters, hospitals, evacuation points, and other facilities).

2-1

ARES relies on the services of amateur radio operators who volunteer their time, equipment and expertise for the benefit of the community and the public good.

THE HISTORY OF ARES

ARES was created by the ARRL in 1935. ARES was subsequently was embraced by Radio Amateurs in Canada first under sponsorship by the Canadian Radio Relay League (CRRL) and then by the Radio Amateurs of Canada Inc. (when that body was created out of the CRRL and the Canadian Amateur Radio Federation in 1993).

In 1980, Radio Amateurs in Canada agreed to provide communications for the Canadian Red Cross. This agreement was put in place following successful cooperation during the Mississauga train derailment and evacuation.

ARES and the National Traffic System (NTS), which was part of the CRRL, now operate under the auspices of RAC's Field Services Organization. In fact, ARES operates under the guidance of RAC using a structure parallel to that used in the US. ARES management and ARES emergency coordinators (EC) must be RAC members.

Radio amateurs volunteer their time, expertise and equipment by registering as members of the ARES and providing communications when needed during time of disaster or emergency. There are now more than 70,000 ARES members throughout North America.

THE VALUE OF AMATEUR COMMUNICATIONS

Technology and the culture of communications are changing faster now than ever before. The 'democratization' of advanced communications technologies is transforming the role that amateur radio and ARES has traditionally played in emergency communications.

While advanced communications systems have become ubiquitous in the commercial and public service worlds, their sophistication and reliance on shared commercial networks increases the probability of 'system overload' during crises (such as the Dawson College incident), the potential for the loss of a range of services if cell and communication towers fail, or a complete loss of service if communications infrastructure is lost to natural disaster.

In addition, while first responders typically have primary and secondary communication systems, this is not true of many support agencies. The primary roles of those agencies don't justify the same level of communications capability or even interoperability with the more sophisticated systems used by the public service sector.

This means that ARES is still important in times of disaster, although now in a different way and for different reasons. The value that ARES offers in today's context is flexibility, survivability, and scalability:

Flexibility

ARES communications capabilities can be tailored very quickly to meet unusual needs. Amateur radio is unique in that the radio operators are also skilled in the installation,

2-2

configuration and even repair of the radio systems that they use, and are able to easily adapt those technologies and systems to meet unforeseen requirements. ARES can create high-capacity ad-hoc networks anywhere that those networks are needed, with very little lead time. Connectivity can be delivered into virtually any location, regardless of coverage by existing repeaters and trunking systems.

Survivability

Systems survivability is a real issue in situations where extreme weather affects physical communications infrastructure, or where commercial electrical power is interrupted for extended periods.

Some entities have very robust and redundant communications systems. But many communications systems that are important during an emergency may be affected by power outages or physical damage to antennas and buildings (for example, commercial radio systems, cell sites, wireless data services, and even landline telephone service). In the near future, survivability will also become an issue for systems that rely on the Internet for data transport.

ARES can serve as a Plan B option when primary communications systems are challenged or disabled. While ARES relies on technologies similar to those used by commercial and government agencies, the diversity of equipment, the training of operators in repair, installation and customization, and the range of frequencies and operating modes available to ARES guarantees that communications can continue even in worst-case scenarios. Even in the most extreme conditions, it is expected that a significant percentage of ARES stations would continue to operate in some capacity.

Scalability

Emergency planners balance cost versus benefit, which means that emergency plans provide communications capacity to meet most needs in most situations. Problems occur, however, when emergency demands exceed the planned capacity, or when the emergency itself affects the availability of key communications resources needed to manage that emergency.

Provincial, municipal and other agency communications systems, although robust and well suited to most emergency requirements, are not easily scaled up in times of emergency. Extra transceivers, repeaters, frequencies, and personnel familiar with communications procedures may be difficult to obtain in time to be useful.

ARES is one possible solution in the event that the demand for communications exceeds capacity. The amateur radio community provides a large pool of experienced telecommunications operators and equipment. Also, frequency diversity available to ARES far exceeds anything available on commercial or government radio systems.

THE ARES ORGANIZATION

The Chief Field Services Officer is elected to carry out policies as set out by the RAC Board of Directors, and maintains liaisons with other organizations at the national level.

2-3

The Section Manager (SM) is elected by the RAC members within that section. The SM manages the field organization activities in a specific RAC section. There are eleven RAC sections in Canada. The SM is responsible for ensuring that RAC capabilities (traffic handling, emergency communications) are maintained in that section. The SM is also responsible for on-air bulletins.

The Section Emergency Coordinator (SEC) is appointed by the SM. The SEC is responsible for the same RAC section as the SM, but focuses strictly on emergency communications. (Non-emergency communications traffic is the responsibility of the Section Traffic Manager.) The SEC is also responsible for promoting ARES activities among local groups, and for recommending policies and planning and encouraging large-scale activities.

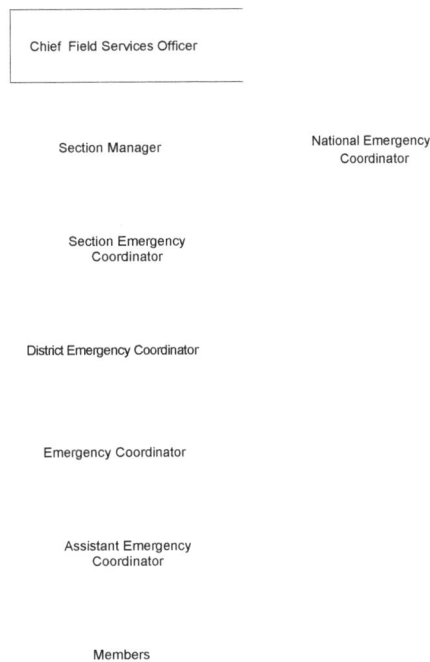

Chief Field Services Officer

Section Manager   National Emergency Coordinator

Section Emergency Coordinator

District Emergency Coordinator

Emergency Coordinator

Assistant Emergency Coordinator

Members

Emergency coordinators (EC) are appointed to handle the direction of all ARES activities in a given area. ECs are responsible for promoting ARES, coordinating training and organizational management, and conducting exercises. ECs are also responsible for establishing links to other organizations that may require assistance, setting up nets, conducting pre-planning sessions, and developing a local ARES standard operating procedure (SOP) manual.

Assistant Emergency coordinators (AEC) are appointed by ECs to assist with all of the duties of the EC. An EC can appoint as many AECs as are required to do the job. AECs do not have to be RAC members.

The District Emergency coordinator (DEC) is appointed by the SEC to supervise a group of ECs in a concentrated population or region. The DEC is responsible for coordinating EC activities, interfacing between ARES and local emergency plans, and recommending EC appointments.

The National Emergency Coordinator (NEC) is responsible for coordinating cooperation between RAC Sections and between the RAC (ARES) and the American

Radio Relay League (ARRL) ARES when mutual assistance is required and requested in case of disaster or emergency. The NEC's function is not to manage emergency communications operations within Sections but to coordinate them with the respective SMs and SECs, acting as a liaison when mutual assistance is requested. In preparation, the NEC will take measures to promote and support such assistance within RAC Sections so as to ensure understanding, readiness and standard procedures by ARES members.

The National Training Coordinator (NTC) initiates and coordinates ARES training. The NTC researches, creates and manages the distribution of consistent training methods, documents and other training support to RAC ARES units and members.

Finally, ARES members are by far the most important participants in the ARES organization. ARES requires active and dedicated members to make it all happen. ARES members do not need to be RAC members.

YOUR PARTICIPATION

Should you become an ARES participant?

Becoming an ARES participant means:

- Having a genuine desire to assist

- Reading all the literature about ARES

- Attending ARES meetings

- Participating in public service events and simulated exercises

- Checking into nets

- Getting involved in training others

- Taking on a specific role.

What ARES expects from you

What is expected from you when you volunteer with ARES? The answer: Whatever you want to offer.

ARES is a flexible, volunteer-centric organization. It serves as an envelope that the amateur community can use to deliver emergency communications services to the community. There is no minimum level of participation. All our documented procedures, protocols and rules are guidelines, intended to facilitate cooperative communications and to communicate best practices.

You should not feel pressured to participate to a greater extent than you are comfortable. Your work with ARES is not a job, or an obligation.

2-5

We do ask that you show respect and consideration for other ARES participants, who are also volunteers. We're all in this together.

What you can expect from the ARES organization

ARES 'management', including your emergency coordinator, assistant emergency coordinators, trainers, and most of the RAC organization are also volunteers. Their work with ARES is not a job. They do not get paid, and they donate their time to benefit the community.

However, even though ARES is an all-volunteer organization, there are certain things you can expect from ARES:

- Your privacy will be protected with regards to any information that is not in the public domain and may be sensitive or confidential.

- Your time and effort will be respected. ARES will try not to waste either.

- Your effort during exercises and emergencies will be recognized and acknowledged.

- ARES will do its best to protect your safety and security during operations. (That being said, the final responsibility is yours, and you must be cautious of your safety at all times. Refuse any assignments or duties that you feel may be too hazardous to your safety.)

- You will have an input into how ARES is run, and the practices that are used. While ARES groups try to use best practices garnered from other ARES groups and ECOM organizations and operations, remember that your ARES group is your organization, and will also reflect your views and preferences.

SECTION 3: ARES IN CONTEXT

This section provides a discussion of the changing role of ARES.

Once you complete this section, you will be able to:

- Explain the difference between a disaster and an emergency

- Outline potential served agencies

- Identify other amateur emergency communications organizations

- Discuss emerging technologies

- Discuss the relevance of ARES today.

WHAT IS A COMMUNICATIONS EMERGENCY?

A communications emergency is a situation in which normal communications infrastructure and processes are unable to meet the communications demands associated with an unusual event, potentially putting people, property or public safety at risk.

THE NATURE OF DISASTER COMMUNICATIONS

Disasters and emergencies

Emergency services train for emergencies and respond to them every day. On the other hand, a disaster is something that emergency services rarely train for, since disasters occur very rarely. Disasters can overwhelm the capabilities of communities and emergency responders, and often cause great suffering, and even the loss of property or life.

A *state of emergency* is a government declaration made in response to a disaster situation. The declaration of a state of emergency leads to mobilization of a wide range of support services and agencies. The specific response to a state of emergency depends on the scope and type of disaster and the size of the region affected. Examples of localized disasters include tornadoes, chemical spills, explosions, and flooding. Regional disasters might include wildfires, pandemics, or a loss of infrastructure such as power or telecommunications.

Communications during disasters

During a disaster, one of the first essential services to be compromised is often communications. Communications can fail in a number of ways: equipment, batteries, power grids and generators can fail. Frequencies may be incompatible or overloaded. Collaboration between agencies that do not normally work together may be hampered by an inability to share communications channels. Personnel not trained or accustomed to two-way communications may not be able to pass information reliably or efficiently. Key individuals, locations or organizations may become unreachable.

3-1

Failures of communications can make the effects of a disaster much worse. Such failures can also lead to ineffective disaster response, with the worst-affected regions receiving little or no aid because they are unable to ask for it. Miscommunications caused by poor practices or system failures can also lead to misunderstandings about what is needed, and where. Information about community conditions, evacuees, casualties, the need for supplies, and resources is critically important during a disaster. That information has to be delivered to decision-makers quickly and accurately.

Disasters can last for a very long time. While some localized disasters can end quickly, larger, destructive disasters can require a disaster response lasting for weeks or even months. The need for communications support can extend from the first alert to the end of the disaster response and the beginning of disaster recovery.

Disaster response

Organizations and personnel

The response to a disaster will vary depending on the nature and scope of the disaster. The response will usually involve a range of agencies and organizations in cooperation, working under a local or regional government authority. However, some disaster responses may involve multiple jurisdictions working in parallel, or agencies with overlapping responsibilities (such as the Salvation Army and the Canadian Red Cross). During a significant disaster, a large number of organizations may become involved, including police and fire departments, search and rescue teams, hospitals and municipal governments, the SPCA, church and social welfare organizations, and of course ARES. In addition, disasters often lead to an uncoordinated response by individuals in the affected region. In fact, an excess of volunteers (particularly untrained, undisciplined volunteers) can create serious problems during a disaster response.

There will also be a presence of organizations and individuals not involved in the disaster response itself. A large or sustained disaster may lead to the arrival of members of the general public from outside the affected area, looking for affected family members or friends. The media is also likely to become actively involved during any disaster situation.

Equipment and supplies

Typically, a disaster response will suffer from either too little in the way of supplies and equipment, or too much.

Equipment must be available in advance of a disaster and transported to its place of use despite the limitations imposed by the disaster. In addition, personnel have to be trained to use the equipment properly.

The proper allocation of supplies will be an ongoing challenge throughout almost any disaster response.

Communications and information

Effective communications is essential. Without reliable, up-to-date information decision-makers are unable to manage the disaster response. Responding agencies and organizations may not share information effectively. In the absence of reliable information, rumours and misinformation can lead to serious harm.

Infrastructure and logistics

Logistics and transportation are always major issues during any disaster. In many cases, a failure of logistics is what defines the disaster.

Failures of infrastructure also characterize disasters. These failures can also degrade the ability of responders to function in a disaster area. Responders may be forced to innovate and work outside their plans. Past examples of responders 'thinking outside the box' include:

- Using dumpsters used to transport essential supplies

- Using train locomotives to provide electricity to evacuation centers

- Using municipal trucks to transport flood victims

- Using airport terminals as hospitals

- Using breweries to supply water for thousands of people

- Using roads as landing pads and jails.

Command

The Incident Command System (ICS) is used to organize most disaster responses. ICS deals directly with many of the critical management, safety and logistical issues that arise during a disaster. Unfortunately, different agencies use different versions of ICS. In general, agencies use only the parts of ICS that they like, disregarding the rest. New positions and titles are added to keep people happy or to reflect the normal organizational structure.

Nature of amateur radio

Amateur radio can be extremely useful during disasters. However, most disaster response managers do not know what amateur radio is, or how it can be used. Only when communications systems fail completely is amateur radio considered as an alternative.

Amateur radio offers a number of advantages:

- Amateur radio operators do not need to stage from a common marshalling area. In fact, they do not need to physically converge at all.

- Amateur radio communications infrastructure is dispersed, which helps during damage assessment. Amateur radio can be used to define the exact boundaries or scope of a disaster.

- Amateur radio stations are less likely to be forced off the air, since they benefit from equipment redundancy, alternate power supplies and operators with the willingness and skills needed to solve technical problems.

- Amateur radio is not tied to specific locations, agencies, or types of disaster, and can be used in many different scenarios.

Amateur radio also suffers from some disadvantages:

- Amateur radio is a scarce resource. Although there are thousands of amateur radio operators, many are too old or physically unfit to respond, and many have never participated in any emergency training.

- Amateur radio is not user friendly for served agencies. For example, it often is not clear what destinations can be reached using amateur radio, and served agency personnel may find themselves forced to use NTS forms.

- Messages sent by amateur radio are much less likely to produce a response.

SERVED AGENCIES - OUR CLIENTS AND PARTNERS

Our served agencies may include:

- Canadian Red Cross

- Emergency management organizations

- Municipalities

- Law enforcement agencies

- Salvation Army

- Other disaster relief organizations.

OTHER AMATEUR RADIO EMERGENCY COMMUNICATIONS ORGANIZATIONS

ARES may also interoperate with other amateur radio emergency communications organizations, including:

- SATERN, the Salvation Army's disaster communications group

- VECTOR, Vancouver's communications group

3-4

- PERCS, British Columbia's communications group

- EMCG, New Brunswick's EMO communications group

- RACES, a communications group in the United States.

EMERGING TECHNOLOGIES

A number of emerging technologies are likely to affect amateur radio and ARES in the near future.

GPS and APRS

The integration of GPS, APRS and packet capabilities into mobile and even handheld radios is imminent. This will turn position reporting into a 'turnkey' application that almost every operator can use, without the complexity of current packet or APRS installations.

Bluetooth

Device-to-device networking using Bluetooth is already commonplace between laptops, printers and other computer peripherals. It's also used to connect wireless headsets to computers and cell phones. Expect to see amateur transceivers (even handheld ones) equipped with Bluetooth modems that will allow connection to wireless headsets or handheld computers, making voice and packet operation and programming much easier.

Spread spectrum

Spread-spectrum technologies are in common use now in digital cell phones, trunked radio systems, and military communications. Spread spectrum works by transmitting a signal that is smeared out over a wide range of frequencies, rather than being focused on a single, coherent frequency (like a CW, AM or FM signal). Ironically, this smearing makes the signal more readable at lower power levels, and more resistant to interference from other spectrum users. In fact, with spread spectrum, the 'user capacity' of a given piece of spectrum can be multiplied many-fold. Spread spectrum effectively removes the need for frequency coordination.

Spread spectrum will have two impacts on amateur operations: amateur equipment that incorporates spread-spectrum capabilities will become commercially available, and the use of spread spectrum by both amateurs and 'competing' frequency users will allow amateurs to share frequencies with other users, without losing spectrum or access privileges.

Smart antennas

Microchip-based 'smart' antennas using phased-array technology will allow order-of-magnitude increases in the efficiency of small, broadband antennas used in mobile and handheld radios.

3-5

Multitask transceivers

Software-based radio technologies will allow amateurs to re-use next-generation business band, aviation, or marine radios, or even cellular phones, as all-band amateur transceivers, making it much more likely that amateurs will have amateur-capable transceivers available when and where they're needed. Once software-based radio technology matures, you may even be able to transmit and receive on your laptop or handheld computer.

Fuel cell batteries

Fuel-cell battery technology developed for laptops and other portable devices will make their way into portable and handheld amateur transceivers. This will allow higher transmit power levels and extended operations, with 'recharging' required after weeks, not hours. Fuel cells will also remove the need for noisy, dirty, unreliable gasoline-powered generators at portable stations and emergency sites.

Miniaturized transceivers

Transceivers are getting smaller and smaller to the point where they will soon become 'wearable' technology. (Even now, you can purchase wrist-watch UHF transceivers for the FRS band.) Expect transceivers to shrink to coin-sized units, as better batteries, antennas and voice-control systems become available.

Robust ad-hoc wireless networks

A problem with current digital communications systems is their fixed hierarchical structure. A mobile node (a transceiver, cell phone or mobile computer) must be able to directly see a 'tower' or cellsite in order to work. In the amateur realm, you need to be able to reach the receiver or repeater directly from your transceiver. In the case of packet, you need to manually redefine your path if you can't 'see' the next node.

However, a new form of ad-hoc network called a MANET will allow nodes to intelligently carry traffic between sender and receiver, adapting to changing 'topology' and making it far more likely that your message will get through. In a MANET, if your handheld can't reach the repeater, but it can reach another transceiver in the parking lot that can in turn reach the repeater, the transceiver in the parking lot will automatically relay the traffic (without any intervention by the operator). Packet traffic will get to its destination without any manual routing on the part of the operator (much like the current Internet). MANETs are critically important in emergency situations, where infrastructure is damaged or users are operating in areas that are signal-hostile.

Convergence of radio, wireless and Internet communications technologies

As wireless devices such as handheld computers and cell phones become more able to access Internet services, and as those services grow to include a variety of communications applications, the line between radio communications and Internet communications will blur. Internet applications already exist that mimic (or obsolete) packet services, dispatch radio, long-haul radio, voice networks, SSTV, and voice repeaters. When everyone with a pocket PC has access to this range of communications

3-6

services, both for business and personal use, the privileges of amateur operation become less meaningful. Looking at this shift from an ARES perspective, our technologies and infrastructure becomes less important, and the value of ARES will lie in our operating practices and our communications discipline.

WHAT TO DO TODAY

Despite the changing technologies and the evolving role of ARES and amateur radio in emergency communications, we still need to train and prepare for the emergencies of today and tomorrow. Things that we can focus on in order to add value and invest in our abilities include the following:

- Practice our voice operating skills for both tactical and formal messaging handling

- Learn packet and use it in exercises

- Think about robustness and survivability when building your station and designing systems

- Keep up to date with digital and wireless communications technologies, even those that do not seem to relate directly to amateur radio (for example, wireless digital telephony, wireless computer networking, and Internet-based communications)

- Be aware of the lessons learned elsewhere in the world by emergency communications agencies, including other ARES groups

- Be professional in all our interactions with community stakeholders, emergency officials, government representatives, and the media

- Be ready to serve.

3-7

SECTION 4: UNDERSTANDING EMERGENCY OPERATIONS

This section provides information about emergency operations and how they are managed.

Once you complete this section, you will be able to:

- Describe the phases of disaster assistance

- Explain when ARES may become involved

- Discuss emergency operations roles and sites

- Discuss telecommunications needs during a disaster

- Discuss the role of amateur radio during disasters

- Consider your participation in roles other than communications.

ASSISTANCE PHASES

Most municipalities base their emergency planning on four phases of response:

Phase 1 - Preparedness

This is the period in which emergency plans are drawn up and tested, and other arrangements are made to deal with a disaster should one occur. It is during this phase that both primary and secondary Emergency Operations Centers (EOC) are established and arrangements made for mutual aid. Training and the exercising of plans are major parts of the preparedness phase.

Phase 2 - Immediate response

The immediate response phase begins with the onset of the disaster and remains in effect until initial recovery begins. The immediate response can run from a few hours to 30 days. It is during this phase that 'responders' are activated and the emergency plan implemented.

Phase 3 - Initial recovery

The initial recovery phase follows the immediate response phase and sometimes overlaps with it. During initial recovery, temporary installations are used to provide services and mitigate harm in preparation for longer term recovery and restoration.

Phase 4 - Long-term restoration

Once the disaster is over, long-term restoration begins. This can include such things as the restoration of transportation and telecommunications systems, the rebuilding of damaged equipment, and the reconstruction of buildings, roads and other infrastructure.

4-1

ARES INVOLVEMENT

ARES could be called upon to assist in any phase, but is more likely to be involved during Phase 1, Phase 2, and possibly parts of Phase 3.

ARES only becomes involved in an disaster when prompted by a served agency.

EMERGENCY OPERATIONS

Disasters come in a variety of types and sizes, each requiring a specific type of response. There are, however, certain basic elements of a response that are common to virtually all disasters. Some of these are as follows:

Designated disaster areas

There are always one or more 'designated disaster areas'. These are usually the areas directly affected by the disaster.

Site manager

There is always a 'site manager', usually appointed by a regional authority (for example, a City Manager or Mayor) to be in overall charge of the disaster site. Where several sites are involved, there will be a site manager for each site. All disaster related initiatives at a site go through the site manager. (When the Incident Command System is being used, there will also be an incident commander who manages the overall response to the disaster.)

Emergency operations centre (EOC)

In virtually all disasters, an EOC is established. That EOC is usually a pre-designated room where senior officials meet to coordinate the response and support those at the disaster site. EOC personnel facilitate and coordinate the response efforts of officials at the disaster site.

Incident command post (ICP)

The ICP is the onsite location where the incident commander controls the incident. The ICP may be as simple as the tailgate of a vehicle or as sophisticated as a large complex with extensive communications services.

Command post (CP)

A CP may be established within any section of the ICS Operations Section. CPs can be used as a central control location within the ICS organization. This can be used to centralize command, control and communications.

4-2

TELECOMMUNICATIONS

Telecommunications between the disaster site and the EOC are critical. Without reliable communications, it is impossible for the EOC to know what is going on, let alone coordinate activities. These telecommunications facilities are normally provided using systems operated by the responding agencies (for example, the police and fire radio systems). Typically, the communications facilities are pre-installed and tested periodically to ensure that they will operate during a disaster.

Disaster response personnel have largely adopted cellular telephones and handheld computers as a backup to the telecommunication facilities used by primary responders. However, when cellular facilities become overloaded or unreliable, alternate telecommunications facilities are needed (for example, rented commercial radios).

ROLE OF AMATEUR RADIO

Amateur radio operators who understand the process and are properly trained and regularly exercised can be of tremendous assistance during emergencies.

When properly trained in formal message handling, amateur radio operators can be used to transmit a wide variety of messages on behalf of participating agencies – particularly those who do not have their own telecommunications resources. These messages could include operational messages requesting equipment needed at the site. Logistic and supply messages are often used to arrange for food and supplies at the site. Personnel and administrative messages dealing with the replacement of shift workers are also important.

Amateur radio operators can replace communications systems that have failed, augment systems that are overloaded, or simply carry lower priority traffic that would otherwise not be communicated at all.

Served agencies direct operations

Served agencies direct our operations. We manage communications to meet their needs, but the served agencies define those needs and identify their communications requirements to us. We are there to serve their needs.

It is important that ARES personnel remember their place in the overall organization. Do not try to take over a situation. Your role is to communicate, not to lead.

4-3

Depending on the nature of the emergency, the location where you are deployed, and your skills, capabilities and willingness to help, you may find yourself taking on responsibilities over and above those of a radio operator. For example, you may be called upon to drive a vehicle, help transport other workers or the public, keep watch over an entrance, site or piece of equipment, or even serve soup in a field kitchen.

There has been a lot of debate about whether amateurs should allow themselves to be tasked with non-communications tasks during an emergency. (In some cases, amateurs have been asked to serve roles that have nothing to do with communications.) In general, volunteers are expected to be willing to take on a range of responsibilities. (For example, the Canadian Red Cross expects volunteers to be cross-trained and willing to perform whatever function is needed at a particular site.)

While the choice to take on additional responsibilities is solely your own, based on your comfort with those responsibilities, your evaluation of associated risks, and your own moral compass, in general ARES encourages you to lend whatever aid and support is needed at your place of deployment.

Consider the following guidelines when deciding whether to accept additional responsibilities:

- If the role you are being asked to serve is of greater benefit to the site than your role as a communicator, please consider accepting the request.

- Do not accept a responsibility for which you are unqualified or unsuited. (For example, do not offer to drive a school bus during an evacuation if you do not have a school bus license.)

- Ensure that the site manager is aware of and in agreement with any request that may compromise your ability as a communicator, and that the site manager understands the possible effect on site communications.

- If your new responsibilities will limit your ability as a communicator (for example, by taking you away from your station or distracting you from traffic), contact the net controller, communications supervisor or emergency coordinator to ensure that they are aware of changes in availability.

It is the emergency coordinator's responsibility to ensure in advance of actual emergencies that an understanding exists with served agencies, including the Canadian Red Cross, to ensure that when a request is made for ARES support, it is made in good faith to meet a communications need and not a general need for volunteers.

SECTION 5: ARES SERVICES

A number of specific services are available to ARES clients, letting them tailor ARES communications support to fit their organizational and operational needs.

Once you complete this section, you will be able to identify the types of support that ARES can make available for supporting emergency communications.

EMERGENCY COMMUNICATIONS STATIONS

This is the most commonly requested service. Emergency communications stations provide voice and data communications between specific locations (for example, emergency operations centers, aid stations, shelters, hospitals, and other key locations). These stations augment existing communications, adding capacity and flexibility. (In the unlikely event that existing communications infrastructure fails, these stations can also serve as a backup.)

SHADOWING

Shadowing involves attaching telecommunications operators to specific 'high-value' personnel in an organization. This ensures that key personnel are kept in touch, regardless of location, communications overloads or failures, or other factors.

MOBILE COMMUNICATIONS SERVICE

ARES *mobile communications service* attaches telecommunications operators to mobile units (such as evacuation buses, assessment units, search and rescue teams, or other mobile units requiring communications support). Telecommunications operators ensure connectivity between the mobile units and EOCs or coordination points.

Mobile communications services could also use a mobile positioned to act as a relay station when there is poor coverage on simplex or repeater networks.

DATA MESSAGING

Data messaging service is provided using D-STAR, ad-hoc packet radio LANs, Wifi networks, and point-to-point Ethernet radio links (using higher power and gain antennas in the shared amateur radio portions of the 900 MHz and 2.4 GHz bands). Data messaging stations are set up at key sites such as evacuation centres and EOCs, allowing the efficient transfer of large quantities of data.

In situations where you need to move formal data or files from one site to another and the Internet is not available, ARES data messaging may be useful. ARES data stations at each site use data radio channels and networks to send text messages (such as lists of names) or actual files.

While the data rate of traditional packet radio is quite low, the AX.25 protocol is very efficient and when combined with B2F compression used with Winlink 2000 or FBBS type bulletin boards, throughput efficiency can approach that of dial-up ISP connections.

5-1

D-STAR in Digital Data mode can approach the capability of commercial "DSL-Lite". Wifi or Ethernet radio links can approach the efficiency of a wired LAN.

For a more detailed discussion of digital communications, see "Digital communications" on page 17.1.

RAPID COMMUNITY ASSESSMENT

During many types of emergency, getting information about conditions in the community at large can be crucial. The ARES network provides an easy way to get basic information very quickly. During community emergencies (for example, during severe weather events), the ARES network can provide rapid assessment of conditions at a large number of locations throughout the region.

The types of information that could be requested include the status of electrical and telephone service, wind and weather conditions, road conditions, or even reporting of physical damage (for example, flood damage).

This service augments existing procedures for community assessment, providing rapid feedback of basic data from a large number of points.

BACKUP COMMUNICATIONS

ARES *backup communications service* places ARES emergency communications stations at or near existing high-value communications stations (such as those at City Hall, EOCs, hospitals, etc.) to provide backup service in case of problems or overload in key communications links. In this mode, the backup communications stations and networks are staffed and ready but idle unless needed.

INTEROPERABLE COMMUNICATIONS (INTER-AGENCY BRIDGING)

In situations where aid, response and recovery efforts are being hampered by incompatible communications systems, ARES can assist by providing a communications 'bridge'. This need may arise when:

- groups that do not normally work together are required to communicate, but are using different radio systems or incompatible frequencies

- a key system used to interconnect communications system becomes overloaded by traffic levels

- communications systems are working normally, but a back-up solution is required in case of failure or overload.

WIDE-AREA COMMUNICATIONS RELAYS

ARES can provide communications connectivity outside the local area when required. This service is useful during emergencies that disrupt telephone and Internet communications over a wide area.

5-2

SECTION 6: ARES ROLES

This section outlines ARES roles and responsibilities.

Once you complete this section, you will be able to:

- Describe the tasks performed by ARES operators and stations playing various operational roles

- Understand the duties of EMO communications officers

- Understand the role played by ARES emergency coordinators

- Understand the duties of communications supervisors

- Describe the duties of other ARES operational roles.

ARES OPERATORS AND STATIONS

ARES operators are radio operators who are familiar with ARES procedures and are included on ARES and provincial EMO callouts.

Net Control Stations

Emergency net controllers serve as net control stations during emergencies or exercises. A net control station will take control of a specific channel (typically a repeater channel), and will maintain order and ensure efficient communications between stations on that channel.

Official Emergency Stations

Stations and associated licensees may be designated as Official Emergency Stations (OES). An OES designation means that the station is fully prepared to provide enhanced capabilities during emergencies.

Telecommunications operators

Telecommunications operators are individual amateur radio operators who participate in ARES nets using either their own handheld or mobile equipment, or equipment at designated Official Emergency Stations.

Telecommunications operators handle radio traffic and message forms in order to send messages from the site that they are supporting, or to receive messages for that site. Telecommunications operators may also be attached to vehicles (for example, a city bus being used for evacuations), or an individual person (for example, *shadowing* a relief coordinator).

Relay stations

Relay stations are located away from supported sites and EOCs, but contribute by relaying traffic from one channel or medium to another. A relay station may be

6-1

designed to carry traffic between a local VHF channel and a provincial HF net. A relay station may move traffic between voice and packet channels, or arrange phone patches. In situations where communications between endpoints is hampered by poor propagation, jamming, or other problems, a station able to communicate with both endpoints may be assigned the task of relaying traffic between those endpoints.

COMMUNICATIONS OFFICERS (DCO, PCO)

The Provincial Communications Officer (PCO) directs EMO communications support activities at the provincial level.

Note: In some jurisdictions, a PCO performs a public relations function rather than a telecommunications function.

The District Communications Officer (DCO) manages communications resources at the local level, when tasked by the PCO.

EMERGENCY COORDINATORS FOR ARES

The emergency coordinator (EC) performs a number of tasks, most of them in preparation for emergencies and exercises rather than actually during an emergency. The EC establishes working relationships with various regional agencies that might need communications support. The EC addresses the training, organization and emergency participation of interested amateurs. The EC also creates an emergency communications plan, communications networks, and site operating procedures.

Training for emergency coordinators is addressed in Volume 3 of this training manual.

Assistant emergency coordinators

Assistant emergency coordinators (AEC) perform many of the tasks that an emergency coordinator performs. The AECs assist by offloading responsibilities from the emergency coordinator.

COMMUNICATIONS SUPERVISORS

Communications supervisors manage communications requirements during an exercise or emergency. Communications supervisors are often ECs or AECs, but any qualified operator can act as a supervisor. Supervisors have the following responsibilities:

- Monitoring active communications channels and 'troubleshooting' any problems that arise

- Managing shift changes of net controllers and operators, in accordance with schedules provided by an EC or AEC

- Responding to ad-hoc communications needs that arise

Training for communications supervisors is addressed in Volume 2 of this training manual.

6-2

STATION MANAGERS

A station manager is similar to a site manager, except that the station manager is responsible solely for the communications station at a site, and coordinates with the designated site manager (or site coordinator).

The station manager is responsible for opening a station at the beginning of an exercise or emergency, or when directed by authorities. The station manager stays onsite or visits regularly to ensure that individual operators are available and are rotated, that equipment works properly, and that logistics support (such as electrical, food, comfort and transportation) is provided as required. The station manager is also responsible for closing a station at the end of an exercise or when ordered to do so.

The station manager will normally be required by the EOC, onsite and support agency clients to provide copies of the station log and message traffic handled by the station.

The role of station manager does not have to fall on one person. The role can be handed off from person to person as required with shift changes. The station manager, in most cases, will also serve as a back-up operator or runner.

It is advisable for staff to rotate between positions in a communications centre to reduce fatigue and stress. However, the site manager should always be a qualified ARES operator.

RUNNERS

Runners are responsible for carrying messages between an ARES station and personnel elsewhere onsite (for example, carrying messages between the City Hall ARES station and the Mayor's Office in City Hall). Runners also perform other support tasks as required, ensuring that the telecommunications operators are able to give their full attention to nets and traffic handling. Runners do not have to be licensed amateurs, although telecommunications operators may take breaks by serving as runners periodically.

The runner could even be an evacuee. However, the runner must be trustworthy, and must be thoroughly briefed on the requirements for confidentiality.

At some locations where FRS/GMRS or telephone communications are used to link parts of the site, a runner may assist by passing traffic between end users and the telecommunications operators using FRS/GMRS radios or telephone message handling. For this reason, it is preferred that runners be familiar with message handling, protocols for working with end users, and the use and interpretation of message forms.

MESSAGE CLERKS

Message clerks, like runners, manage message delivery and collection. However, message clerks usually work alongside radio operators at the communications station, typically behind a desk or counter. Message clerks help clients fill in message forms, and ensure that messages are delivered only to those authorized to receive them.

6-3

REPEATER MANAGERS

Repeater managers are the owners or technical contacts for specific area repeaters that may be important to emergency communications. A repeater manager is someone who may or may not actually be involved in ARES or in any specific exercise or emergency, but can be 'on-call' to troubleshoot problems during emergencies. A repeater manager is also the point of contact for requesting permission to use a repeater during exercises.

TECHNICAL SUPPORT PRIMES

In some situations, technical support might be required (for example, to restore repeater operation during power outages, or to establish antennas or emergency power as specific locations). Technical support primes are people who volunteer to perform technical support where and when it is needed. Support primes do not have to be licensed amateurs (although in most cases they probably will be certified).

Section 7: Emergency preparedness

This section provides information about emergency preparedness and what you need to do in the home, the office and your car to ensure you are safe, secure and available during an emergency.

Once you complete this section, you will be able to:

- Discuss the need for preparation

- Prepare your car, home and workplace for emergencies.

Need for preparation

Chances are good that when an emergency arises, you will either be at home or at your place of work. You need to be prepared for emergencies when at home or at work, to ensure you're equipped to respond when situations arise. This means having radio equipment available and ready for use, along with supporting materials like paper and pens, a flashlight, and other useful items. It also means having a kit that contains anything you may need during a 24-hour period without support (things like medications, water, chocolate bars, and spare batteries).

Preparation goes beyond simply your ability to operate. You should also prepare your family, your home or your business so that during an emergency you will be free to participate in ARES. Discuss your role in ARES with your employer so that they will understand the need to give you time off if you are needed during a disaster.

In your car

In many emergencies, your car will become essential transportation. In many situations, it may become your operating post. The following guidelines suggest steps you can take to ensure that your vehicle is ready for an emergency situation:

- Keep the gas tank above the halfway mark at all times.

- Install proper winter tires (and not all-season tires) in the fall.

- Keep snow chains in the trunk during the winter (and learn how to use them).

- Keep sand bags and a snow shovel in the trunk during the winter.

- Keep the following items in the car or in a Ready Kit:

  - 12v power cables for all your portable radios (including handhelds)
  - Empty coffee thermos
  - Bottles of drinking water (except in winter)

7-1

AT HOME

The first priority in home safety is ensuring the safety of your family and property. By preparing in advance, you'll ensure that you'll be available for ARES operations and that your family and home will be safe in your absence. Consider the following recommendations:

- Keep bottled water available (2L per day per adult, 1L per day per child).

- Keep an alternate heat source available (for example, a catalytic camping heater) in case an electrical outage turns off your heat. (DO NOT use any devices that emit carbon monoxide within the home!)

- Give every member of the family the number of a family friend or relative outside the region. This way, that person can serve as a point of contact in case your family members cannot reach each other.

- Ensure that you have flashlights at strategic points in the home, so that you can move around safely during a night-time power outage.

- Have at least one POTS phone (a phone that does not require a power adapter) in the house. A power outage will disable cordless and 'full featured' phones.

- Keep a small battery powered AM/FM radio in the kitchen where it can be easily found during a power outage. (A radio capable of receiving TV audio is very useful during emergencies, if one is available.)

- Have an evacuation bag prepared, in case your family needs to leave in a hurry. The bag should contain a change of clothes for each family member (old or out-of-style clothing can be used), warm clothing in wintertime, a flashlight with spare batteries, spare car and house keys, small bottles of water, extra doses of any essential medication, and photocopies of identification, insurance papers, prescriptions, phone numbers, and special medical instructions.

- Keep any pet carriers near the evacuation bag.

- If you have FRS/GMRS radios, know where they are so you can throw them into the evacuation bag. FRS/GMRS radios may be used to keep your family coordinated in chaotic situations at shelters or evacuation points.

- If you have a generator, do not try to connect it to your house wiring without the assistance of a professional, certified electrician.

- During an emergency, try to keep telephone calls to a minimum (including dialup Internet calls).

7-2

AT WORK

If you do not take your car to work, prepare a small ready pack that you can leave at your desk or in your office.

If you are willing to participate in callouts during your working hours and need to explain your ARES involvement to an employer, contact your emergency coordinator to ask about obtaining an employer letter. An employer letter, issued either by the emergency coordinator or preferably by a served agency official or emergency preparedness coordinator, explains briefly what ARES does for the community, and the value of your involvement in it. (Such a letter does not compel your employer to give you time off or facilitate your participation in ARES, but it may help your employer understand the benefit your participation brings to the community and allow the employer to justify the expense of supporting you.)

EQUIPMENT

Ensure that your equipment is complete, appropriate, and reliable.

For more information about equipment selection and configuration, see "Equipment selection and configuration" on page 14.1.

7-3

SECTION 8:   ACTIVATIONS AND MOBILIZATIONS

This section provides information related to ARES activations, mobilizations, and deployments (the activities that occur at the beginning of an exercise or disaster).

Once you complete this section, you will be able to:

- Describe how callouts are triggered

- Understand how activations and mobilizations occur

- Understand how frequencies are selected for ARES operations.

CALLOUTS

At the beginning of an exercise, or when a need for ARES support is identified during an emergency, a callout is performed to activate the local ARES group. The EC and AECs call their assigned operators to warn of a possible mobilization, to ask operators to monitor a net frequency, or to actually deploy operators to locations.

In situations where telecommunications has failed, or where a community emergency has been declared but ARES has not been specifically activated, available ECs or AECs may decide to perform a limited (warm-up) or full activation in the expectation that a request may be received.

Types of activation are described below. If you receive an activation call, see "When you get an activation call" on page 8.4.

ACTIVATION AND MOBILIZATION

This section describes the types of activation, and the activation processes. It also provides information about what to do during exercises and emergency activations.

There are two general types of activations:

- EMO activations, triggered by the provincial EMO

- ARES activations, triggered by served agencies or events that have occurred within a region or community

In some situations, these activations may both occur, perhaps even at the same time.

ARES activations

Types of ARES activation

ARES has several levels of activation, providing flexibility in situations that may not require a full mobilization of personnel.

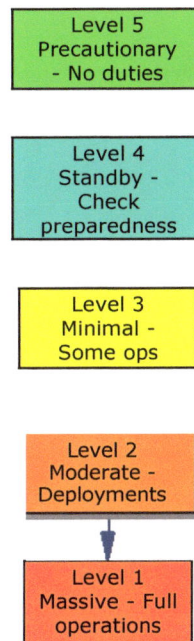

```
┌─────────────────┐
│    Level 5      │
│  Precautionary  │
│   - No duties   │
└─────────────────┘

┌─────────────────┐
│    Level 4      │
│   Standby -     │
│    Check        │
│  preparedness   │
└─────────────────┘

┌─────────────────┐
│    Level 3      │
│   Minimal -     │
│   Some ops      │
└─────────────────┘

┌─────────────────┐
│    Level 2      │
│   Moderate -    │
│  Deployments    │
└─────────────────┘
         │
         ▼
┌─────────────────┐
│    Level 1      │
│ Massive - Full  │
│  operations     │
└─────────────────┘
```

Activation Level 5 - Precautionary . Under a Level 5 activation, ARES is triggered spontaneously by a community situation (for example, a power or telecommunications outage, or an event such as an industrial explosion). A Level 5 activation is usually a response to an unexpected event that has occurred without warning. The EC begins monitoring the group's primary frequency (often referred to as TAC1), and ARES operators may decide to check for ARES activity on that frequency. There is no formal callout or net initiation, and the EC acts as a coordinator, providing any information that is available and asking other ARES stations coming on frequency to stand by.

Level 5 will be rescinded when the EC decides that ARES support is not likely to be needed. The EC broadcasts a message to all operators on TAC1, standing down ARES operations.

If ARES support may be needed, the EC escalates to Level 4, Level 3, Level 2 or Level 1 as appropriate.

Activation Level 4 - Standby . Under a Level 4 activation, ARES volunteers are asked to prepare for a possible deployment. Depending on the situation, volunteers may be notified by phone, email, or radio.

ARES operators are asked to monitor TAC1. No net is initiated.

ARES volunteers are asked to check their level of preparedness. Checking preparedness means:

- Checking family members to ensure that they are secure

- Checking schedules and availability

- Checking batteries

- Testing primary and backup equipment

- Checking Ready Packs

- Checking vehicle readiness

- Filling gas tanks.

Activation Level 3 - Minimal Deployment. Under a Level 3 activation, the EC assesses the need for volunteers. The EC contacts key ARES volunteers in order to gather scheduling information.

Operators are asked to continue monitoring TAC1. A net is initiated on TAC1 only if required. An ARES net controller begins making periodic announcements on TAC1, and prepares to initiate an ARES net.

If needed, the EC will dispatch ARES operators to key sites (such as an EOC).

A second callout is performed to contact any operators who did not respond to the initial callout.

Activation Level 2 - Moderate Deployment. Under a Level 2 activation, at least one EC is on duty at the primary EOC. ECs start the callout to ARES volunteers for a 72-hour schedule.

An ARES net is initiated on TAC1. The EC dispatches operators to sites as required. Initial deployments may be up to 12 hours in duration.

However, be prepared for longer deployments in a larger emergency, as relief may not be available.

Activation Level 1 - Massive Deployment. Under a Level 1 activation, the EC schedules operators to meet site and net control requirements for up to two weeks. All ARES resources are made available to client agencies.

All available ARES operators are asked to check in to the ARES net on TAC1, and are dispatched to specific locations and assigned duties.

Additional ARES nets are initiated on additional frequencies as required. All nets and sub-nets observe strict net protocols until Level 1 is rescinded.

8-3

When you get an activation call

When you get a call for an emergency callout, you will be told the emergency channel that is being used. In some situations, you may also be immediately dispatched to a location. On activation:

- Begin monitoring the emergency channel and stand by for instructions.

- Call the personnel on your own ARES callout page, if you have been assigned callout duties.

- Check into the emergency net during the next general call for check ins.

- Prepare your emergency pack (add charged batteries, cell phone, etc.) and stand by for deployment.

When you hear about a community emergency or telecommunications outage

When you hear about a community emergency or telecommunications outage, begin scanning the ARES frequencies and stand by to join an emergency net.

If the community emergency is not serious enough to warrant ARES or EMO activation, the net may not convene.

If the emergency is serious, or if the telecommunications outage is likely to affect critical services, an EC or district communications officer (DCO) will initiate the emergency net and call for check-ins.

If you discover a widespread telecommunications outage and believe that your EC may not be aware of it, take steps to notify your EC using whatever means are available.

When you are deployed to a location

When you are deployed to a location, take your Ready Pack and enough food, water and medication to operate comfortably for at least 24 hours.

If you require transportation, advise the EC/AEC or DCO when they call to activate you, or inform the net controller when the controller requests information about your status and availability.

When you arrive at the location

At a location that does not yet have an ARES communication station

1   Seek out the location site manager and tell them that you have arrived. (The location of the senior officer is often indicated by a flashing green light.)

2   Ask them where you are to set up the station (or if operating handheld, where you should place yourself).

8-4

3   Check into the emergency net and notify the net controller that you are on station and in contact with appropriate parties.

4   Wear a name badge that clearly says Communications Operator.

5   If practical, put up a sign identifying your post or station as a communications station.

6   If you are equipped with an FRS handheld and are at a location where FRS is being used by officials, turn it on to channel 9, with privacy codes (CTCSS) turned off.

At a location that has an ARES communication station

1   Seek out the station manager (or location site manager, if you are the first ARES operator to arrive).

2   Find the communications station.

3   Refer to the Communications Station Operating Procedures in the ARES binder at the station and follow procedures to activate the station.

4   Check into the emergency net and notify the net controller that the station is activated and ready for service.

5   Wear a name badge with your first name, clearly indicating ARES.

FREQUENCIES FOR ARES OPERATIONS

Frequencies used during ARES operations will depend almost entirely on the repeater systems and communications plans in place within your region. In addition, the frequencies used during ARES operations may vary depending on the available surviving repeaters, on the area where communications support is needed, and on the number of channels needed to meet end-user requirements.

ARES 'channels' are divided into four types:

1   VHF/UHF FM frequencies

2   'Exotic' frequencies on bands or modes that will not normally be used, but may be required for special applications

3   HF SSB frequencies for NVIS applications

4   HF/VHF/UHF frequencies for digital communications

8-5

SECTION 9: WORKING WITHIN THE INCIDENT COMMAND SYSTEM

This section provides information about working in an Incident Command System (ICS) environment. This is a summary for use by ARES personnel, and is intended to provide only a basic understanding of terminology and concepts associated with ICS. This training module does not replace or supersede formal ICS training provided in your region or by your served agencies.

During smaller incidents, a subset of ICS's full structure will likely be used.

In some regions, ICS is modified or combined with other protocols (for example, with Emergency Site Management protocols in New Brunswick), and there are significant deviations from standard ICS practices.

Once you complete this section, you will be able to:

• Describe how ICS works

• Understand how radio communications fits within the ICS structure.

ABOUT ICS

ICS is an organizational system used to help manage planned or unplanned events that require a response by emergency service or disaster response personnel to minimize loss of life or damage to property or natural resources. The system features a standardized approach to incident management, a modular, scalable organizational structure, and common terminology and practices. It develops from the top down, based on the size and complexity of the incident. In fact, ICS is used to manage incidents ranging from small, everyday events to massive disasters.

The system increases the efficiency and effectiveness of mutual aid while maximizing safety and minimizing opportunities for confusion. It also provides for an orderly escalation, if needed. ICS can be scaled up to include several thousand people without compromising effective supervision.

Unified command

The Incident Commander (IC) sits at the top of the IC organizational structure. The IC manages the incident and defines operational objectives. The IC has overall responsibility for the incident, though some duties may be delegated to others.

Unity of command
Unity of command means that each worker has only one supervisor. This eliminates confusion and the possibility of conflicting orders.

Span of control
Span of control means that no one individual is required to supervise or manage more than seven other individuals (and ideally, only five). Chain of command

9-1

Chain of command

Chain of command means that there is a clear line of authority, with lower levels subordinate to and connected to higher levels. In most cases, the chain of command consists of:

- Command

- Resource.

As responses expand, the chain of command also expands to include, from the top down:

- Command

- Sections

- Branches

- Divisions or groups

- Units

- Resources.

Unified command and multiple jurisdictions

Unified command allows multiple jurisdictions to agree on objectives and strategies. ICS makes this possible without any loss of authority, responsibility or accountability. Under unified command:

1   There is only one IC for any event.

2   A single, coordinated Incident Action Plan (IAP) is used, including the following elements:
    - What are the objectives of the team or what do we want to do?
    - Who is responsible for accomplishing what tasks?
    - How does the team communicate?
    - What is the team safety plan or how do we take care of a person who becomes injured?

3   One Operations Section Chief will have responsibility for implementing the IAP.

4   One Incident Command Post (ICP) will be established.

Management functions

The success of ICS relies on two key elements:

- Management by objectives

- Organizational structure

ICS positions fall into five types of management:

Command
The IC is responsible for all activity. The size and complexity of the incident determines which other management functions are needed. The command staff assists the IC and reports directly to the IC.

Operations
Operations directs tactical actions. There is only one Operations Chief (if activated by the IC), but the Chief may have deputies.

Planning
The Planning function collects, evaluates and reports information about the incident. Planning also keeps track of resources, and prepares the IAP and other documentation.

Logistics
Logistics ensures that adequate services and support are available to responders and other ICS personnel.

Finance & Administration
Finance & Administration manages incident-related costs, tracks personnel, and maintains equipment records. It also administers any procurement contracts associated with the response.

Scalable organization

Each functional area of ICS can grow into additional organizational units with any delegation of authority. In turn, elements that are no longer needed are deactivated. The size of the ICS organization is determined through the IAP process.

Each activated functional group must have a designated supervisor. A single supervisor may initially be in charge of more than one unit.

Personnel and roles

The following personnel report to the IC:

- Command staff

- Safety Officer (command staff)

- Liaison Officer (command staff)

- Public Information Officer (command staff)

- Operations Chief

- Planning Chief

- Logistics Chief, responsible for

    - Communications
    - Medical unit
    - Food unit.

- Finance/Administration Chief

ICS locations

ICS locations include:

- Incident Command Post (ICP): The field location at which the primary tactical-level, on-scene incident command functions are performed. The ICP may be collocated with the incident base or other incident facilities.

- Base: The location at which primary Logistics functions for an incident are coordinated and administered. There is only one base per incident. (Incident name or other designator will be added to the term *base*.) The Incident Command Post may be collocated with the base.

- Staging Area: Location where resources can be placed while awaiting a tactical assignment.

- Camp: A geographical site, within the general incident area, separate from the Incident Base, equipped and staffed to provide sleeping, food, water, and sanitary services to incident personnel.

Incident documentation

Incident action plan (IAP)
The IAP provides supervisors with instructions to guide them throughout the response. The IAP may be written or verbal (but written plans are preferred).

Communications plan
The communications plan can be very simple or even verbal, or it could be complex enough to become part of the written IAP. The communications plan lists the communications methods to be used for the response.

After action report
While you are on assignment, keep notes on what you did while there so you can provide your team leader or sponsoring agency with information for an After Action Report or Review (AAR).

An AAR typically contains:

- Tasks/duties or items to keep

- Task/duties or items to change

- Task/duties or items to add

- Task/duties or items to delete.

When providing your input to the AAR, be honest and sincere. However, do not take your frustrations out on the team leader or on sponsoring agency employees.

9-5

RADIO COMMUNICATIONS WITHIN ICS

ICS does not alter the way any unit (including ARES) performs its internal function. ICS does not dictate how the police does its policing, how firefighters fight fires, nor how communications units accomplish their tasks. ARES methods and procedures remain unchanged.

However, ICS does provide an organization and reporting structure, with a clearly defined chain of command and span of control. Within ICS, communications falls under Logistics.

Within the ICS communications team, there will be a Communications Unit Leader (COML), who manages:

- A Communications Technician (COMT)

- An Incident Communications Centre Manager (INCM)

- A Radio Operator (RADO).

Not all of these positions will be filled during every response.

This structure allows for the management of any incident, regardless of size. ICS also allows for the expansion of the organization if needed to maintain the span of control (providing between three and seven – ideally five – subordinates per supervisor).

An ARES operator may be assigned to the COML, or they may be assigned as a Technical Specialist in another area. ARES operators may also be asked to perform non-ARES activities, and could conceivably be assigned anywhere. If an operator is assigned to a non-ARES unit, operators need to comply with the directions of the unit supervisor, understand the mission, and report actions back to that unit supervisor.

Amateur radio groups deployed as units should be structured into groups of three to five operators under one ARES unit supervisor. For example, if a unit has 20 members, the leadership needs to break the unit down into four or five units. This could be based upon geography (where the units will be deployed), time of day (shifts), specific function (HQ unit, field unit 1, field unit 2, etc.), or any other reasonable, manageable division of labor. Instead of one ARES leader getting status or providing direction to 20 members, the one leader interacts with only four subordinates, and those four interact with three to five operators. This allows a much faster and more manageable method of communications and control. Smaller units are also able to be re-assigned and moved more quickly than large units, so the smaller units also give ICS more flexibility in the use of overall resources.

ICS requires the use of plain English in all communications. Avoid special codes, prowords or jargon.

9-6

SECTION 10: EMERGENCY OPERATIONS

This section provides basic information about radio operations during emergencies.

Once you complete this section, you will be able to:

- Describe the types of net used during emergency operations

- Understand the types of traffic carried over ARES nets

- Describe best practices for voice communications

- Describe best practices for formal message handling

- Understand how to use cross-band repeaters

- Work with and replace other ARES operators.

TYPES OF NETS

Depending on the nature and duration of the emergency situation, more than one net may be operating at any given time, either on repeaters or on simplex channels.

Two general types of net are used in ARES operations:

1   Directed net. A formal net with a net controller, who directs all communications on the net. Stations request permission from net control before calling other stations or passing traffic.

2   Open net. A net that allows informal communications, with or without a net controller. If there is a net controller, the controller acts to provide coordination, recordkeeping, and other support. On an open net, stations do not need to get net control permission before calling or passing traffic.

The specific types of net that may be initiated include the following:

- Operational net. This is a directed net that carries the bulk of the traffic for the client agencies.

- Task-specific nets. If a need exists for subnets dedicated to specific client groups or tasks (such as inter-municipal EOC communications), new net frequencies will be selected and specific operators will be moved to the new frequencies. Task-specific nets may be an open net or a directed net.

- Standby (availability) net. This is a directed net that is a point of first check-in for operators who are announcing availability to participate. Operators are kept on this net until deployed to a location or role and moved to the operational net.

- Support net. This is an open net used to provide technical and procedural support to operators, and ARES resource coordination (for example, finding spare handhelds). The purpose of the support net is to keep 'maintenance' traffic off the operational net.

10-1

TYPES OF TRAFFIC

The types of traffic that ARES communications stations can carry include the following:

Tactical voice traffic

Tactical voice communications is used in situations where messages need to pass back and forth between stations without delays, and do not need to be formal. Examples of tactical traffic include:

- Requests to mobile stations for location or operational status

- Traffic that has not been originated by third parties (such as coordination between telecommunications operators or ECs)

- Informal discussions between officials

- Informal information requests

- General broadcasts from one station to many other stations (point to multipoint)

Formal voice message traffic

Formal voice communications is used in situations where messages need to reach their destinations without any errors, need to be logged and recorded, or are being relayed by intermediate stations. Examples of formal voice message traffic include:

- Formal requests or directives sent to a specific individual or office

- Formal reports or responses sent to a specific individual or office

Digital data messaging

Like formal voice message traffic, digital communications is used in situations where messages need to reach their destinations without any errors, and need to be logged and recorded. Digital messaging is particularly well suited to formal traffic that is lengthy in nature. Examples of tactical traffic include:

- Evacuee lists sent from evacuation shelters to the Canadian Red Cross

- Detailed reports sent from shelter managers to the Canadian Red Cross

- Supply requisitions sent from an emergency measures office to aid agencies

- Public bulletins sent from City Hall to local radio and TV stations

10-2

Automated traffic

Automated traffic is any form of communications that does not involve operators at both ends of the connection. Current examples of automated traffic include:

- Vehicle location coordinates (GPS data sent over APRS packet)

- Weather data sent over packet

- Site photos or video sent over SSTV or amateur television (ATV)

BEST PRACTICES FOR VOICE COMMUNICATIONS

The following recommended voice operating practices work well in emergency communications contexts:

- Know what you are going to say before you transmit.

- Listen carefully before transmitting to ensure that you understand the net and that you are not 'speaking over' another station.

- Speak clearly and slowly.

- If the message needs to be written down, speak more slowly.

- Pause after logical phrases.

- Speak at an even pace

- Speak across the microphone, and not into it.

- Key the microphone a second or two before speaking, to ensure that repeater and receiver squelch has opened.

- Identify using your callsign or tactical callsign at the beginning of any transmission.

- If using a handheld, do not move around while transmitting.

- Acknowledge any instructions directed at your station. If you understand the instructions, reply with "acknowledged". If you wish to indicate that you will comply with the instructions, reply with "will comply". If you do not understand the instructions or need more information, request that the sender repeat or clarify the instructions. (Do not say "repeat". Instead, use "say again".)

- Do not use the word "break" when you pause. It is confusing, wastes time and has another meaning in formal message handling. Merely unkey and pause. If the other station has questions, they should key up and make their request known. This also permits other stations to break in if they have emergency traffic.

- Do not make any angry or sarcastic comments on the air. On-air humour is not recommended. During an exercise or emergency, amateur radio becomes a profession, not a hobby. Sound professional.

10-3

Q codes

Do not use Q codes (such as QSY, QSL or QTH) during emergency operations.

Tactical call signs

Use tactical call signs once you have been assigned a task or location. A tactical call sign is a label that identifies either your duties (for example, *Fire One* for an operator attached to the Fire Chief) or your location (for example, *RC* for a station at the Red Cross building). Tactical call signs reduce confusion.

Use your own call sign periodically in order to satisfy Industry Canada identification requirements, but do not over-use your own callsign. (For example, normally say "EOC this is RC", and every 15-30 minutes during traffic, say "EOC this is RC, VE9ZYX at the Red Cross.")

Phonetics

The only phonetics that are acceptable during emergency communications are those of the NATO/ITU phonetic alphabet. This is the phonetic alphabet recommended by Industry Canada, and in general use in amateur radio.

Table 1:   NATO/ITU phonetic alphabet

A	ALFA	M	MIKE	Y	YANKEE
B	BRAVO	N	NOVEMBER	Z	ZULU
C	CHARLIE	O	OSCAR	1	ONE
D	DELTA	P	PAPA	2	TWO
E	ECHO	Q	QUEBEC	3	THREE
F	FOXTROT	R	ROMEO	4	FOUR
G	GOLF	S	SIERRA	5	FIVE
H	HOTEL	T	TANGO	6	SIX
I	INDIA	U	UNIFORM	7	SEVEN
J	JULIETTE	V	VICTOR	8	EIGHT
K	KILO	W	WHISKEY	9	NINE-ER (or NINE, if reception is clear or the meaning of the number is trivial - such as the nine in VE9ZYX)
L	LIMA	X	X-RAY	0	ZERO

Note: Do not use other phonetics. "Made up" phonetics, such as "Victor Echo Nine Henry America Kilowatt," are not acceptable. The use of improper phonetics makes it difficult for receiving stations to copy the traffic, even under normal conditions, and also makes ARES operators appear unprofessional to other emergency responders and agencies.

10-4

Frequency designations

Use frequency designations (for example, **F3**) instead of lengthy frequencies or repeater names.

> *Note: Frequency designations are not an attempt to 'conceal' frequency information. (Anyone able to monitor a channel will be able to find other channels easily.) Frequency designations make it easy to communicate frequency information quickly and accurately, and are a best practice in emergency communications.*

TACTICAL VOICE PROCEDURES

Net operations

This section provides guidelines for participating in an ARES directed net as an ARES station.

Best practices

The following recommended net operating practices work well in emergency communications contexts:

- If you call net control and do not receive a reply, wait a minute or two and call again. (The net controller may be handling off-air or off-frequency activities.)

- Do not relay for another on-net station unless you are asked to do so by the net controller.

- If you move off the net frequency for any reason, try to maintain a watch on the net using a second receiver, in case you are needed on net.

- Stay off the air unless you are certain that you can be of assistance.

Checking in without traffic

When the net controller calls for check-ins, respond with your callsign only. Wait until you are acknowledged, and then stand by for further instructions from the net controller. If you are not acknowledged, wait until the next call for check-ins.

For example:

NCS: This is ARES Net Control. Any new stations, check in now.

VE9FK: V-E-9-Foxtrot-Kilo

VE9BES: V-E-9-B-E-S

VE9ZYX: V-E-9-Z-Y-X

NCS: Acknowledging V-E-9-F-K, V-E-9-B-E-S. Any further check-ins, come now.

10-5

VE9ZYX: V-E-9-Zulu-Yankee-Xray

NCS: Acknowledging V-E-9-Z-Y-X

Checking in with traffic

When the net controller calls for check-ins, respond with your callsign and identify your traffic (either with a brief description, or with a destination). Wait until you are acknowledged, and then stand by for further instructions from the net controller. If you are not acknowledged, wait until the next call for check-ins.

For example:

VE9FK: V-E-9-Foxtrot-Kilo

VE9ZYX: R-C with traffic for E-O-C.

NCS: Acknowledged V-E-9-F-K, acknowledged R-C. R-C, call E-O-C.

VE9ZYX: E-O-C this is R-C with traffic.

VE9BES: Send for E-O-C.

VE9ZYX: E-O-C this is R-C. Coordinator here is asking for an extra generator at St.Rose, if one is available.

VE9BES: Acknowledged R-C, extra generator for St. Rose. Will reply shortly. E-O-C out.

VE9ZYX: R-C out.

NCS: This is ARES Net Control. Any new stations, check in now.

Breaking in with urgent traffic

If you have urgent traffic and need to interrupt ongoing communications, wait until an end of transmission and then break in.

For example:

VE9BES: Blah blah blah blah.

VE9FK: Blah blah blah blah.

VE9ZYX: VE9ZYX, traffic.

NCS: Send traffic.

VE9ZYX: Site 0-5 with priority traffic for E-O-C.

VE9BES: Send for E-O-C.

10-6

VE9ZYX: E-O-C this is Site 0-5. We've had a power failure at St. Joseph's Hospital. Generators are urgently required.

VE9BES: Acknowledged Site 0-5. Stand by.

NCS: All stations stand by.

VE9BES: Site 0-5 from E-O-C.

VE9ZYX: E-O-C send.

VE9BES: Two five thousand kilowatt generators are being sent now. Time to delivery is 20, two-zero, minutes.

VE9ZYX: Acknowledged E-O-C. Thank you. Site 0-5 out.

VE9BES: E-O-C out.

NCS: This is ARES Net Control. Any stations with traffic, check in now.

Breaking in with information

If you have information that will be of value to two stations that are currently communicating, wait until an end of transmission and then break in with information.

For example:

VE9FK: *Ongoing.* We need to have an ambulance or first aid team here at this site. We have a number of elderly here and some medical support may be needed.

VE9BES: Understood. We are checking into available first-aid teams.

VE9ZYX: Info, VE9ZYXX.

NCS: Send info.

VE9ZYX: E-O-C, this is Site 0-5. EMTs have been dispatched to all evac centres.

VE9BES: Acknowledged, Site 0-5. Site 2-0, stand by for now. Notify us when you receive your EMT.

VE9ZYX: Will comply. Site 2-0, out.

VE9BES: E-O-C out.

NCS: This is ARES Net Control. Any stations with traffic, check in now.

Letting third parties speak with each other on-air

If you are providing tactical or command communications, there will be times when the most effective way to facilitate communications is to allow third parties to speak directly with each other over the amateur radio channel.

10-7

When this is required, consider changing to an alternate channel that is not used to carry formal message traffic.

Establish contact with the other station before handing over the microphone to the third party.

Be sure that the third party is comfortable with the use of the equipment before the conversation begins.

Once the traffic is completed, take back the microphone, sign off in the normal way, and return to your designated channel.

Remember that you are in charge of the station and that you are responsible for all transmissions from that station.

If you have concerns about the content of the traffic (for example, due to the use of offensive language, or possible commercial traffic), politely terminate the exchange, ask the other station to stand by, and explain the 'rules of the road' to the third party.

Log any informal traffic in your station log, noting time, participants, and a brief description of topic or content.

FORMAL MESSAGE HANDLING

Formal message handling can be done using voice, packet, or even CW or RTTY. Formal message handling involves a simple process at the sending and receiving stations to ensure accuracy, delivery, and tracking.

The sending station transcribes the message onto a radiogram form (or has the sender fill in the form themselves).

If you are sending the message across the NTS, use the standard RAC ARES radiogram form. (See "ARES forms and stationery" on page 33.1 for an example of an ARES message radiogram form.)

If you are sending the message locally, use the RAC ARES radiogram form unless the served agency has supplied its own customized message forms.

The sender keeps one copy of the radiogram for message processing and record keeping, and can give another copy of the form back to the sender if required. (At some locations, copying an be done using a photocopier; at other locations, carbon paper may be useful. Operators who do not have carbon paper or a photocopier could fill out a second copy of the form themselves, if required.)

The operator then transmits the message to another station for delivery. In most cases, the message will be transmitted to a station that is capable of directly delivering it to the recipient. In some cases (for example, where the NTS or a relay operator is needed), the message is sent to another station (or series of stations) that in turn transmit it to a station capable of delivering it.

If a message cannot be delivered, a second message is sent back to the originating station, notifying it that the message could not be delivered. Depending on the situation, the cause of the delivery failure, the precedence of the message, and the preference of

10-8

the sender, the originating station then either attempts retransmission, or abandons the attempt.

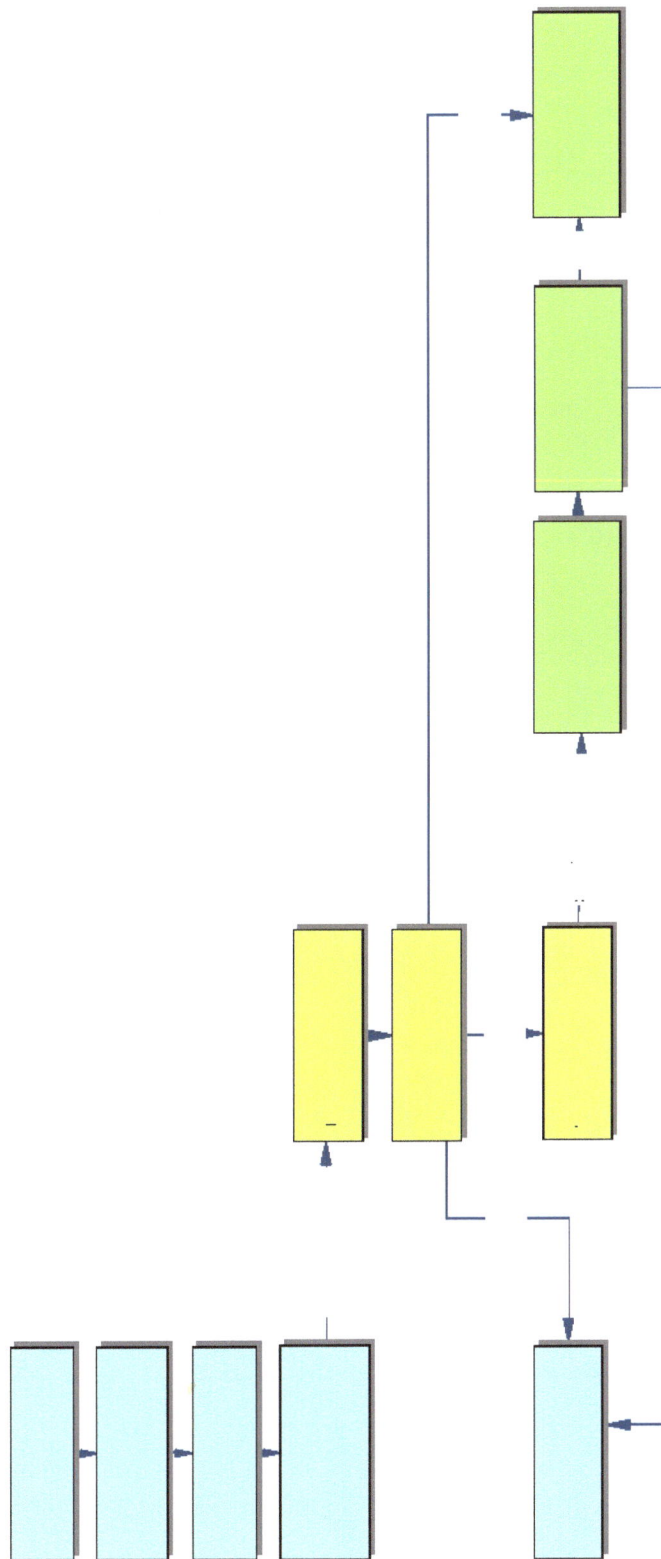

Elements in a formal message (radiogram)

A formal radio message contains the following information elements:

- Preamble

- Address

- Message body

- Signature

Preamble

The Preamble block contains all of the handling and routing information for the message, including the message's urgency.

- **Number**. The number is the originating station's counter for traffic. The number begins at one for the first message sent during an operation.

- **Precedence**. This is the urgency of the message. Emergency or immediate traffic is handled with the highest priority. Priority traffic is handled with maximum dispatch and care. Routine traffic is handled when there is no emergency, immediate or priority traffic waiting. Finally, welfare traffic is handled when there is no other traffic waiting. (EMO EMCG stations in the Maritimes do not use the Welfare precedence, and use Immediate instead of Emergency.)

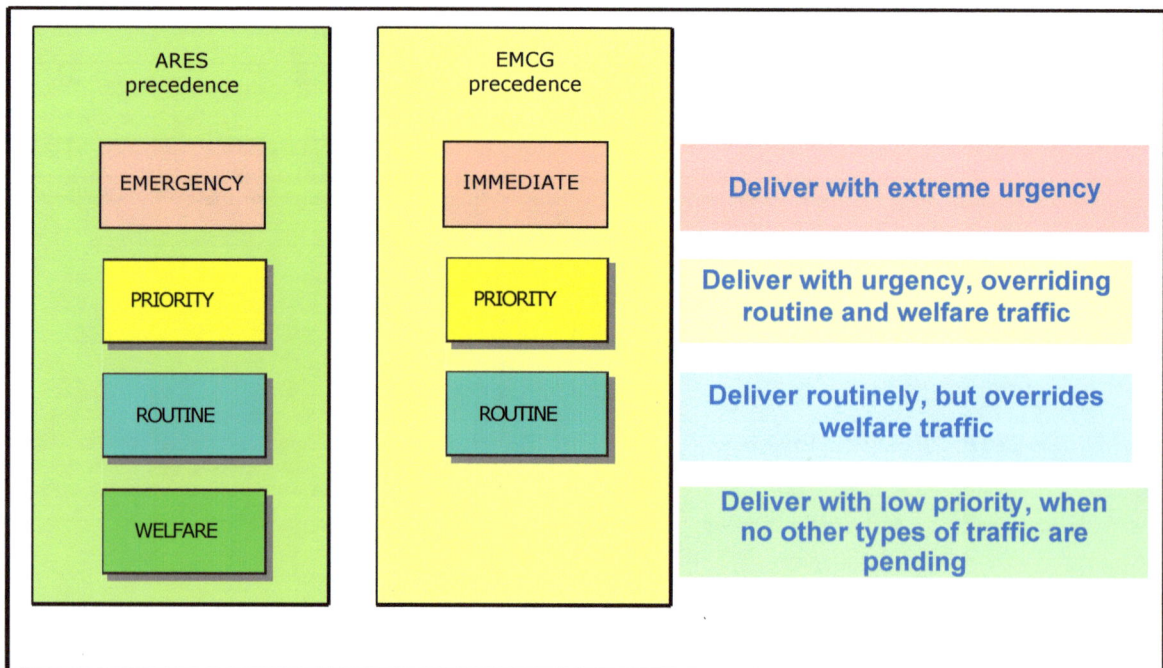

ARES precedence	EMCG precedence	
EMERGENCY	IMMEDIATE	**Deliver with extreme urgency**
PRIORITY	PRIORITY	**Deliver with urgency, overriding routine and welfare traffic**
ROUTINE	ROUTINE	**Deliver routinely, but overrides welfare traffic**
WELFARE		**Deliver with low priority, when no other types of traffic are pending**

10-10

- Precedence codes are:

  - E: Emergency (ARES only) - written out in full
  - O: Immediate (EMCG only)
  - P: Priority
  - R: Routine
  - W: Welfare (ARES only)

    EMCG messages can have dual precedence (if sent to more than one recipient). Each recipient can have an associated precedence.

- Handling instructions (HX). This may be optional, depending on the situation. This category provides a statement of what is to be done with the message when it arrives at the delivery point (for example, make a collect call to recipient, or discard if any problems are encountered).

- Station of origin. The call letters or tactical callsign of the originating station. This provides a path back to the originator in case of a problem or a request for confirmation.

- Check. A count of the total number of words making up the message. This ensures the message is intact, like a parity check in data. Count individual words, punctuation signs, and letter/number groups. Remember to perform the wordcount check very carefully. The loss of a single word could have a radical effect on the meaning of the message.

  Note: The total message should be limited to less than 25 words if possible. This helps reduce errors, and shortens the handling time at each transport point. In the case of a Disaster Welfare Message, there are seven preset messages that can be used.

  Note: Word counts are not used by some communications organizations with which ARES interacts, including EMCG.

- Place of origin. The location (City and Province, or tactical site) where the message originated. If a message originates at a site and given to the ARES station over the telephone, the *place of origin* is the site, not the station.

- Time filed. ARES only. An optional entry stating the time when the message was submitted to the originating station for transmission. (Use 24-hour military time format. Use either local time or UTC, as instructed by the emergency coordinator, communication supervisor or net controller at the beginning of operations.)

- Date-Time Group (DTG). EMCG only. A code representing the time and date when a message was originated. The format is DDHHMM MONTH YR (for example, 281430 AUG 05 representing 1430 hours, 28th August 2005).

- Date. The month and day when the message was submitted to the originating station for transmission.

10-11

Address

This must be as complete as possible. Include the postal code and the telephone number, or any other information needed by the receiving station to deliver the message to the recipient.

Message body

This is the content of the message itself. Keep this as short as possible, preferable under 25 words. The total message should be limited to less than 25 words if possible. This helps reduce errors, and shortens the handling time at each transport point. In the case of a Disaster Welfare Message, there are seven preset messages that can be used.

Signature

This identifies who sent the message.

Accepting messages for transmission

When you accept a formal message for transmission to another station, you must collect the following information from the sender:

- The exact title and address of the addressee. This is extremely important to guarantee the accurate, prompt delivery of the message.

- The exact title of the sender, so that if any return traffic is required, the addressee will know who should receive the message.

If you are handed a written message to send, do not modify it. Send the message as it is written by the sender. You do not need to understand the message content.

Record the date and time when the sender dictated or delivered the message to you.

If the originator has not already assigned a message number to the message, assign a message number yourself. The message number should be the number of the last message you assigned, plus one. As soon as you assign the number, record the number in the station message log.

Fill in the radiogram form, if it has not already been filled out. If the sender has not specified a priority, assign the message a ROUTINE precedence.

ARES INTERNAL TASKING (ORDERS) AND INFORMATION MESSAGES

In addition to passing messages for third parties (our served agencies), ARES operators will also send and receive messages to provide other ARES stations with important information, or to provide tasking (orders, instructions or rules of operation). This 'internal' ARES network traffic is not intended to go to any third party, but may be just as important as third-party traffic if it impacts ARES operator safety or the health of the ARES communications network.

10-12

Examples of **ARES internal tasking and information messages** might include:

- An instruction to shut down an ARES station, or move that station to a different location

- An instruction to impose radio silence for a period of time

- A notification that relief operators have been dispatched to a station

- A request for a station's operational status

- A bulletin providing an update of the overall emergency, intended to provide ARES operators with situational awareness.

ARES internal tasking and information messages may be formal or informal. Informal messages are suitable when the sender is certain that errors in reception of the message will not have a significant operational or safety impact, and no formal record of the message is required. Formal message handling is required when errors could have a significant impact, or when a formal record is required.

Format for tasking instructions (orders)

If you are a communications supervisor or emergency coordinator, you will issue 'orders' to ARES operators or stations to set up, maintain and manage the ARES communications network.

As an ARES operator or station manager, you will receive orders for you or your station.

When possible, these tasking messages should be delivered in person, rather than by radio. Do not interrupt during tasking. Wait until the instructions are complete before asking questions. .

The format for orders is broken in to several distinct units:

1 Situation
2 Mission
3 Execution
4   Coordinating instructions
5   Service and support
6   Command and communications
7 Safety
8   Time check (self explanatory)

Situation

A brief overview is given of the current situation and expected changes during the current operational period.

Mission

- An overview of what is to be a accomplished during the operational period

- Any attached agencies

- Agencies you will be attached to or working with

Execution

- Details of what is to be done

- By whom

- When

- How

- Why

Service and support

- Transportation

- Meals

- Special equipment required

- Availability of air support etc.

- Accommodations if required

- Location of medical services

Command and communications

- Who is in command

- Location of command or CP

- Chain of command

- Where and from whom command instructions will come from

- Where information, situation reports, etc. are to be passed

- Radio frequencies/channels, tactical callsigns

- Emergency procedures and frequencies

- Radio frequencies/channels, tactical callsigns of adjacent units/agencies/sectors

- Special signals, whistles, warnings, etc.

- Nicknames for reference points

- Code words or phrases for confidential messages if required

Coordinating instructions

- Information of who you will be working with

- Meet points, identification if required

- Entry and exit routes

- Timings

- Time and place of debriefing

- Boundaries and control points

- Priorities of work

Safety

- Must include daily safety briefing

- Emergency procedures and instructions

- Weather forecasts

- Possible hazards in area

- If a forest fire, forecasted fire behavior

- If air support is available, safety procedures

CROSS-BAND REPEATING

If you are using cross-band repeating, remember the following guidelines:

- Count 1001, 1002 before talking after pressing the PTT switch. The 1001 provides time for your radio to transmit and bring up the repeater. The 1002 provides time for the repeater to bring up the cross-band repeater.

- In bi-directional repeat, repeater tails will lock you out until the tail drops. (The cross band radio will not drop out until the repeater tail drops.)

- Other users can slip in before the tail drops, keeping the person using cross band from getting in.

10-15

- Amateur radios are not designed for heavy use. Configure your radio to minimize transmit power. Consider using a computer CPU fan to keep the CBR transceiver cool.

- Use CTCSS to keep out intermod or other users on the same frequency.

- Make sure your radio is capable of cross-band repeating, and that you know how to set it up.

WORKING WITH AND REPLACING OTHER OPERATORS

When you are replacing another operator at a site or station (or when you are being replaced), ensure that the handoff of responsibility goes smoothly by discussing:

- Basic procedure, policy, net, and stations

- How messages are routed, and local delivery procedures

- Who the location manager is, and where

- Any equipment concerns or issues

- General activities within the location

- Planned activities over the next shift or 24 hour period.

SECTION 11: ON-DUTY ETIQUETTE

This section provides some basic guidelines that should be followed during any ARES exercise or emergency.

Once you complete this section, you will be able to discuss the issue of on-duty etiquette.

WHEN YOU DEPLOY

It is likely that during emergencies and even some exercises you will find yourself dealing with officials or individuals who have not had experience with ARES, and do not understand who you are or why you are onsite. The fact that ARES is a volunteer organization puts you at a disadvantage when working around professional teams during an emergency. Volunteers are often perceived as a liability, and may be seen as unprofessional, untrained and unvalidated. This perception can lead to mis-use or nonuse of your services, suspicion of ARES operators who are trying to enter secured areas to reach their posts, and other counterproductive reactions on the part of officials and disaster recovery personnel.

You can take some steps as individuals to mitigate this effect (although you should also learn to expect and accept it). The following common sense do's and don'ts may help:

- Even during the most urgent callout, take five minutes and change into clothing that is appropriate to the situation (for example, business casual for an EOC, shadowing role or onsite post, or hiking boots and hunter orange for a search and rescue situation).

- Remember to check your ready pack or kit to ensure that you have what you'll need. It looks bad if you try to set up onsite and have to return home to get things you've forgotten.

- Remember to take any ID or 'ARES-wear' that has been provided to you, and to wear it when onsite.

- If you feel ill for any reason, inform the EC that you are unavailable for onsite duties. Unless there are no other operators available, it is best for anyone who is under the weather to operate from home, to minimize risks to others and to maximize their own comfort and effectiveness.

- This should be obvious, but **never** consume alcohol or any drugs that will impair your judgement or performance before reporting to duty. A good rule of thumb is that if you would not be allowed to drive, you are not ready to perform an ARES function.

- Don't speed when you drive to your duty station. Obey all traffic laws.

- If you have some sort of flashing tow light or similar gear for your vehicle, don't use it. (In many regions, use of these lights is illegal except under specific conditions.)

- Park legally, if possible.

11-1

- Be patient and professional at checkpoints, controlled entrances, or other barriers.

- Don't arrive at your duty station with a coffee in hand, unless the station has already been established and this is a routine shift change.

- Do not eat at your duty station unless there is no alternative.

- When eating at an emergency site, consider others around you. (For example, do not start eating MREs in front of evacuees who are being fed only coffee and energy bars.)

- Keep your workstation as tidy and clean as possible.

- If you are working with other operators or personnel at a station, keep your conversations discrete and be aware that serious, sometimes somber business is being conducted around you.

- Whenever served agency personnel approach you, be polite and helpful, even if the situation becomes exceptional. Do not get angry, emotional or confrontational.

- If you are getting tired, request relief. If it isn't available, try to take a break for five or ten minutes and go off-station. A short walk may help.

- If you need to sleep onsite, try not to do so at the duty station itself. Find a discrete corner, and let officials know where to find you if they need you.

- Do not operate emergency services scanners while onsite.

- Try to blend in as much as possible to the working environment in which you find yourself. Be part of the team, without intruding on the team.

ON AIR

When you are on the air during an ARES exercise or emergency:

- Maintain a professional demeanor at all times.

- Do not make personal observations or comments, unless specifically requested to do so by a net controller or other authority. (Your role is that of a radio operator, not an appraiser, assessor, surveyor or official.)

- Keep non-essential communications to an absolute minimum.

- Do not ragchew or chatter, even if you are on a secondary or ad-hoc channel.

- Remember that during an emergency, there are likely to be media and even private citizens monitoring your communications.

- Use lowest workable power levels.

- Listen before transmitting.

- Use tactical call signs when assigned.

11-2

- Use only formal (NATO/ITU) phonetics.

- Use frequency and location designators.

- Do not use Q-codes.

AT AN EOC

If you are on station at an EOC:

- Maintain a professional, serious demeanor.

- Do not move away from the communications station except when taking breaks or carrying traffic.

- If you need to change batteries, or if you must take a break and do not have a replacement operator at the site, contact the net controller and temporarily sign out of the net.

- Stay out of executive and operational areas of the EOC unless invited by officials.

- Keep noise levels to a minimum by turning down volumes or using headphones, and by minimizing any conversation that might disrupt neighbouring workstations or areas of the EOC.

- Keep the communications station as tidy as possible. File all forms and papers so that work areas are clear.

- Do not take photographs or video.

- Leave when your shift ends. (If you are waiting for transport and are no longer assisting at the station, wait outside the EOC if it is safe to do so.)

WHILE SHADOWING

If you are assigned to an official in a 'shadowing'

role: • Dress appropriately and professionally.

- Stay quiet. Do not participate in conversations or activities except those related to passing traffic to or from the shadow. (You are not the shadow's 'partner' or advisor; you are their telecommunications operator.)

- When passing extended traffic, try to be discrete so that you do not disrupt the shadow.

- Follow any instructions provided by the shadow.

- If you are carrying a cellphone, set the phone to private, vibrate or quiet mode so that its ringer is disabled.

11-3

- If possible, use a headset or earphone to prevent radio traffic from being overheard (unless the shadow has asked to hear the traffic).

- Monitor your assigned channel closely in order to maintain 'situational awareness'.

- Request radio checks only if you are in a fringe area or have reason to believe that you may no longer have coverage.

- Do not tune around or move off your assigned channel.

- Take advantage of your shadow's comfort breaks (rest, eating, toilet, and other breaks).

- Do not take photographs or video.

- If your shadow indicates that you are no longer needed, leave the shadow but check in with the on-duty EC or AEC before leaving the site.

- If you must leave to meet personal commitments, request a replacement by contacting the on-duty EC or AEC, and wait until the replacement takes over. Introduce the replacement to the shadow to ensure that the shadow understands that a shift change has occurred.

WHILE DEPLOYED

If you are deployed to a shelter, support station, search site, or other emergency location:

- Dress appropriately. (For example, for a search site, bring weather gear and hiking boots.)

- Bring and wear your ARES identification vest. You need to be easy to find. (See "Tactical and identification vests" on page 14.18.)

- Wear or carry your ARES Photo ID – and, if applicable, any locally issued ID – to identify you as a trained and authorized emergency communications operator.

- Keep yourself neat and tidy. You must look professional if you want to be taken seriously.

- Do not 'geek out'. Deploy the radio equipment you need, and keep the rest in a bag or out of the way. (Someone bristling with antennas and headsets might look great at a hamfest, but won't be taken seriously at an evacuee shelter.)

- Do not wander unnecessarily. Find a location that is near the site manager or command function, without being in the way.

- When you arrive onsite, introduce yourself to the site manager or command personnel so that they know you are available, and what your function will be. (Once you have introduced yourself, stay out of the way until you are needed.)

- Put up signage, if possible, identifying your function.

  Note: A large, bilingual RAC ARES banner is available from RAC for less than cost. (One has been supplied to every Section at no cost.)

- If you are not fully occupied with radio communications tasks, be willing to do tasks that are not radio-related. (For example, you may be asked to 'work the phones', use non-ARES radios, participate in a search, provide assistance to evacuees, serve soup, or wash a floor. Unless you are busy on the radio, do it.)

AROUND THE MEDIA

Do not make any statements to the media or the public about any emergency. The Public Information Officer (PIO) for the served agency is the only person authorized to make statements.

Ensure that you understand your group's operational guidelines regarding the media. Typically, you are allowed to provide the media and the public with information about amateur radio, if you have time and they ask, but be sure not to stray from that topic.

Never provide information about the use of modes, frequencies or traffic volumes.

Never provide information about damage, injuries or fatalities to the media or the public without explicit instructions from the primary served agency.

Media representatives can be persistent. If challenged, check with your served agency and consider using the following statement:

ARES is the Amateur Radio Emergency Services. These are volunteer Amateur Radio communicators who are aiding local law enforcement, fire, EMS and other agencies with auxiliary or supplemental communications due to the current overload or difficulties due to high volume of traffic or other unusual conditions. We currently have (XX #) operators in places like the EOC, communications centers, Red Cross shelters and other places where additional communications are required.

11-5

SECTION 12: PARTICIPATING IN A NET

This section provides guidelines and information that will be useful when you are asked to serve as a net controller.

Once you complete this section, you will be able to:

- Describe the types of nets used in ARES operations

- Describe the requirements associated with the role of net controller

- Use best practices for net control

- Participate in NTS traffic nets

- Understand the requirements and practices associated with CW nets.

TYPES OF NET

Types of net control

Directed nets

A directed net is a formal net with a net controller, who directs all communications on the net. Stations request permission from net control before calling other stations or passing traffic.

A directed net is used when there is a large volume of traffic that cannot be dealt with on a first-come first-served basis. The net controller determines who will use the frequency at a given time. Random conversations between stations are not permitted. The net controller will assign tactical call signs to facilitate traffic handling. Stations having traffic not suitable for the net are diverted to alternate nets.

Open nets

An open net is a net that allows informal communications, with or without a net controller. If there is a net controller, the controller acts to provide coordination, record keeping, and other support. On an open net, stations do not need to get net control permission before calling or passing traffic.

A typical open net permits any kind of traffic or communications. Open conversations are allowed on the net provided they break every so often to allow incident-related traffic to pass. Stations are not required to contact the net controller before making a call to other stations, and incident-related traffic may be handled on a point-to-point basis.

12-1

Purpose or audience specific nets

Operational net

This is a directed net that carries the bulk of the traffic for the client agencies. The operational net is typically the first net established during an emergency, and remains the *primary net* throughout the operation.

Task-specific tactical nets

If a need exists for subnets dedicated to specific client groups or tasks, new net frequencies will be selected and specific operators will be moved to the new frequencies. A task-specific tactical net may be an open net or a directed net.

Examples of task-specific nets include the following:

- a command net, to provide communications among 'executives' at municipalities, aid agencies, and other stakeholder organizations

- a Red Cross net, to interconnect Canadian Red Cross aid stations and Red Cross headquarters

- a transport net, to allow coordination of transportation assets

Standby (availability) net

This is a directed net that is a point of first check-in for operators who are announcing availability to participate. Operators are kept on this net until deployed to a location or role and moved to the operational net.

This net is also a holding area used for non-ARES trained stations who wish to participate during the emergency. The net controller of the availability net issues regular bulletins regarding the status of the emergency, and broadcasts information about ARES procedures in preparation for including non-ARES trained operators in ARES activities. The net controller maintains a rollcall of available stations so that needs for operators can be met when they arise.

Formal traffic net

This is a directed net that is used to carry formal message traffic.

Support net

This is an open net used to provide technical and procedural support to operators, and ARES resource coordination (for example, finding spare handhelds). The purpose of the support net is to keep ARES 'maintenance' traffic off the operational net.

12-2

DUTIES OF A NET CONTROLLER

The basic duties of a net controller are:

- Taking charge of the net while the net is in session. You are responsible for controlling who uses the frequency. This needs to be balanced with the fact that you are managing a group of volunteers. You need to determine whether tight net discipline is required for the incident.

- Keeping track of which resources are on the net and who has cleared the channel. You are also responsible for knowing what types of traffic each resource is capable of handling.

- Ensuring that there is a backup net controller, in case you are indisposed or experience an equipment or propagation failure. (For some nets in some situations, this may not be required.)

- Keeping a written record of net activity, stations and

traffic. WHAT YOU NEED

To serve as a net controller, you should try to fulfill the following prerequisites:

- Speak with an air of authority, without sarcastic overtones or being overbearing.

- Develop a sense of control and self-assuredness.

- Be decisive and mature.

- Develop a knowledge of band characteristics.

- Develop a knowledge of common equipment.

- Develop good basic communications skills and a fluent command of the language.

- Know ICS.

- Maintain a physical condition that will allow you to tolerate high stress for extended periods of time.

- Be a strong team player and organizer.

- Maintain good ear-to-hand copying skills.

- Maintain decent (readable) penmanship.

- Develop computer keyboard skills - touch typing.

- Be willing to take and carry out direct orders.

- Consistently demonstrate above average operating technique.

- Have a general understanding of all MOUs with served agencies.

12-3

When you serve as a net controller, you need the following items and resources:

- Good coverage of the area served by the net (for a net on a repeater, a solid signal into the repeater)

- Good received audio (preferably a headset)

- Good transmitted audio

- Backup transceiver (to use to call for help on alternate channels when required, or as a backup in case of equipment failure)

- A comfortable way of writing down notes and traffic (for example, a notepad, a typewriter, or a laptop)

- If available, a tape recorder and tapes

- If available, a second operator onsite to keep notes and transcribe traffic, handle phone calls, and spell you during breaks

NET CONTROL BEST PRACTICES

- Speak slowly in a calm voice at all times.

- Pause before transmitting to allow break-ins.

- Periodically announce the designation and purpose of the net to ensure that new check-ins and monitoring stations understand that purpose.

- Keep a written record of net activity, and a list of traffic for each station. If you don't use an organized recording system you will get confused as the traffic gets heavier.

- Discourage idle chatter courteously, until all traffic is cleared. Do not however, make the net cold, stiff, and formal except at times of high traffic density, or during real or simulated emergencies.

- Remember that other people will have to read your notes. Write clearly and in clear text (no special symbols or short forms).

- Make instructions clear and precise. Use as few words as possible. Use clear text.

- Send traffic as fast as you would write it down. Tactfully remind other stations to do the same when necessary. Break every five words or so to allow stations time to catch up. Request that stations ask for fills at the end of each paragraph.

- Use tactical callsigns and enforce this rule with other members on the net. Tactical call signs are legal as long as periodic ID requirements are met.

12-4

- If a station's traffic is not appropriate for your net (for example, safety traffic on a support net), direct the station to the appropriate net, or to the primary net.

- When receiving multiple checkins or breakers, acknowledge all the stations that you heard. Then yield the channel to a single station, (usually the first one you heard, unless there is prioritized traffic). When the first station has passed their traffic, call in the next station on your list.

- Do not solicit new traffic until your current traffic list has been completed.

- Minimize contacts to their bare essentials. Try to operate without wasting any motions.

- Remain cool, calm, and collected. Never allow yourself to become frustrated or angry.

OPENING A NET

When opening a net:

- Politely break in to communications currently on the repeater or frequency, explain the situation and the need to open a net, and request use of the repeater or frequency.

- Once you have control of the repeater or frequency, introduce yourself, with your callsign, as net controller.

- Clearly identify the net designation (for example, ARES logistics net) and explain the net's purpose.

- State that the repeater or frequency will be used solely for net operations for a period of time.

- Briefly review 'rules of the road' for net operations.

- Call in any stations that you know are waiting to check in (such as stations that you know have been assigned to the net).

- Solicit other check-ins.

To open a net, use the following prompts:

1   Introduce the net.

    For example: *Good evening, this is VE9ZYX Net Control for this evening. My name is Don and I am located in Fredericton. This is a National Traffic System Net operating daily at 19:00 hours local time on or about a frequency of 3.742 MHZ. This is a directed net specializing in formal traffic using the standard NTS format complete with full address and telephone number. A postal or ZIP code is often helpful. Traffic should be limited to 25 words if possible, and use of ARL numbered text is encouraged. All stations checking in to the net are asked to stay on*

12-5

frequency for the duration of the net unless excused by the net controller. If you must leave the net please inform the net controller before so doing. All stations are invited to take part in the activities of this net.

2   Call for any station with emergency, priority or welfare traffic.

> *Note: Note, this traffic must have absolute priority over all other net business. It must be moved as soon as a station is available to deal with it.*

3   Ask if there is an ECN (Region) representative on frequency.

4   Ask if there any stations wishing to list ECN (out of province traffic) on frequency.

5   Ask any net liaison stations to check in, call signs only.

6   Ask for any stations with formal traffic to check in, call signs only.

7   Ask for stations with or without traffic to check in.

MANAGING CHECK-INS

Activation check-ins

Initially, accept check-ins on the primary net frequency. Once the primary net becomes an operational net, and a standby net is established, make periodic announcements directing newly activated stations to wait on the standby net until directed to return to the operational net.

Check-ins by non-ARES operators

Divert any non-ARES stations that wish to assist to the standby net. By 'parking' non-ARES stations on a secondary channel, you keep the operational net free for traffic.

NATIONAL TRAFFIC SYSTEM NETS

Traffic routing

Local traffic is routed to a section net, then to a region net, then to an area net, and finally to TCC. It then returns to another area net, then to a region net, then to a section net, then to a local net.

For example, a message destined for Vancouver is listed on the Ontario Phone Net. It will be picked up by the region net (ECN), sent to the area net (EAN), taken across Canada by the Trans-Continental Corps, taken down to the Pacific Area Net, to RN7, and finally to a B.C. section net for delivery.

With good band conditions, and reasonable access to the addressee, you could have an answer the next day. Complete cycles occur twice each day, 365 days per year. In the case of very high volume or emergency periods, four complete traffic cycles are already designated by the NTS.

12-6

Assigned net representatives (net liaison stations)

A local net may ask for a representative to go to another net such as a section net or to a higher net. For example, the OQN (CW) NCS, may ask one of its stations to be liaison to the OPN. Net control will also ask for liaison stations to go to other nets either locally or to higher level nets. The NCS on the section phone net may ask for a representative to go to region net (in this case ECN).

It is also customary for NCS to call for net liaison stations from other nets. Remember that you are only net liaison from another net if the other net NCS or the Net Manager has assigned you that task. Furthermore, if you appear as assigned liaison to a net the NCS expects you to remain on the net until you are excused.

Freelance traffic

The handling of out-of-section traffic not routed through NTS is discouraged on an NTS net. The NTS does not object to stations handling out-of-section traffic, since this is often both convenient and a courtesy to the originating station. However, such traffic should be directed to appropriate informal nets.

If there is time, and the amateur listing the traffic is not familiar with NTS regulations, the traffic could be handled; however, the listing station should be politely told that a formal NTS net must route traffic via the normal pathway. Failure to maintain this standard on a regular basis would soon cause the traffic handling system to break down. Amateurs who feel otherwise may wish to route all their traffic through independent nets.

Digital NTS is now a fully integrated part of the North American NTS. Although digital NTS does not rely on traditional NTS's four cycles, it is very efficient in moving traffic and operates 24 hours a day, 7 days a week (including "unattended" operation in assigned spectrum areas to move messages automatically).

Running an NTS voice net

When running an NTS traffic net, remember the following best practices:

- Clear regional traffic as quickly as possible, allowing your representative to move to the region net.

- Clear any stations for which there is no traffic early in the net.

- Always call the receiving station first.

- Remember to call for stations with or without traffic at regular intervals. A station from an area you need to access may be listening.

- Pass traffic on the net frequency, when practical. (This is different from the practice of moving off-net to pass traffic on CW nets.)

12-7

Counting and reporting net traffic

The traffic handled by each traffic net is reported to the Section Traffic Manager (STM) monthly by the Net Manager. These reports are normally sent to the STM in the form of a formal message.

The number of net sessions, the number of check ins for the month, and the monthly total number of pieces of traffic handled by each Canadian Net are reported each month in Field Organization Reports.

Net Control Station report

A sample NCS report is shown below:

```
SAMPLE NCS REPORT
NR 30 R VE3MNI 19 VERONA ON DEC 25

DAN VE9ZYY
BREAK

(COUNT)        (1) (2)          (3)        (4)       (5)
  (5)        OPN| 240000Z| VE3MPX  |   X       |CHECK |
 (10)        INS| 25     |   TFC   | 14/12     | TIME
 (15)         22| MINS |VE9ZYY/LN| BBB/GBN | GT   |
 (19)        TO| ECN    |   X     |  73       |

                      BREAK
                   DON VE9ZYX
              END OF MESSAGE NO MORE
```

The report is laid out with the bracketed numbers to assist with the word count. It is much easier to word check if groupings are set out in five items to the line.

Interpretting the NCS report. TFC 14/12 means that 14 pieces were listed, but only 12 were handled, VE9ZYY/LN means that VE9ZYY was liaison from LN, 240000Z, means that the net was held on the 24th day of the month at 0000Z or if you prefer U.T.C. (or in really old terms, Greenwich Mean Time), time 22 mins, means that the net lasted 22 minutes, and the VE3MPX following 240000Z, means that VE3MPX was net control. Note that a count of 11/17 could equally well appear, meaning that although only 11 pieces of traffic came into the net, after relays etc., 17 messages actually went out of the net. Thus, some messages had to be relayed and so were handled more than once.

Participating in an NTS net

Any licensed amateur can participate in the NTS. Listen to NTS nets to familiarize yourself with the practices and culture of NTS traffic handling and net operations.

Prior to participating in an NTS net, obtain the "pink card", *Operating Aid FSD-218*.

Checking in

When checking in to an NTS traffic net, remember the following best practices:

- Listen to, and comply with, all instructions of NCS.

- If you are waiting to check in to the net and have no traffic (even if you have identified traffic that you are able to clear), delay your check-in until the stations with listed traffic are recognized.

- When the appropriate time arrives, send your call sign only. Net control normally acquires a list of check ins, then calls in each station individually.

- Do not say "break" when checking in.

- When you are called in, speak clearly and slowly, remembering that NCS is making notes with reference to your transmission.

- Always list your call and location when checking in and list your traffic at that time or if you have no traffic say "This is VE3MPX, Kitchener, no traffic", or if you have traffic say "VE3MPX Kitchener, I have 2 ECN, and 1 Ottawa".

- Be very careful to "zero beat" the NCS. The NCS cannot move. The NCS is always on the "right frequency". Ensure that your RIT is turned OFF.

- List out of province traffic by routing (for example, 1-ECN), and not by destination. ECN listed traffic is understood to be going out of section and will be routed by the Region representative.

- Stay on frequency until you are excused.

Listing traffic

Traffic for out of province/territory is listed for the Region Net. (for example, *I have 1 ECN*). Traffic for within the section is listed by town or city (for example, *I have one Owen Sound*). If you are listing other than routine traffic, state the priority when listing (for example, *I have one priority Toronto*).

Listings with a priority above routine will always be cleared first.

Transmitting a message

When sending a message:

- Speak slowly and clearly. Remember the receiving station has to write down everything you say.

- If you are transmitting VOX, there is no need for fills at the end of the message.

- If you are using PTT, lift your thumb off the button at regular intervals and give the receiving station a chance to break for fills.

- End the message with "End of message, no more", or "end of message, one to go".

12-9

-

- Use international phonetics when requested by the receiving station. Do not use phonetics unless the receiving stations requests you to so do.

- Spell unusual words. If they are very difficult, spell them twice.

- Before you spell a word, say *I spell* (for example, *I spell "dirkwartz" D I R K W A R T Z*).

- If you are going to repeat a word, say *I say again.*

- If you are going to spell a word again, say *I spell again*

- Indicate a group of numbers by saying *number group.* ....

- Indicate a letter-number group by saying *number* (or if you prefer *figure*) *letter group*. If the letters precede the numbers, it is common practice to say *letter number group.*

Copying a message When

copying a message:

- Start writing after the transmitting station says *Number.*

- Write down everything sent, accurately and legibly.

- If you have missed a part of the message, don't panic. Just leave a bit of extra space, and when the transmitting station pauses, ask for fills. For example, "word after birthday", or "all between Mike and red", or "in preamble, all before Brantford".

- If you are unsure about a word or number say *confirm* (for example, *confirm 'bar bells'*). You will be answered with *confirmed*, or if incorrect, with the corrected text.

- Never guess at the message contents; our job is to be 100% correct.

- Be sure to check the word count in the preamble, and do not acknowledge receipt of the message until you agree with the check, or the transmitting station agrees that the check should be changed.

- Some stations will be asked to clear traffic off the net frequency. The NCS will suggest a possible frequency to pass the traffic. The receiving station is responsible to find the frequency nearest to the suggested frequency where the station can reasonably hear, and then the receiving station calls the transmitting station and receives the message. They should clear their traffic as quickly as possible, then return to net frequency and let NCS know they are back by simply sending their call signs. Remember, when off net frequency, to exchange call signs as in normal non-net operations.

- When you have cleared or received your traffic, simply stop transmitting.

- Do not use QSL or other Q signals on voice nets.

12-10

Table 2:   Example code table for challenge-response station authenti

At the end of each month, before the fourth or fifth day of the month, all traffic handlers should file a station activity report with the STM. Most messages handled count only as a single point, but there are some exceptions as you will note in what follows. Credit is given for each of the following classes: ORIGINATED, RECEIVED, SENT, and DELIVERED. Some messages will count for two points each. Some examples are as follows. When you ORIGINATE a message for some one else, count one point; when you actually send the same message, count a second point. Other messages counting for two points are: RECEIVED.... SENT, or RECEIVED ...DELIVERED. Any message bearing your own signature can only count for ONE point, and is counted in the SENT category only. This message demonstrates only the text of the message. Remember you need a preamble and address.

```
SAR VE3MPX JANUARY X ORIGINATED

1 RECEIVED 10 SENT 10

DELIVERED 2 TOTAL 23 X

73

BREAK
```

Some amateurs tend to report only *big number months*, but you are strongly encouraged to report every month, even if you handle no traffic. That way the STM can identify available resources. In a time of emergency, this can be very helpful.

Sending a service message

It is proper practice and common courtesy to send a service message back to the originating station if a message can not be delivered within 48 hours of receipt of a message at destination.

> *Note: Sometimes a message is received garbled, and a service message will need to be sent for this reason. It is the responsibility of the station receiving the message for delivery to originate this message, not the responsibility of the station from which the message is received.*

Proper service message format requires the use of the full name, address and telephone number of the originating station. (This is easier if you have online access to a callsign database.)

Use ARL standard text – ARL SIXTY SEVEN: *Your message number blank undeliverable because of blank. Please advise.* The second blank (after *because of*) might consist of one of the following: "*No phone number given, no number listed*", "*No record of blank in this area*", "*Addressee has moved, location unknown*", "*need more complete address*", etc.

Make every reasonable effort to deliver the original message without resorting to a service message.

A service message uses the following format:

```
NR 73 R VE3MPX ARL 14 BROCKVILLE ON 2300Z JAN 8
DAVE VE9FK
LEPREAU NB
BREAK

ARL SIXTY SEVEN 34 NO
TELEPHONE NUMBER GIVEN X TELEPHONE
NUMBER UNLISTED X
73
BREAK
GEORGE VE3MPX
```

> *Note: It is not necessary to list message precedence after ARL SIXTY SEVEN since it is implied in the ARL text. A precedence other than Routine should be entered. SVC does not appear in any league traffic handling publication, the content of the message makes it obvious that it is a service message, and the use of abbreviations in amateur to amateur communications – although not formally recognized in published NTS literature – is generally accepted by operating practice standards.*

NET CONTROL OF A SUPPORT NET

Unlike standby and operational nets, a support net normally does not require full-time net control. If you are assigned to control a support net, consider the following guidelines:

- Monitor the net and be ready to step in to provide coordination when it is required.

- Make a periodic announcement (perhaps every 15 minutes) on the net. The announcement should state that a net is taking place, and explain the purpose of the net. You may also consider listing key stations that are permanently on net. Keep the announcement brief so that you do not distract monitoring operators from other tasks.

NET CONTROL OF CW TRAFFIC NETS

In the unlikely event that you are required to run a CW traffic net (for example, in situations where propagation is too poor for voice communications, and digital modes are not available), use the following guidelines:

Calling a net
Remember that the NCS is always on the right frequency. Zero beat the NCS carefully. If you are not on the correct frequency you may not even be heard.

12-12

Net call-up or preamble

The call up varies slightly from net to net. It tends to be abbreviated on the higher level nets.

This sample is sent in the generally accepted form:

KA OSN OSN OSN ONTARIO SECTION TRAFFIC TRAINING NET DE VE3MPX QND PSE QNZ OSTTN QTC? QNI K.

> *Note: KA stands for "beginning of work".*

In the example above, the NCS identified the net by its short form OSTTN, then announced the net's full name. QND indicates that the net is directed, which means that you will only transmit when invited to so do.

PSE is the abbreviation for *please.*

QNZ means you must zero beat your frequency with the

NCS. The net short identification is sent again.

QTC? calls for stations with traffic only. Do not check in until stations with traffic have been acknowledged.

QNI is an invitation to check in to the net (though the first set of QNI right after the preamble should be limited to stations with traffic).

Checking in QNI

Stations with traffic are asked to QNI first. After this process is complete, the NCS will resend the short form of the net name, send the NCS's own call sign, and send QNI.

The preamble is now complete and stations with traffic have checked in and listed their traffic. NCS would now call OSN DE VE3MPX QNI K. At this point send a single letter – usually one from your call (for example "B"). NCS will reply B. Now send your own call followed by QNI QRU K or QNI QTC and list your traffic. NCS would reply GE GEORGE R AS. This simply means *Good Evening George I copy you stand by.*

Do not use BK when checking in. Some stations choose to use the two or three letters of their call suffix on initial check in. This is proper but not necessary.

A sample check-in follows:

----OSN DE VE9FK QNI K ----B (Sent by QNI)

B (Sent by NCS)

VE3MPX GE QNI QRU (Sent by station checking in).

> *Note: "QNI" means I am checking in to the net and QRU means "Do you have any traffic for me?"... whereas QRU from NCS with nothing following it means "I have no traffic for you.")*

12-13

VE3MPX GE R AS (Sent by NCS and means *good evening Larry, I acknowledge you, please stand by*).

The net will proceed in this manner until NCS clears all traffic or determines that some can not be cleared. As soon as NCS is reasonably sure there is no traffic for your area or that you can relay to another net he or she will send VE3MPX GE TU QNI 73 QRU QNX. (QRU means *I have nothing for you...* QNX means *you are excused from the net.*)

Reply with TU GE DE VE3MPX. Many really expert traffic handlers will just reply GE Dit Dit or just send a single "Dit".

If it is evident to NCS that the net will be short he or she may not QNX individual stations but rather may close the net after 4 or 5 minutes with no QNI or QTC. Closing the net is done as follows: OSN QRU QNF TU QNI 73 DE VE9FK GE. (QNF means the net is free, no longer controlled.)

Listing traffic on a section or local net

Once NCS has called for stations *QTC,* QNI. If you wish to list traffic send the brief letter group you have chosen to use to access the net. (It is good practice to always use the same group because it often helps the NCS to know who is calling). Then list your traffic.

For example, the NCS sends:

OSN DE VE3FGU QTC? QNI K

You then send B.

NCS replies B.

You reply VE3GOL QNI QTC WINDSOR 1 AR. This means VE3GOL checking in I have one for Windsor. The AR after Windsor indicates that is all you wish to list.

Assume now that you wish to list several pieces of traffic. You might want to list Toronto 1 EMERGENCY Ottawa 1 P ECN 2 Brockville 1 AR. They should be listed in order of precedence. EMERGENCY is always listed first and should be cleared immediately. P and W traffic are listed next and they too will be handled as quickly as possible. Out-of-province traffic for the Region Net is listed next and will be cleared before in-province routine traffic. Traffic listed without a precedence is assumed to be routine and will be dealt with last.

Transmitting the message

The NCS will usually send stations off net frequency to clear messages. If the NCS wishes to clear traffic on frequency he or she will call VE3AAA VE3BBB QNK Kingston 1 HR K. A more normal procedure is for the NCS to send VE3AAA VE3BBB QNY UP 5 Toronto 1 K.

Reply G or GG for Gone or Going. Many experienced stations send only a single "dit" to acknowledge NCS.

12-14

Note that the first call sent will be that of the receiving station. Both stations then move up 5 kHz to the nearest clear spot for the receiving station. The receiving station selects the frequency – since he or she has to find a clear spot where the receiving station can hear the message – and calls the transmitting station.

Be careful not to move too close to the net frequency and QRM net. Send your call two or three times followed by the sending stations call and stand by. Wait for a few seconds and if nothing is heard repeat the call – for example "VE3BBB VE3BBB VE3BBB DE VE3AAA VE3AAA VE3AAA K". VE3BBB should reply VE3AAA DE VE3BBB GE ED QRV? *meaning good evening Ed Are you ready to copy?*

The receiving station now sends GE SAM QRV meaning *good evening Sam I am now ready to copy the message.*

The sending station should carefully zero beat the receiving station. After the message has been sent the receiving station will send QSL NR X.

If fills are needed, it is common practice to send DIT DIT SPACE SPACE DIT DIT. The receiving station then indicates what is lacking (as in "WB hammer" meaning *Word Before hammer* or "AA tent" meaning *All After tent* or "AB cat" meaning *All Before cat and dog etc.*

The transmitting station reviews the message and retransmits the word before the requested fill followed by the fill.

Check back

Assuming that you have QNYed to receive or clear traffic, it is very important to check back into the net as soon as you have finished. This is done by moving back to net frequency X carefully zero beating NCS and waiting for an opening. NCS will send "OSN QNI K", then you will send the suffix of your call. NCS will reply *callsign* R AS. This means *I acknowledge that you have returned to the net please stand by.* If the NCS is certain that your presence will no longer be required when you are sent off frequency, he or she will probably send you both off frequency: *callsign callsign* QNY UP 5 TORONTO 2 BOTH QRU QNX TU GE K.

This means VE3BBB and VE3AAA move up 5 kHz VE3BBB to receive 5 pieces of traffic for Toronto.

QRU means *I have nothing further for you. You are both excused from the net.*

In this situation, there is no need to check back in to the net.

Traffic routing

Messages move through a carefully structured system. Traffic areas are divided as follows, local net to section net to region net to area net to TCC to area net to region net to section net to local net.

In Ontario the setting is this local net; that is, OLN to section net OSN or OPN to ECN to EAN to TCC etc. This assumes that the traffic is moving across North America. Traffic for the Caribbean and Australia is moved through Earl WX4J in Florida for relay through NTS-D, although it can be relayed through ECN.

12-15

The majority of NTS digital traffic is moved on Pactor-I and Pactor-II.

QNK, QNV and QNQ

QNK means *Transmit messages for "Amateur Call" to "Amateur Call"*.

QNK means that the message is to be transmitted on net frequency. Except in the case of QNK, the NCS usually calls the receiving station first.

QNV means establish contact with *callsign* on this frequency and if successful move to new frequency and send traffic for "wherever". The purpose of QNV is to ensure that, under poor band conditions, two stations are going to be able to pass traffic without a relay station. If the receiving station sends QNP then NCS should find a station who copies both to act as relay between them. NCS should call a station he feels can copy both stations and ask him if he QNJ's one and then the other.

For example, VE5AAA calls QNP VE5BBB after an attempted QNY and he returns to the net frequency. The NCS should try to find a station midway between the two stations that might QSP. The NCS then sends the following exchange. "VE5DDD QNJ VE5AAA K". VE3DDD answers "C" if he is able. NCS now asks "VE5DDD QNJ VE5BBB K". VE3DDD replies "C". NCS now sends "VE5BBB VE5AAA QNY D 5 VE5BBB 1 K".

> *Note:* QNJ means *Can you copy me* and QNP means *I am unable to copy you.*

QNQ means Move frequency to "blank" (NCS will suggest a frequency) and wait for *callsign* to finish handling traffic then send him traffic for "blank" the destination you have a piece of traffic for). Assume that VE3BBB is up 5 receiving traffic for ECN from VE3AAA. VE3CCC now lists traffic for ECN as well. NCS will send VE3CCC QNQ UP 5 VE3BBB ECN 1 K. This means VE3CCC move up 5 kHz and wait for VE3BBB to finish receiving traffic from VE3AAA.

When VE3AAA has finished sending and VE3BBB QSLs send VE3BBB DE VE3CCC K. VE3BBB will reply to your call VE3CCC DE VE3BBB K. Now send QRV ECN 1?

VE3BBB will answer QRV and you may then send your ECN traffic.

Remember that QNQ does not QNX you, so when your traffic is clear, check back into the net. When you arrive back on net frequency wait for NCS to invite QNI then send your call suffix. NCS will reply with your suffix and send AS asking you to stand by or if there is no more traffic for you will QNX.

An example re-check to net follows. You hear OSN DE VE3MPX QNI K and send BDM (Your call has the BDM suffix). NCS will answer BDM R AS meaning VE3BDM I acknowledge you have reQNIed please stand by, or may send VE3BDM GE GEORGE QRU QNX 73 at which time you are free to leave the net. Acknowledge with GE or Dit Dit.

Out of province traffic

Out of province traffic listed on a Section Net is listed for the Region Net. In the case of Ontario the region net is ECN. Assume a piece of traffic is listed on OSN destined for BC. It is listed as follows "QTC ECN 1 K". Do not list the traffic as BC 1 etc. It would be taken to ECN where it would be listed as EAN traffic since this is the correct routing for BC. The message will in fact go to EAN via a station designated as EAN TX by ECN NCS or by EAN NM. Some times the EAN station will go from ECN as EAN TX/ RX meaning that he is there to both transmit and receive traffic.

It is common to find that the region net NCS will also go to the area net. For example the ECN NCS usually is the EAN TX/RX station. The AREA net rep will often receive and send messages for all three North American Areas. The EAN meets at 2030 local time and a station assigned by the director of TCC will be on EAN to receive traffic for PAN and he will QNI as PAN RX. He will meet with a west coast TCC station at a predetermined frequency and time. The west coast TCC station will appear on PAN as TCC TX and relay the message to a PAN RX liaison station. The message will then move to region net to section net and finally to destination. On rare occasions a TCC (Trans Continental Corps) rep will appear to list traffic on lower level nets. These operators are very hard working and traffic listed by them must have priority over all but EMERGENCY or Priority traffic. QNX a TCC rep as quickly as possible. Traffic for adjacent area nets should not be handled at Area net level. If you are assigned liaison to ECN from the section net receive the traffic then group it together by destination for listing on region net. For example you receive messages for BC AB NB and ME 2. They would be listed on ECN as follows VE9FK QNI OSN TX/RX QTC APN 1 EAN 4 AR. APN traffic is the only piece that will stay in the coverage area of ECN and thus does not have to go to a higher level net. NCS of ECN will check in VE9FK as OSN rep and have him QNY or QNQ to the frequency where EAN rep is taking traffic. Note that NCS on a region net must always be sure that the Area Net rep is able to get to the Area Net on time. Do however clear stations with high traffic counts QNY etc. ASAP so these busy traffic handlers are not sitting there twiddling their thumbs. VE9FK would then be asked to QNY to receive any traffic coming down to the Ontario Quebec Net. When ZZZ QNIs the next OSN he will QNI as ECN/RX.

Going to the area net

If you are competent at the Region Net level and can operate at 25 wpm, you can participate in the Area Net. The request to go to the Area Net MUST come from the NCS or the region net manager. In Ontario, the Area Net is EAN. On EAN you should find six region nets represented by TX and RX stations. Several TCC reps will also be present to receive and bring down traffic from other Area Nets. TCC stations will accept traffic for relay to CAN and PAN. Alternate TX/RX stations may QNI from all of the above.

If EAN NCS uses QNA, check in in prearranged order, you will have to wait for his call. In Ontario you would wait for NCS to send ECN, then send VE3MPX ECN TX QNI 1RN 1 3RN 3 4RN 1 PAN 2 AR assuming you are listing traffic for those areas. NCS will send VE3MPX R AS. Stand by for QNQ QNK QNV and QNY instructions. Be alert and try to keep your own list of other QNI and their traffic. Such a list will alert you that traffic is about for your Region and you will be prepared to QNY to pick it up.

Circle the call signs of stations with REGION traffic. Regions appearing on EAN are 1RN 2RN 3RN 4RN 8RN ECN ARN CAN and PAN. When listing traffic do so in the above order only.

Remember that most traffic moves across North America CW through these Nets. Remember to indicate precedences since if no precedence is listed traffic is considered

12-17

to be Routine. A sample QNI to a REGION Net follows: "VE2EDO QNI ECN TX QTC 1RN 1 3RN 3 4RN 4 PAN 1 EMERGENCY 1P 2R AR N".

Traffic for Western Canada will go CAN or PAN.

Look at the National Traffic System Routing Guide in the PSC Manual. Make a copy of this table and keep it near your operating position for reference at region or area net operating level.

Note that international traffic should be routed via EAN for Earl WX4J in Florida for relay through NTS-D. It would be best to make your own traffic routing table.

Make headings for Regions 1, 2, 3, 4, 8, ECN ARN CAN and PAN. Under each heading write the provinces/states/territories covered.

Remember that although all stations at this level are capable of higher speed operation, 100% copy is still the rule. Do not bluff your way through a message and QSL when you are not certain. QRS is a useful tool and a good TX station will send at the speed of the RX station and will slow down when the band is poor.

NCS records and methods

There are probably as many ways of recording and running nets as there are NCS stations. If you have adopted a method that works for you do not change. A commonly used method is to mark off 4 liberal columns on an 8 1/2 by 11 sheet. The four columns are marked as follows Column 1 QNI, Column 2 liaison, Column 3 QTC and column 4 QNY. The first couple of lines might read as follows. (This sheet could represent one used by an NCS on OSN) Only the first two lines are shown:

```
VE2EDO  | ECN TX | ECN 1 BRAMPTON 1R THOROLD 1P | UP 5

VE3MPX      | EAN RX| TORONTO 2 EMERGENCY TRENT 1 | D 5
```

It is important to know at all times who is on board and to where stations are QNYed. In this case as the net has progressed NCS has sent VE2EDO up 5 to receive ECN 1. A Toronto QNI has arrived so VE3MPX is QNY down 5 to pass the Toronto. NCS knows he is down there so when he gets a QNI that can QSP Trent he QNQs that station down 5 to receive the Trent. Note that VE3MPX will get EARLIEST POSSIBLE service tonight because he is holding EMERGENCY traffic. When traffic is cleared simply draw a line through that listing. On the sheet list QTC in a column one above the other for easy reading. When a station checks back into net cross off the last column QNY and make a new entry in column one. When NCS spots a potential handling station for a listing he draws an arrow from the listing station in column one to the prospective traffic listing in column three. Keep a circled list of the number of pieces of traffic handled on the left side of column two.

If QNB relays are necessary count one for the TX to relay station and another for relay to the receiving station. When you close the net write down the closing time in UTC and record net length in minutes.

As soon as net is QNF write your report for net manager.

Call the net on time. Stations standing by for net to start if NCS does not appear in three minutes someone must QNG or take over as Net Control Station NCS. On most nets someone will QNG after only one minute without an NCS. NCS is unlikely to be upset if you start up the net after a couple of minutes. Do not waste time waiting for someone else to take the net.

Collect QTC stations first then liaison stations then general QNI so you have stations on board to handle the traffic. Keep on calling for QNI regularly. Move traffic quickly. QNX the QNI ASAP or in 15 minutes maximum if possible.

On Region nets it is common practice for NCS to go EAN as ECN RX.

Always clear TCC reps immediately even if you have to take the traffic yourself and QSP it. Then get your EAN TX moving. He will need the available time after net to organize the traffic before EAN QNI.

Net reports

When net is QNF your job is not yet done. Please do your Net Report immediately. QNS means *The following stations are in the net* followed by a list.

Net manager needs to know QNS for each net. Report date, time started, NCS call sign, QNS, number of pieces of traffic listed/over number handled, liaison stns/reps, and any other info that might be useful like the name and QTH of a new QNI.

Ask the net manager how he likes his QNS reports formatted. On ECN the normal report lists stations representing a net followed by a slant bar and the net. The text only of a Net report follows in this case for the OSN:

```
(INSERT PREAMBLE ADDRESS ETC.)

OSN 232300Z VE9FK X QNS

W3OKN VE3MPX EAM FGU/OPN WV/OLN

BDM/OBN KK VE2EDO X QTC

7/5 TIME 12 MINS X

VE3MPX ECN TX SELF RX

73

BT

DAN
```

OSN means that the net in this example is the Ontario Section Net. 232300Z means net session was on 23rd day present month at 2300 UTC. VE9FK means VE9FK was NCS. Then follows a list of QNS grouped by call area. Only the first call area is identified followed by other call suffixes from that area. TFC 7/5 means 7 pieces were listed 5 cleared. Time is obvious and in minutes. VE3GT went ECN Transmit and SELF VE9FK went ECN Receive.

12-19

```
        SAMPLE REGION NET REPORT:

        (PREAMBLE etc.)

   ECN 232345Z VE3FGU X QNS

   APN VE1WF TX VE1AMR RX

   OSN VE3MPX TX VE9FK RX

   OPN VE3BCZ TX/RX X TFC

   16/12 TIME 22 MINS X

   VE3ORN EAN TX SELF RX X

   73

   B T

   M I K E

   A R   N
```

SECTION 13: ON-AIR AUTHENTICATION

In some situations, you may be required to authenticate with another station. For example, if you are transmitting mission-critical information or instructions and the receiving station needs to make sure you are actually an authorized ARES station, the receiving station will ask you to authenticate.

Once you complete this section, you will be able to:

- Request authentications from other stations

- Respond to requests for authentication

- Change to new code tables

- Resolve authentication failures.

The process of authentication is simple. The station that requests the authentication chooses a challenge code at random from a code table (a printed matrix of unique, secret codes called a one-time pad). The station that has been challenged to authenticate has the same code table, and finds the matching response code. The challenged station reads the response back to the challenger, who then checks their code table to ensure that the response is correct. If the response is correct, the challenger knows that the challenged station has the correct code table and is therefore authorized to send or receive traffic.

Most ARES stations will be provided with a standard set of code tables. For specific high-sensitivity links between specific stations (for example, between an EOC and a command centre), additional code tables may be provided that are available only to those stations, providing an extra layer of authentication. (For procedures regarding *restricted authentication*, see the Communications Station Operating Procedures at your post, if available.)

13-1

Authentication codes - sheet 3 - issued 2004-08-01

Challenge	Response	Challenge	Response	Challenge	Response
388	11C8EJ	6MN	29IX9K	DJY	DIDJ3I
4JJ	CEWWNC	A3J	329I2D	F22	5KXKWN
58C	R2IMCK	A9N	OKPOKX	FT4	CUI4KS
5SI	NNREKS	BQL	JICWOE	H0J	C4ID99
683	TE3JC8	CLL	DJCFIJ	Q90	KLKZLK

Codes are sorted numerically and alphabetically, down the left column, then down the middle column, and then down the right column.

Any authentication code is used only once. All stations that hear an authentication (even if they are not participating) cross out the challenge-response code on their code table so that the code is not used again.

When most of the codes on a code table have been used, the net controller will retire the pad, asking all stations to begin using the next pad in the series.

The following procedures will help you perform authentications. Suggested on-air scripts are provided, but you can use your 'own words' so long as the overall protocols are followed.

Procedure 13-1: Request authentication from another station

Do not overuse authentication: Request authentication only when demanded by the traffic you are sending, at the request of the originator or recipient, or if you have reason to believe that you are being 'spoofed'. During an emergency, not all ARES stations will have current code tables, and some stations may have only a limited number of code tables. Once a code is used by any station, it cannot be reused. In addition, a repeated failure of a station during authentication usually results in the disposal of the current code table by all stations. Authentication should be an exceptional event that happens primarily during the set-up of operations, and not routinely.

1. If you have been off-net for a period of time (either off the air or on a frequency without a net controller), check in to the primary net or a secondary net and ask for confirmation of the current code table. The net controller will read out the current code table's sheet number and date (found in the upper left section of the table). Make sure that you are using the code table that the net controller identifies. Return to your working channel.

2. Pick an unused challenge-response pair from the current code table.

13-2

3. Ask the other station to authenticate, and read the challenge code. *For example, say, "VE9FK, this is VE9ZYX, please authenticate, Whiskey-8-3".*

4. Stand by while the other station looks up the response on their code table.

5. If the other station responds, "Challenge expired," cross the challenge-response code off your code table and return to Step 2.

6. If the other station responds, "Challenge not found," compare the sheet number and date they read you with the sheet number and date on your own code table. If your code table is 'newer' than theirs, ask them to update to the new code table. If your code table is 'older', update your own code table to match theirs. Then return to Step 2.

7. If the other station reads back a response code, validate it using your code table.

8. Cross off the challenge-response pair on your code table so you do not use it again.

9. If the response is valid, reply "Authenticated", and proceed with traffic handling.

10. If the response is not valid and you have tried to authenticate less than three times, return to Step 2 and try again.

11. If you have tried three times without success, reply "Authentication failed", and go to Procedure 13-3: "Responding to an authentication failure".

Procedure 13-2: Respond to a request for authentication from another station

1. When you are asked to authenticate, write down the challenge code and look it up on your code table.

2. If the challenge code is crossed out (meaning it has already been used), respond, "Challenge expired, please try again", and return to Step 1.

3. If you cannot find the challenge code on your code table, respond, "Challenge not found," then read back the sheet number and date of your code table (see the upper left section of the table), and return to Step 1.

4. Reply to the challenging station with the response code that appears beside the challenge code in the code table.

5. Stand by while the challenging station verifies your response.

6. If the challenging station asks you to authenticate again, return to Step 1.

Procedure 13-3: Responding to an authentication failure

1. If you are a net controller, go to Procedure 13-7: "Resolving authentication failures".

1. If you are not on a net controlled channel, ask the failed station to move to the primary net for follow-up, and then go to the primary net yourself.

13-3

2. Ask the net controller for assistance to resolve an authentication failure.

3. If you are asked by the net controller for the issue number of your code table, read back the sheet number and date from the upper left portion of the table.

4. If you are asked by the net controller to change to a new code table, securely destroy your current code table and open the new code table contained in your code table envelope.

5. Follow any other instructions provided by the net controller.

Procedure 13-4: Monitoring a challenge-response between other stations

1. Each time a challenge code is used, find it on your code table and cross it out. This ensures that you do not use that code yourself later on.

2. If a challenge-response fails, make a note of the callsign of the failed station. (If you are required later to communicate with the station that failed authentication, you may want to authenticate them yourself.)

3. If your code table has only three unused codes remaining and you are on a frequency without a net controller, move temporarily to the primary net and notify the net controller that a new code table is required.

4. If you are a net controller on a secondary net and your code table has only three unused codes remaining, contact the net controller on the primary net (either directly on a second transceiver, or using a relay station) and notify them that a new code table is required.

5. If you are the net controller on the primary net and your code table has only three unused codes remaining, or you are notified by another station that a new code table is required, go to Procedure 13-5: "Ordering a change to a new code table".

Procedure 13-5: Ordering a change to a new code table

Use this procedure if you are the net controller on the primary net and your code table has only three unused codes remaining, or you are notified by another station that a new code table is required, or you decide to order a new code table to resolve an authentication failure (which might occur if two stations are using different code tables).

1. Securely destroy your current code table.

2. Take the next code table sheet out of your code table envelope.

3. Write down the sheet number and date of the new code table (see the upper left section of the code table).

4. Broadcast an instruction to all stations on the primary net, asking them to change to the new code table with that specific sheet number and date.

13-4

5. If there are secondary nets in operation, contact the secondary net controllers directly using a second transceiver, or by way of a relay station, and ask them to make the same request to their net stations.

Procedure 13-6: Changing to a new code table

Use this procedure when you are asked either by a net control station or a challenging station to change to a new code table.

1. Write down the sheet number and issue date of the new code table.

2. Securely destroy your current code table.

3. Remove the new code table (identified by its sheet number and issue date) from your code table envelope.

4. Begin using the new code table immediately for any authentications.

Procedure 13-7: Resolving authentication failures

Use this procedure if you are an active ARES net control station and are requested by another station to resolve a failure to authenticate.

1. Get both stations on frequency together.

2. Query both stations for their code table sheet number and date.

3. If one of the stations is using an incorrect code table, ask them to update to the current code table and try again.

4. If you suspect an operator competence problem (for example, if an operator has been on duty for an extended period at the failed station and is exhausted), consider asking the failed station to change operators, to go off-air and take a break, or to cease operations.

5. If you suspect that spoofing or malicious interference may be taking place, cease communications with the failed station and broadcast an alert regarding the situation to all stations involved in the ARES operation.

13-5

SECTION 14: EQUIPMENT SELECTION AND CONFIGURATION

This section provides guidelines to help you choose and prepare equipment and deployment kits. The information provided here is intended to help you make your own decisions about what to include in your ARES emergency packs, based on the equipment you own, your transportation, your ability to carry gear, and the various scenarios for activation.

Once you complete this section, you will be able to:

- Take steps to protect and recover equipment

- Set up shared stations

- Build emergency packs (ready packs) and kits

- Prepare your equipment for emergencies

- Make decisions about buying and configuring equipment for ARES use

- Select appropriate battery types

- Plan alternate power sources, such as generators.

LABELLING AND RECOVERING EQUIPMENT

During times of emergency, it's quite likely that you will become separated from some of your equipment (for example, during shift changes at stations, while loaning items out to other operators, or simply during transit). It is very important that you clearly label all equipment to make sure that it finds its way back to you at the end of the operation. Any valuable piece of kit should be marked with your callsign. You may also consider labelling your equipment with:

- your name

- your phone number

- your email address

Tip: You can stick a white Avery label on the equipment and write the information on it, or you can use a label-maker to make a semi-permanent label.

Labelling packs, bags and containers

You should also label or tag any packs, bags or containers you are likely to use during an ARES operation (including your Ready Pack and any 'subpacks' within it). Use Avery labels or adhesive equipment labels on any 'hard' items like Pelican cases or briefcases. Use luggage tags on any soft items.

14-1

SETTING UP SHARED STATIONS

A shared station is:

- a station that will be manned by more than one operator at a time, or

- a station at which operators will work in shifts using a consistent equipment configuration

If you are asked to set up a shared station, see "Station configuration" on page 15.1.

EMERGENCY PACKS AND KITS

Ready Pack (emergency pack)

A *Ready Pack* is a portable package of equipment and supplies that will let you operate comfortably from any location for at least 24 hours (and hopefully longer). You should keep the Ready Pack somewhere accessible, such as the closet close to your front door, or in your car's trunk (so that it is accessible while you are at work).

Suggested contents:

- backup handheld radio with antenna, microphone or headset, and spare alkaline or high-capacity batteries for 12 hours operation

- speaker mike with earphone, or a headset

- 2m magmount (or mini-magmount) with antenna adapters for handhelds

- extra 25' of coax cable with connectors (more is better!)

- barrel connector to mate mag mount cable to extra coax

- cigarette lighter cord & extra fuses

- cigarette lighter female to car battery adapter

- printed copy of ARES procedures

- printed ARES/NTS forms

- reflective identification vest or tactical harness/vest

- ziplock bags (for packaging and for preventing exposure of gear to water, weather or contamination)

  - If you are working outside in wet weather, a ziplock bag over the radio and an elastic band around the antenna will keep the equipment dry. After the assignment, remove the radio from the bag to air out and dry it.

- water for 12 hours (2 litres)

14-2

- any required medications

- snack food for 12 hours or longer (snack bars, chocolate, trail mix, etc.)

- single-serving sugar packets

- sunhat or ball cap

- sun block and sunglasses

- insect repellent

- small first-aid kit

- 'disposable' rainwear (sold by Canadian Tire for about $3)

- flashlight and spare batteries

- large pad of paper, pens x3, mechanical pencil, black heavy permanent marker

- clipboard

- electrical tape

- duct tape

- basic set of tools

- Swiss army knife or multi tool

- 3m string

- 10m of #10 wire

- Velcro adhesive 'buttons' or strips

- permanent black marker with fine and coarse tips

- set of FRS/GMRS handheld radios with batteries

- breath mints

- nametag

- good photocopies of photo identification (such as your driver's license)

- any identification cards or documents provided to you by ARES or EMO

- business cards (or some sort of cards with your name, phone number and email address)

- regional street map

- $60 in cash (useful for coffee, snacks, etc.)

14-3

At the time of deployment, remember to add the following items to your Ready Pack:

- primary radio equipment, antennas, microphone or headset, power supply and spare batteries

- cell phone and spare batteries

- ARES access keys for designated station, centre, location or vehicle (if any keys have been issued to you)

Consider adding the following items, if convenient:

- garden tractor battery (if it can be transported safely), gel cell, or other portable battery system

- charger for your battery system

- simplex repeater module

- GPS

- second flashlight (preferably a long-life LED type)

- 12-to-120V auto inverter/adapter for your power supplies

- disposable camera

- tape recorder with batteries and tape

- wet naps or wash napkins

- blanket

- foldout seat

- sleep mask (the type provided on long-distance flights to aid sleep)

When deciding what to include in your Ready Pack, remember that you may have to carry your pack some distance, depending on where you are deployed. Try packing your Ready Pack with everything you would take on an actual emergency, and then take a 10 minute walk with it to make sure you will be comfortable carrying it when the time comes.

If you are not comfortable carrying the pack, and cannot minimize the contents of the pack, consider leaving it in the trunk of your car. In most situations, you will use your car to get to your deployed location.

14-4

You can also break out groups of items into 'subpacks' within your Ready Pack, so you can remove them easily when they are not needed, letting you re-organize your pack quickly. For example, you may bundle your gel cell and trickle charger in a bag within your Ready Pack so you can pull that gear out quickly if it is not needed, or is too heavy to carry to your destination.

> **TIP:** Zip lock sealable bags are great for packaging the content within your Ready Pack. Not only do they let you see their contents at a glance, they open and reseal easily and provide an additional layer of weatherproofing.

Another technique is to keep a small, minimal Ready Pack within a larger Pack. The smaller Pack contains the most essential gear, and can be carried easily. The larger Pack contains the gear that is less essential. In a situation where you may have to carry the Pack for an extended distance, you can leave the larger Pack behind in a safe place.

You may also be able to use a suitcase cart, granny grocery cart, or hand cart to move your equipment.

Extended operations kit

In some situations, you may be asked to provide services for longer than 24 hours, or you may volunteer to provide emergency communications outside your normal operating area. In these situations, you should take additional supplies, hardware and comfort items to meet the needs of the situation and to allow you to operate for longer periods or in situations where you may not have immediate support. Suggested items include the following:

- change of clothes (two changes, if possible)

- any medications you might need during extended operations

- sleeping bag or bed slip

- eyeshades and earplugs

- basic toiletries

- paperback books or other entertainment materials

- maps for any areas in which you may be called to operate

- plastic coffee cup

- dry soup packets, hot chocolate, etc.

- canned food and high energy snacks

- can opener

- spoon and cup

- first aid / medication / toilet kit

- deodorants

- moist towelettes

- Purell (waterless hand wash)

- extra cash, including small bills and coins for public phones

- fanny-pack or back-pack

- space blanket

- small refillable water bottle

- large trash bags

- tools

  - Swiss army knife and/or Leatherman-type tool
  - screwdrivers: Phillips and flat
  - needle nose pliers
  - vise grips
  - electrical tape
  - digital voltmeter (DVM)
  - duct tape (rolls in different colours)
  - crimper and wire stripper
  - butane-powered soldering iron
  - butane-powered micro torch (for soldering antennas, grounds, Powerpole connectors, etc.)
  - assorted adapters, connectors, screws and nails

- radio gear

    - photocopy of amateur radio license
    - backup radios
    - spare battery packs (charged)
    - AA-cell battery adapter
    - spare speaker-mic (needed for third-party communications when shadowing)

        A speaker mike makes a handheld radio easier to use as a "base" radio. It also keeps the operators hands free when using it when walking, driving, etc. In some cases, a small speaker can be used to advantage as it will give clearer and louder audio than the built-in speaker.

    - spare headset (recommended for discrete shadowing)
    - switching power supply (A/C)
    - 50 feet extension cord
    - multi-outlet AC power strip
    - assorted Powerpole cables and connectors
    - dual-band mag-mount antenna
    - 50 ft RG8X coax with UHF connectors
    - BNC or SMA to PL259 adapters
    - female-female UHF-UHF barrel adapters
    - 12V gel cell (75 A/H recommended, if possible) with charger
    - spare fuses

- HF accessories

    - key
    - headphones, ext speaker
    - NVIS antenna (NOT a mobile vertical)
    - 75m dipole with ladder line or 130 ft of wire or equivalent
    - antenna tuner with built-in SWR meter
    - insulators
    - guy rope
    - pegs for guys
    - weight and 50 ft light line for tossing over tree branches. (A plastic water bottle can make a good weight, since you can adjust the weight by pouring out water.)
    - bright marking tape to warn passers-by of guys and lines.

- power

    - generator kit: generator; fuel; oil; outdoor-grade three-prong 12-14 gauge power cable (50 ft); block of wood to place generator on (if used on damp earth); small tarp, two 2-ft wood pegs, two 3-ft wood pegs; 80 ft nylon rope (used to provide some protection against theft, and to set up a generator rain

14-7

shelter); reflective safety tape to cordon off generator area and mark cables and rope.

- small fire extinguisher
- solar kit: soar panels with protection diodes, Powerpole connectors
- auto power kit: vise grips (for loosening and tightening battery connections); 100 ft heavy duty 12v cable; battery clips with Powerpole connector; Powerpole connector block or distribution panel; reflective safety tape to mark cables; spare ignition key for car.
- chargers for equipment
- deep-cycle battery with charger
- spare fuses

- portable field gear:

  - canopy or shelter tent
  - umbrella (sun or rain)
  - table
  - folding chairs (2+)
  - portable light
  - materials for ad hoc antenna tower: five 5-ft 2x4 wood sections that can be bolted or screwed together; 150 ft of light nylon rope; 6 tent pegs or tie-downs; antenna base mounts; 50-ft coax (one for each antenna that might be installed); power screwdriver or torque wrench to install screws or bolts.

- hardship field gear:

  - camp cooking equipment and fuel; food ratios or MREs; water (4L per person per day) -- may not be needed if deployed to a shelter or other site with its own canteen or feeding station

- extended hardship field gear (for deployments of days or weeks at a site without accommodation or amenities):

  - sleeping tent. (You do not want to be sleeping at the radio station during an extended posting with other operators.)
  - sleeping bag
  - wash basin, dish soap, face soap, shampoo
  - wash towel
  - solar water heater shower bag

Auto kit

You should keep a limited kit in your car, separate from your Ready Pack, to facilitate in-car operations. The auto kit should include the following items:

- mag-mount 2m antenna (if your car does not have an installed antenna)
- auto power adapter

14-8

- fused female cigarette lighter plug with large alligator clips for direct-to-battery connection, with a cable long enough to reach into the cabin through a window or body seam. (Equip this cable with in-line Powerpole connectors.)

- detailed road maps for the province

- pads of paper and pens

Station kit

If you are responsible for station setup at a specific location, you need additional equipment and supplies specific to that location and the equipment that will be used there. For example, your station kit may include the following items:

- any equipment (transceivers, antennas, power supplies, batteries, etc.) specifically intended for use at that station

- fold-up table or card table (if the location does not provide an operating position)

- ARES forms and procedures

- paper pads, pens and pencils

- a backup VHF radio for operator talk-in

- signage

- comfort items, if appropriate:

  - coffeemaker or kettle, with coffee or tea
  - hot chocolate packets, in cold weather
  - folding chairs

- bottled water

- additional tools and hardware

- voltmeter

- soldering iron (battery or butane powered), resin-core (electronic) solder, desoldering wick or solder sucker

- selection of Slot, Phillips, Robertson and Torx screwdrivers

- selection of pliers - long nose, adjustable, mini-vise grip, wire cutters, crimping tools

- hookup wire, wire-nuts, tape, crimp connectors

- splice kits, 1/4 in. phone jack plugs, mini phone plugs, RCA plugs and adapters

- alligator clip jumpers

-

- generator and fuel

- extension cords

- trouble lights or lanterns

- 2-prong plug adapters to 3 prong (AC receptacle)

- 1 to 3 plug adapters (AC receptacle)

- 12 V power supply(s) for HF/ VHF / UHF rig(s)

- extra battery packs, Gel Cell(s), Ni-cad cell(s)

- cigarette lighter adapter

- spare fuses for rigs for AC line and DC cables

- mobile power cords, adapters, wire nuts, tape

- variable voltage AC to DC power supplies and plugs

Field pack

If you are responsible for setting up an in-field station, bring the following items:

- large tent (sleeps six or more) for operations and sleeping shelter

- a second tent, if one is available, for multi-shift stations

- boundary or trail-marking tape

See "Station configuration" on page 15.1 and "Station management" on page 19.1.

Search and rescue pack

At this time, regional ARES involvement in SAR is limited. It is expected that ARES may be used only in large-scale SAR operations (such as a passenger jet crash), but this may vary from Section to Section.

If you are interested in volunteering for deployment on possible search and rescue exercises or events, you need to build an additional pack with gear you will need during SAR operations. Your SAR Pack should include the contents of your Ready Pack, and should also include the following items:

- extended-length flex antennas for handhelds (cannot be fragile)

- regional road and topographical maps

- outdoor clothing suited to the season (including hiking or snow boots, reflective 'hunter wear', hats, etc.)

14-10

Consider adding the following items, if available:

- GRS (CB) handheld transceiver with earphone, flex antenna and alkaline or high capacity batteries

- FRS/GMRS handheld with spare batteries

- GPS with spare batteries (GPS should be capable of displaying MGRS and UTM coordinates)

- waist or fanny pack for equipment and batteries

- orange 'anti-hunter' vest or clothing

GENERAL PREPAREDNESS GEAR

Home

- Blankets or sleeping bags

- Warm clothes

- Additional prescription eyeglasses

- Extra pairs of house and car keys

- Cash and change

- Manual can opener

- Baby supplies: formula, bottle, pacifier, clothing, blankets, diaper wipes, disposable diapers, canned food and juices

- Additional medical prescriptions

For pets

- Water

- Food

- Blankets

- Spare leash and collar

- Medications

- Carrying case

- Favourite toy

14-11

Auto

- Blanket

- Booster cables

- Cash and change

- Change of clothes, rain gear and sturdy footgear

- Fire extinguisher

- Maps

- Shovel

- Road Flares

- Tire Repair Kit

HANDHELD EQUIPMENT

Choosing handheld radios

When you are buying a handheld radio, you may wish to consider features and accessories that will be useful during emergency operations:

- long-life batteries

- AA battery adapter or case

- external power/charger input that allows power and recharge while in use

- headset or earphone

- BNC connector or SMA-to-BNC adapter (for connection to external antennas)

- BNC-to-PL259 adapter (for connection to onsite, fixed antennas)

- belt clip or lanyard

- switchable high and low power

- weather resistant shell or case

It is recommended that you have two handhelds: one primary radio that you use regularly, and a backup radio that normally stays in your Ready Pack and can be used in case your primary radio dies. (A backup radio may also be useful in situations where you wish to monitor more than one channel, or wish to loan a radio to another operator.)

14-12

Accessories for handheld equipment

- Antennas

- Power packs

PRIMARY RADIOS

Your primary radios should be ones that you use on a regular basis, and should be kept charged and ready for use at all times. Recommended features and configurations include:

- programmed with local repeaters and ARES channels

- able to function on battery/auto/emergency power for extended periods

- headset, or speakermic with headphones

- effective portable antenna (extended-length whip for handhelds, or an external mag-mount 1/4-wave or better)

BACKUP RADIOS

Your backup radios should be ones that you do not need on a regular basis, but that are in working condition. Recommended features and configurations include:

- programmed with local repeaters and ARES channels

- AA alkaline compatible battery packs, or external battery input with an external AA battery pack

- effective portable antenna (extended-length whip for handhelds, or an external mag-mount 1/4-wave or better)

- a BNC antenna jack, or an SMA jack with an SMA-to-BNC adapter

- headset, or speakermic with headphones

POWER

Batteries

Batteries are one of the most crucial elements of your radio system. During ARES operations, most operators will spend most of their operating time running from battery packs or battery systems.

When choosing batteries, you need to consider how they will be used. Equipment that is used and recharged regularly can benefit from batteries that have high capacity but may self-discharge (run down without being used). Equipment that is used infrequently benefits from batteries that do not self-discharge, or can be replaced quickly in the field.

14-13

Most handheld radios come with their own internal or clip-on battery packs, and you may not have much choice regarding capacity or chemistry (the elements used within the battery that determine a battery's characteristics and capacity).

Chemistry

The following types of battery chemistry are common:

- Lead acid

- Gel Cell lead acid

- Nickel Cadmium (NiCd)

- Lithium Ion (LI, Lion)

- Nickel Metal Hydride (NiMH)

- Alkaline

- Rechargeable alkaline

- Carbon

Lead acid batteries are suitable only for use at fixed stations, as backup supplies (or where they are normally found, in automobiles). They are not recommended for use in other mobile applications.

Gel Cell lead acid batteries are useful in mobile situations, but are often too heavy for man-carried packages (such as backpack radio kits). Gel Cell batteries have high capacity but must be charged carefully to prevent battery damage.

NiCd batteries are commonly used in internal battery packs, and are useful for external packs in their AA, C and D formats. NiCd batteries have moderate capacity and can be charged or discharged with little memory effect, so long as they are not COMPLETELY discharged or overcharged. NiCd batteries are recommended as a cheap, rechargeable battery for external battery packs (or internal AA battery cases).

LI batteries are commonly used in laptop computers and in some radio systems. LI batteries have very high capacity, but a limited charge-cycle life. LI batteries also require specialized charging circuits to avoid severe damage. LI batteries do not self-discharge. They are not recommended for any equipment that is not designed specifically to use them.

NiMH batteries are becoming more common in internal battery packs, but are readily available in AA format. NiMH batteries have high capacity and can be charged with a normal NiCd charger (though an NiMH charger is much preferred to preserve overall battery life). NiMH batteries can have up to twice the capacity of NiCd batteries, and do not suffer from memory effects. NiMH batteries do have a charge-cycle life, but are much hardier than LI batteries. NiMH batteries self-discharge slowly, making them unreliable for backup or low-use equipment. NiMH batteries are recommended as a rechargeable battery for external battery packs (or internal AA battery cases).

14-14

Alkaline batteries are readily available and have good capacity. Unfortunately, regular alkaline batteries cannot be recharged, and tend to be an expensive solution. Two common brands are Eveready and Duracell. Both brands are nearly identical, with the exception that Eveready batteries self-discharge and fail at cold temperatures, and are not recommended for winter use. Alkalines are recommended for use as reserve batteries for occasional (or emergency) use in external battery packs or internal AA battery cases.

Rechargeable alkaline batteries are a little more expensive than non-rechargeable alkalines, but can typically be recharged 25 times (resulting in a great cost savings). Rechargeable alkalines require a special recharger, readily available from Radio Shack. These batteries do not self-discharge as quickly as NiCd and NiMH batteries. Rechargeable alkalines are recommended as a cheap, rechargeable battery for external battery packs (or internal AA battery cases).

Carbon batteries are the cheapest available, but have low capacity and tend to be unreliable on electronic systems. (They are intended primarily for flashlights and other fixed-current devices.) Carbon batteries are not recommended for ARES use, since they may not be able to power your handheld radio on high or even medium power.

Table 3:   Battery chooser

Primary 'regular use' Battery type	equipment	Backup 'occasional use' equipment	Fixed backup power
Lead acid			X
Gel Cell			X
NiCd	X		
NiMH	X		
Alkaline		X	
Rechargeable alkaline	X	X	
Carbon			

Auto power

Cigarette lighter installations

Getting power through your cigarette lighter is fast and convenient. However, you cannot draw more than 5A through the connection reliably, and in many cars the cigarette lighter power is on only when the ignition is on.

If you are going to use low-power equipment powered through cigarette lighter connections, consider installing a second cigarette lighter female connector (or bank of connectors) with a direct, fused connection to your car battery. This minimizes voltage drop and ensures that power is available through the connector even when the ignition is off.

14-15

Anderson Powerpole connectors

Powerpole connectors are highly recommended for use in your auto power installation, in place of or in combination with the options described earlier. It is important to provide a Powerpole plug-in that will allow you to quickly install other ARES equipment into your vehicle.

Battery clip installations

A fast though messy method of connection to your car's 12V power is to use a female cigarette lighter connector with battery clips. This is suitable only for low-power equipment. You must exercise caution to prevent shorts or disconnections. This method is suitable only for short-term use, but allows you to connect to any automobile without causing damage. Powerpole connectors with alligator leads can be used to meet higher power requirements.

Permanent installations

Permanent installations can provide a good solution if you use portable equipment in your automobile on a regular basis, or if you are using high-powered equipment. A number of commercially available systems are available for in-car power, but you can brew your own easily. The simplest installation is to run the power cable for your high-powered transceiver from the cabin into the engine compartment through the firewall, and to connect it via a high-current fuse directly to the battery.

Other options

Other options for permanent installation include:

- a secondary battery, charged from the alternator through a battery isolation diode or an ignition controlled relay

- power distribution points at strategic locations in the car, such as the glove compartment, back-seat floor, or truck camper cab

- an auto-shutdown module to prevent the battery from being run down. (Koolatron sells these through Canadian Tire for about $30.)

In addition to the rechargeable battery the operator should have a power cord for the portable to operate of a 12 volt battery or power supply. A power cord that plugs into a cigarette lighter socket is good for mobile use. A battery case that takes 'AA' batteries is a asset. For emergency power a battery holder that holds larger batteries can be carried in a pouch and used with a power cord. This is great for extended power consumption.

A small 3 amp regulated power supply can be used for most handheld radios. A "wall wart" power supply is not recommended for use as they usually do not have sufficient current and poor voltage control.

14-16

Generators

Generators are extremely useful for ARES operations, particularly for those that involve commercial power failures lasting longer than several hours. A generator is a large investment, so it is not recommended that you buy one just for ARES applications. However, you may be able to justify buying one to power your home (keeping your refrigerator or other equipment operating) during an extended outage.

> *Note: If you are planning on using a generator to power your home, you need to ensure that its capacity is high enough to run any equipment, lighting, heating or other devices that you are likely to want to run. Also, have a qualified electrician make the connection from your generator to the house wiring prior to an emergency, or connect equipment directly to the generator without using the house wiring! (If you connect a generator to your house wiring yourself, you risk voiding your home insurance, burning down your house, possibly injuring power company workers.)*

Handheld generators

Small generators like the Honda 350W can be considered 'handheld', since they weigh only a few pounds and can actually be dropped into ready packs and easily carried to any location. These small generators typically take little fuel (about a litre) and run for several hours on a fillup. They typically run on gasoline with a very low oil mix. They cannot be used indoors, but are safe to use just outside a building, so it is important to pack an extension cord with the generator. The output is not usually a true sine wave, so care must be taken when using cheap chargers or power supplies with the generator. (A DVM will let you check supply or charger DC output to ensure that it is not unusually high or low.)

Portable generators

A portable generator can be transported in a vehicle and carried by one or two people to where it's needed. Portable generators range in output from 1000W to 5000W, and typically run on gasoline. They also require 2- or 4-cycle engine oil. Some generators in this range do not output true sine wave, so care must be taken when using cheap chargers or power supplies with the generator. (A DVM will let you check supply or charger DC output to ensure that it is not unusually high or low.)

Fixed generators

Fixed generators are useful when powering equipment at home or at a fixed emergency site (like an EOC). Fixed generators may run on gasoline, oil, propane or natural gas.

HEADSETS

Headsets are essential in most emergency operating locations. Headsets let you function in noisy environments (like a typical EOC) and also reduce the noise that your station generates. By increasing overall comfort, headsets let you operate longer and reduce fatigue.

For use in an automobile, a single earmuff headset is recommended. (Dual-muff headsets may be illegal if worn by the driver.)

14-17

For use at an EOC or other busy site, a double earmuff headset is recommended.

For use during shadowing or other highly mobile activities, you may wish to use a more discrete headset, like an in-ear bud or audionic headset.

EQUIPMENT CASES AND CARRY BAGS

You need to be able to transport your equipment to locations where it is needed. If you are a mobile or shadow operator, you'll need to carry equipment with you as you move. Equipment cases and carry bags make transportation and operation easier. Tactical vests make it easier to pack equipment on your person.

Equipment bags or cases should be clean and in good condition. Padding inside the bags or cases will protect your equipment from rough handling. You may wish to use a watertight or weather resistant case for high-value equipment.

TACTICAL AND IDENTIFICATION VESTS

Tactical vests should be comfortable even if worn for hours. Camouflage (camo) vests are NOT recommended; they are not suitable for any ARES deployment. Ideally, wear an ARES tactical vest (which is orange, yellow or green with EMERGENCY COMMUNICATIONS, ECOM, ECOMM or COMM printed on it.

Note: Standardized ARES safety vests can be ordered directly from RAC. See http://www.rac.ca/fieldorg/aresvests.htm for more information.

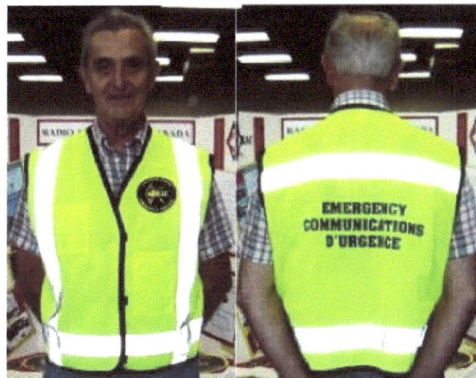

The British Columbia Provincial Emergency Program (PEP) has also designed a vest suitable for ARES use. For more information, see http:// www.cordeoc.ca/CTV-CommunicationsVest-710x533-June-04.htm.

COMPUTERS

Desktop computers

Desktop computers are not usable in situations where you need to relocate to an emergency site. However, if you are serving from home (for example, as a net controller, liaison or relay station), a desktop computer collocated with your station can be very useful. Ensure that your computer is preconfigured with software you can use for logging, record keeping, and packet communications.

14-18

Laptop computers

Laptop computers can be very useful at fixed locations, or where data communications is required. Ensure that spare batteries and the power supply are also packed with the computer itself. Consider using a waterproof case (such as a Pelican case) to ensure protected transport.

Handheld computers

Opinions are mixed on the usefulness of handheld computers (PPCs, Palms, etc.) in emergency contexts. Palm and PPC handhelds are not currently recommended, since they cannot be used easily for packet and data exchange, and are not as suitable as pen and paper forms in mission-critical applications and mixed environments.

SOFTWARE

An important issue is software compatibility and familiarity. Any experienced operator should be able to sit down at your logging terminal or packet terminal and use the most commonly required features.

For packet operations, it is recommended that you have ARESPACK software installed or available. (To find the most recent version of ARESPACK, or equivalent software, search the Internet for "ARESPACK".)

COMPUTER ACCESSORIES

A number of computer accessories may be useful during an exercise or an emergency event. You do not need all these accessories, but if you have them you should consider including them in your emergency pack.

Network and wireless LAN adapters

If you are stationed at an EOC or other facility with infrastructure, there may be a LAN available, and you should be equipped to connect to it. Make sure you have an Ethernet card or port for your laptop. Also consider bringing an 802 Wifi wireless card, in case a wireless network is used.

Floppy disk drive

A floppy drive is invaluable when you need to trade data with other users at your location (for example, when sending or receiving lists of names by packet at an aid station or shelter).

USB Flash Drive

A USB drive (for example, a USB keychain memory) can be very useful if you are working in an ad-hoc situation with a number of computers.

14-19

SPECIALIZED RADIO EQUIPMENT

Cross-band repeaters

Cross-band repeaters are typically mobile VHF/UHF dual-band radios that have a cross-band repeat (CBR) function built into them. The radio receives on a UHF channel and transmits the signal on a VHF channel (or vice versa). These radios can be invaluable during ARES operations.

Simplex repeaters

A simplex repeater is a transceiver that has been configured with a specialized audio module to retransmit any received signals. The simplex repeater records the audio from a received signal on a digital recording chip, and when the signal stops, immediately begins retransmitting that recorded audio on the same frequency (on simplex). This provides a 'dirty', simple way of extending communications range.

A common simplex repeater configuration uses a basic handheld radio with an Icom-compatible mic/speaker jack, and a Realistic simplex repeater (available on clearance from some Radio Shack stores in the US, and from eBay).

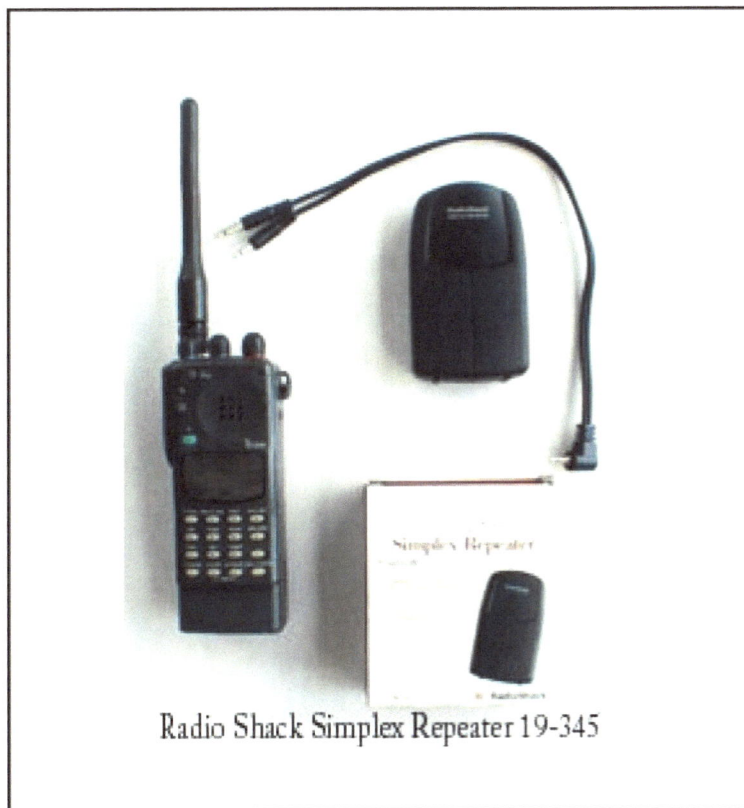

Radio Shack Simplex Repeater 19-345

The Radio Shack simplex repeater can record up to 30 seconds of audio in a single transmission. It runs on four AA batteries, or on external power.

14-20

VEHICLES

With regards to ARES participation, the most important consideration when deciding which automobile to use and equip is reliability. While heavier vehicles (like SUVs or pickup trucks) may seem like attractive choices, they aren't needed for most scenarios. While four-wheel drive vehicles can be invaluable during winter storm emergencies, most cars can be equipped with traction equipment (such as snow chains) to make limited driving possible even in severe conditions. Almost any vehicle capable of getting you to your station or duty location is enough, so long as you can rely on the vehicle to work, and be available, when it's needed.

Remember that having access to a vehicle is not a prerequisite to participating in ARES. If you have restrictions that limit your mobility or prevent you from driving, if you do not own a car, if you share access to the car, or if your car is simply untrustworthy, you're still encouraged to participate. Let your EC know about transport restrictions so that plans can be adjusted accordingly.

Fuel. Vehicles that require diesel fuel may run into problems during an emergency. Access to fuel may be very limited, and the fuel most likely to be available will be regular petrol. If you will be using your diesel-powered vehicle for emergency purposes, try to ensure that the tank is kept filled at regular intervals, and consider storing additional diesel fuel (1-2 tankfulls) at a safe but accessible location.

For petrol-powered vehicles (which will include most cars), fuel may also be an issue, particularly during emergencies that limit mobility (like winter storms) or power outages that disable gas station pumps. It is a good practice in general to keep your tank over half-full at all times, ensuring that you will have at least 200 km of operating range regardless of how much warning you have that an emergency is occurring. Also, keep an empty jerry can in the trunk, to make fuel transfers easier in unusual situations.

Traction. Four-wheel drive vehicles can be invaluable during winter storm emergencies, and if you have a four-wheel drive vehicle you should consider that your primary vehicle for emergency use. However, if you have a regular two-wheel drive car, don't worry. You can take steps to improve your traction and clearance, making it safer to travel during winter emergencies:

- Install proper winter tires (and not all-season tires) in the fall.

- Keep snow chains in the trunk (and learn how to use them).

- Keep sand bags and a snow shovel in the trunk during the winter.

Electrical. Modern inverters can provide 120VAC with fairly high efficiency. It is recommended that you keep a 75 watt (or higher capacity) inverter in your car, in order to operate chargers, laptops or other 120V equipment from your 12V electrical system.

Also have a cigarette lighter splitter (plugging into the cigarette lighter and providing three power plugs instead of one).

If you have a car in which the cigarette lighter power is turned off with the key, consider modifying the circuit to keep power on, or install a second cigarette lighter power plug to allow operation of equipment without having the key in the ignition. See "Auto power" on page 14.15 for more information.

14-21

Antennas. Fixed mounted antennas are more reliable than mag-mount antennas. However, if you have a mag-mount antenna available, you should keep it in the car even if you also have a fixed antenna. The mag-mount can be used as an emergency or secondary antenna, either in your car or at an operating site.

In addition to the rubber-duck antenna the operator should carry a "Roll-up half wave antenna with a 15-20 foot coax that can be used as a "throw-up" antenna. A mag-mount with a 1/2 or 5/8 wave whip antenna is good for mobile use. A collapsable "base" type antenna with 25 and 50 foot coax cables can be used in a fixed situation to get the antenna outside and improve signal quality.

Radio mounts. Even if you don't permanently mount radios and other equipment in your vehicle, you may consider installing mounting hardware so that radios can be securely placed in the vehicle when needed, with little or no installation time. You can even use self-adhesive velcro to provide a temporary mount.

Radio equipment. You may wish to include a range of equipment in your vehicle to allow interoperability and flexibility. 2m radio equipment is essential (either in the form of an external antenna and power point for your handheld, or a full-powered mobile installation). Full-powered mobile HF can also be very useful if combined with high-performance 80m and 40m whip antennas.

Other radio gear that you might include for convenience would include a portable 'bagphone' cellular phone (if you already have one for your boat or business), a GRS (CB) transceiver or handheld (or emergency-type kit), a pair of GMRS or FRS handhelds, and a general coverage VHF/UHF scanner.

Comfort items. It is a good idea to stock your vehicle with items that can make you more comfortable in situations where you are required to operate from within the vehicle. Items may include:

- 12v kettle for tea or coffee

- paperback books or magazines for downtime

- candy bars or snack bars (nonperishable)

- wetnaps or washup napkins

- blankets

14-22

VHF RADIO CONFIGURATION

Configure your radio so that the following operations are easy for you to perform:

- Access all VHF repeater frequencies in duplex mode

- Access all VHF repeater output frequencies in simplex mode

- Access all VHF simplex frequencies

- Access all packet frequencies (if your station is packet-capable)

- Toggle high and low power output

- Cross-band repeat (if your transceiver is CBR-capable; see "Cross-band repeating" on page 10.15)

SECTION 15: STATION CONFIGURATION

This section provides information needed by individual operators responsible for setting up, provisioning and configuring an ARES emergency station.

Once you complete this section, you will be able to:

- Select a location for your ARES station

- Set up and configure a station

- Configuring a home station for ARES.

SELECTING A LOCATION

Before choosing a location for the ARES station, work with the manager responsible for the operations site to find a location that will meet your needs while staying out of the way of other essential functions.

Consider:

- Accessibility

- Antenna erection

- Privacy

- Nearby facilities.

Also discuss with the site manager how messages and communications will be handled by the station.

STATION SETUP AND CONFIGURATION

If you are responsible for establishing a station at a location, there are a number of things you need to consider:

Special site considerations

Some types of sites where you may be asked to establish a station have specific constraints or conditions that may require care.

EOC

If you are setting up a station at an EOC or other operations centre, consider the following recommendations:

- Install or use headsets or earphones to minimize your impact on the EOC.

- Consider RFI when installing antennas, feedlines and equipment. Do not interfere with other communications systems at the EOC.

15-1

- Unless the station has been set up at the EOC prior to the emergency, set it up as quickly and quietly as possible, without making the installation permanent. Use velcro, cable ties and other items that can be 'de-installed' after the operation without damage.

Medical environment

If you are setting up a station in a hospital, at a medical-care senior citizens' home, or in any environment where medical equipment is being used:

- Install or use headsets or earphones to minimize your impact on patients and staff.

- Consider EMI/RFI when installing or using radio systems. Some medical equipment is extremely vulnerable to accidental interference, with tragic results.

- Run antenna systems outside and away from patient areas.

- Shield your radio equipment from the mains power.

- Configure transmitters to operate at their lowest power levels.

- Set up a kill switch (for example, a single switch on a power bar) that can be used to immediately shut down all station equipment.

- Make staff aware of the possibility of interference, so that they know to watch for it and to notify you if it occurs.

Sealed sites

If you are setting up a station in a building or trailer that is sealed (for example, during a chemical or radiological emergency):

- Do not attempt to run feedlines or antennas to the outside. If you do not have coverage from inside, and feedlines and antennas are not already installed, consider using a relay station, or a simplex or CBT repeater in a nearby automobile.

Mobile units

If you are setting up a station in a mobile unit (for example, in a city bus being used for evacuations):

- Do not drill or hard-mount equipment. If you need to temporarily mount equipment, use velcro strips.

- Do not alter the vehicle in any way.

- Keep all antennas, cables and equipment out of the way of the driver.

- Keep in mind the purpose of the vehicle during the emergency, and the activities that will take place on the vehicle. (For example, if the vehicle is being used to transport victims, ensure that your installation will not be in the way of, or vulnerable to injured persons brought onboard.)

15-2

- Do not interfere with any existing radio equipment.

- Do not 'hotwire' into the vehicle power system to get radio power. Use cigarette lighter plugs or temporary clip-on fused cables to get power, or run off batteries.

Antennas

Indoor antennas

Indoor antennas are the easiest to set up, and may work well in many locations. Your choices will be determined by the antennas that you have available yourself, and by the antennas that other operators can loan to the station. Typical indoor antenna types include:

- BNC or SMA rubber ducks or whip antennas

- wall-mounted or window-mounted dipole antennas for 6m or 2m

- mag-mount whips

Outdoor antennas

Outdoor antennas may be required at some locations, but are much more complex to install, even in temporary situations.

Ad-hoc outdoor antennas that you can install in an emergency include the following:

- mag-mount whips

- handheld-style BNC whips or rubber ducks with an 'auto-style' window-mounted extension cable and base

- externally mounted dipoles for HF, 6m, or 2m

- J-pole for 2m

A length of 2 by 4 wood with a cross piece can be inserted into a sewer vent pipe as a temporary antenna mount. Pass-throughs

A pass-through for antenna cables can be made through the walls of EOCs and other locations with a section of 1 1/2 to 2 inch PVC pipes with screw top, clean-outs on the inside and outside of the building wall.

Antenna and power safety

All amateur radio antennas should be grounded whenever and wherever possible. This is particularly important for stations operating during disaster situations, when there may be a tendency to continue operating even during electrical storms.

In fixed installations, use DC grounded antennas whenever possible.

15-3

A grounded antenna still needs a lightning arrestor. In addition, each coax feed line should be connected to ground (at least 2.5 m ground rod connected with minimum #4 AWG bare copper, through a lightning arrestor).

An individual surge protector should be used on each piece of equipment connected to the AC mains.

Both coax feed lines and power cords should always be disconnected from amateur equipment in EOCs and other served agency locations when not in use. Make sure that coax terminations ends are legibly tagged for identification and placed at least 1 m from equipment.

The equipment ground, antenna ground and lightning arrestor should be tied to the same points whenever possible to form a grid.

Tables

The site manager may be able to provide a table or surface on which you can set up a portable station or a working location, if you are at a location with resources. Otherwise, you should consider bringing a small card table or other fold-up table.

Signage

Your services aren't useful if no one can find you. If you are stationed in an EOC or in an operations centre, this won't be an issue. But if you are serving a number of clients, or are located remotely from your clients, you'll need some signage to make finding your station easier.

Local communications

You may want to integrate as much as possible into local communications being used onsite. For example, if you are serving in a large EOC, you may want to adopt a phone extension and make sure that key clients know how to reach you via that extension. You may want to monitor an FRS/GMRS channel (such as Channel 9) so that clients can reach you using the cheap, short-range FRS handhelds that are now commonly available. You may want to bring an Ethernet-equipped laptop so you can plug into the location's LAN in order to facilitate messaging and file transfer.

Comfort

If you and other station operators are going to be operating for extended periods, you'll need some comfort facilities at your station, or at the location you are serving.

Cots and blankets. Being able to sleep at the station allows you to run short shifts with other operators.

Coffeepot or kettle. Access to coffee, tea or hot chocolate will make operations much more comfortable.

> *Note: Do not eat or drink in front of evacuees unless they have also been provided with meals and water.*

15-4

Food. Although each operator is expected to arrive with 12 hours of food and water, any extended operation will require ongoing commissary services for station personnel.

Entertainment. In order to allow operators to rest or take a break without leaving the station, you need to provide light reading such as magazines or recent newspapers. You may also consider providing a small portable TV.

Internet. Although many emergency situations may affect Internet access, you should consider providing an Internet-connected laptop (with a LAN connection or a wireless Internet connection) that can be used by personnel on break to check email or read online.

Bathroom facilities. For any operation of any length, you need to provide access to washroom facilities, and somewhere where personnel can wash up.

Shelter. You may need to provide a tent or other form of shelter.

CONFIGURING A HOME STATION FOR EFFECTIVE ARES USE

Whether you are a skilled ECOM operator, a serious traffic handler, or simply a hobby operator, consider the following suggestions for configuring your home station for ARES operation:

- Designate a room or space for the radio station and ensure that the space is not cluttered with items not related to the station.

- Set up a well-lighted desk or table and a comfortable chair.

- Include an accurate battery clock. (Two are better – one set for local time and one for UTC.)

- Put up a wall calendar.

- Include the following items:

  - A flashlight or other emergency light source
  - Logbooks and note books. (In addition, 3x5" index cards in a file box can be useful.)
  - Extra pens, pencils and a sharpener.
  - A repeater directory, operating guide, antenna books, and copies of emergency plans
  - Maps
  - File folders and cabinets
  - Weather station or outdoor thermometer (properly shaded)
  - An operational notebook in a sturdy binder, containing important names and numbers, frequencies, and other reference information
  - Blank paper, paperclips, pre-printed message pads, and envelopes
  - Headphones.

15-5

SECTION 16: FREQUENTLY ASKED QUESTIONS

This section provides answers to commonly asked questions raised by ARES volunteers.

WHAT CAN I DO TO MAKE MYSELF MORE EFFECTIVE AS AN ARES OPERATOR? The following best practices may make you a more effective ARES operator:

- Start a log. Write down date, time and description of any significant activities, events, or observations. This helps you keep track of your responsibilities during your shift, helps your replacement continue after your shift, and may also help forensically after the operation. Use a pen. Never keep a log in pencil.

- Document as much as you can. Document your own activities, your communications, your observations, and any injuries or traumas you experience.

- Don't expect people to know who you can talk to or how to send messages. Put up big signs that explain your function, let people know who you can talk to, and help them through the messaging process.

- Spend as much time as possible following up on messages and trying to close the loop.

- Get into digital communications. The more you can do here, the more useful you will be in a disaster.

- Assemble Grab and Go bags for your gear. Use one bag for personal gear (waterproof) and one for a single station set-up. Do not over-pack. If one person can't carry it, it is too much.

WHERE AM I LIKELY TO BE POSTED AS AN OPERATOR?

The places where you might be posted during an emergency depend on the nature of the emergency, the number of operators available, and other unpredictable factors. In general, it is expected that you may be posted to locations such as:

- Emergency Operations Centres (EOC) at City Hall, in a police station, or at another government facility

- Incident Command Post (ICP)

- Command posts (CP)

- Municipal buildings

- Hospitals

- Seniors residences and special-care facilities

- Shelters

16-1

- Schools and arenas

- Community centres

- Airport

- Evacuation points

- Transit buses used for evacuations

- Mobile survey or command units

- Police stations

- Your own home (net controllers, relay stations, NTS traffic handlers, and backup operators)

WHAT EQUIPMENT DO I NEED IN ORDER TO PARTICIPATE?

In general, you need a 2m FM transceiver during exercises or emergency situations. Ideally, you need a primary and backup transceiver, to ensure reliability.

If you have packet equipment, you should configure it so that it can be transported onsite. (For example, install packet software on your laptop, and package your station so it can be carried in a briefcase.)

In some situations, we may also make use of HF channels, either using portable stations set up at the time of the emergency, or using home-based HF stations that relay traffic carried over 2m FM.

If you don't have equipment, you can still participate in ARES. Other participants may have spare equipment that can be loaned, or you may be able to assist or operate at an Official Emergency Station (OES).

DO I NEED TO BE ABLE TO DRIVE IN ORDER TO PARTICIPATE?

No. If you do not have access to a car, or cannot drive at the time of an exercise or emergency, alternate arrangements may be available. Let your EC or net control know during the callout about any restrictions on your mobility. If you have permanent restrictions (for example, if you don't own a car), let your EC know so that plans can be adjusted accordingly.

DO I NEED MY OWN RADIO EQUIPMENT IN ORDER TO PARTICIPATE?

If you do not have 2m equipment, or any radio equipment, you can still participate. You may be posted to an onsite location with its own radio equipment, or equipment may be loaned to you by another ARES operator.

16-2

IF I HAVE A PHYSICAL RESTRICTION OR DISABILITY, DOES THAT MEAN I CAN'T PARTICIPATE?

You are welcome to participate regardless of physical restrictions or disabilities. Your ability to operate your radio station qualifies you for ARES participation. Let your EC know about any restrictions or disabilities so that plans can be adjusted accordingly.

WHAT IF I GO ON VACATION OR TRAVEL?

Let your EC know when you are going to be out of town for extended periods. (This is a suggestion, not a requirement.)

WHAT IF I AM REGISTERED WITH ANOTHER EMERGENCY OR DISASTER RELIEF ORGANIZATION, AS WELL AS ARES?

Participation in other emergency and disaster relief organizations does not affect your eligibility to participate in ARES. If you are registered with another organization, please let your ARES EC know so that plans can be adjusted accordingly.

AM I INSURED DURING ARES EVENTS?

Generally, no. ARES does not provide any form of liability, disability or workers compensation insurance.

Check with your own insurance provider to determine whether you are covered by your personal policies during ARES volunteer activities.

Also check with your EC to determine whether you are covered by Workers Compensation or Worker Health and Safety during activations by specific served agencies. In many cases where emergency volunteers are working for a municipal service and are registered with the municipality, the volunteer is covered by the municipal liability insurance and Workers Compensation insurance.

In most provinces, Workers Compensation coverage is extended to all registered volunteers responding during a state of emergency. (This coverage may not apply during training exercises.)

If you are a RAC member, you are automatically covered for liability up to $5 million. Full details are available at http://www.rac.ca/service/insurance/faq-liability_e.php.

Your ARES group may also have purchased RAC liability insurance that covers you during ARES activities.

SHOULD I BRING A CELLPHONE ON A CALLOUT?

Yes. If you have a cellphone, bring it. Cellphones, when they are working, can be invaluable when coordinating an activation or troubleshooting a station setup. In addition, a cellphone may allow your business or work to reach you when needed, which in turn may allow you to take leave from work more easily and remain on station longer.

16-3

SHOULD I BRING A POLICE SCANNER ON A CALLOUT?

No. Although an emergency services (police, ambulance, fire) scanner may be useful to you while at home during an emergency, it is not a good idea to bring an emergency services scanner with you on a mobilization. There are several reasons for this:

- The use of mobile police scanners is illegal in many municipalities.

  Note: In Canada, information heard on scanners – which is not intended as a broadcast for any one listening – must not be divulged to any third party. Amateur radio transmissions, however, do not have this protection.

- Scanner traffic may distract you from your primary purpose (ARES communications) when onsite.

- The scanner may cause clients to mistake your role while onsite, and will detract from the professional image you need to maintain.

- You should get your 'situational awareness' from ARES channels, and not from emergency services channels.

- Traffic on emergency services channels may include highly confidential or sensitive information, especially during a real emergency. You do not want to be responsible for others overhearing this traffic, even inadvertently.

The only exception to this recommendation is the case where you are specifically requested by an EC, communications supervisor or net controller to monitor emergency services traffic. Typically, this role (if required) will be assigned to a home base station in response to a specific need.

WILL WE USE MOSTLY VOICE OR MOSTLY PACKET?

In many situations you will use both, but the degree to which you use packet will depend on the situation and the client needs. Voice communications will be used during all emergency situations. In situations where ARES is carrying extended formal traffic between specific locations, packet will be used to carry that traffic. In many scenarios, the bulk of the traffic will be carried by packet or over other digital modes. However, voice channels will still be used to coordinate those packet communications.

WILL WE USE CW AT ALL?

It is possible that CW may be used in a limited way in the following situations:

- When a message needs to be protected from casual eavesdropping, and digital modes are unavailable

- When a low-power or out-of-range station is unable to check into an HF net using voice

- During extreme propagation events that prevent reliable HF voice communications.

16-4

WHAT IF I AM ASKED TO SEND A MESSAGE 'SECURELY'?

If you are asked to send a message securely, inform the originator that you cannot legally encrypt or code any communications that are to be sent over amateur channels.

If you and the recipient location are equipped with packet, inform the originator that you can send the message digitally, which will provide some privacy from the public and the media. Winlink 2000 and automatic FBBS transfers also offer increased security since the message content is transferred in binary format rather than ASCII format.

If you and the recipient location are equipped with HF or CW, try to pass the traffic over an HF channel or using CW (which is less likely to be monitored).

SECTION 17: DIGITAL COMMUNICATIONS

This section provides guidelines and information that will be useful when you operate a digital station.

Once you complete this section, you will be able to:

- Discuss the use of digital communications during ARES operations

- Understand the use of digital modes in the NTS network

- Describe the use of Winlink

- Discuss the set-up of digital messaging network

- Describe common message formats.

INTRODUCTION

In the context of emergency communications the term "digital communications" refers primarily to the transmission of electronic messages. We can further subdivide the topic into modes used in the HF bands and those used in the VHF bands and above. The development of affordable personal computers with powerful data processors is driving significant and on-going change in the way that digital communications can be exploited by ARES.

There are two important concepts to understand. The first is that the current technological change is not with the underlying radio technology so much as in the development of software applications that allow us to exploit radio communications as never before. The second concept to embrace is the scope of change in the workplace that has resulted from the widespread adoption of information technology and electronic communications. Today emergency management and response organizations simply can't function without it. Our challenge is to understand the scope of the change, how Amateur Radio is adapting to it, and how to exploit digital communications as part of your group is capability.

HF DIGITAL COMMUNICATIONS

The earliest means of radio communication was CW, keying a carrier wave on and off. Radioteletype was the next major advancement, switching the carrier between two frequencies (frequency shift keying or FSK) or switching between two audio tones (audio frequency shift keying or AFSK). This advancement represented a significant increase in transmission speed, mechanized the transmission and reception of message traffic, but it suffered from a high error rate due to radio signal fading and multi-path propagation. Phase shift keying (PSK), where a change in the phase of the transmitted wave is utilized to indicate the shift in logic level, is a third methodology.

The development of "packet radio" in the late 1970s brought significant change (see below). Information was assembled in packets of data that were individually addressed and numbered in sequence. Each packet carried with it the ability to verify that the data was received and decoded correctly, and comparison of the sequence numbers ensured that no data packet was lost. The development of the Terminal Node Controller (TNC) -

17-1

part modem and part radio controller – coupled with the advent of simple personal computers brought about major change. If the receiving TNC successfully decoded a packet it immediately sent an acknowledgement and the next packet was transmitted. If not, it would request a retransmission. In time it lead to routine communication exchanges between automatic stations.

Over the years several transmission schemes progressively improved the ability to decode radioteletype transmissions in marginal propagation conditions. Pactor, a combination of the packet protocol with the error correcting features of AMTOR (Amateur Teleprinting Over Radio, see Wikipedia) has been one of the most successful and today is utilized by the National Traffic System (Digital) and the Winlink System to be discussed below. The Pactor II and III modes take advantage of inexpensive microprocessors to increase both the data transmission rate and the ability to detect and decode very weak signals through digital processing techniques. More recently experiments with computer sound cards, interface devices, and modulation techniques such as PSK, Multiple Frequency Shift Keying, MT63 and others (see Wikipedia: Radioteletype) but to date Pactor has proven the most reliable for speed and bandwidth conservation. One caution: it is generally held within the ECOM community that the reliability of techniques that use computer sound cards, because of inherent technical limitations, lack the assured reliability of hardware TNCs.

VHF/UHF DIGITAL COMMUNICATIONS

The development of microprocessor based TNCs and personal lead to a virtual explosion of Amateur Radio development in digital communications. Utilizing two-metre band radios and the "personal mailbox" incorporated within the TNC the concept of "text messaging" quickly took hold. By the late 1980s local area packet radio networks were well established and Bulletin Board Systems with message forwarding capabilities were becoming commonplace. Sophisticated inter-provincial and international backbone networks, many operating in the 70-centimetre band, were created. These developments peaked in the mid-1990's. The irony is that having been at the forefront developing the concepts and capabilities which lead to the Information Age, Amateur packet radio quickly lost it's lure as interests turned to software development and exploiting the Internet (e.g. the Internet Radio Linking Project (IRLP) and Echolink). Nevertheless, it is the packet radio capability that today is being exploited through a modified *Winlink 2000 System* that gives ARES a new opportunity to be of service to our traditional clients.

NATIONAL TRAFFIC SYSTEM DIGITAL (NTSD)

The NTSD is a component of the NTS. It is organized into three geographic divisions (Eastern, Central and Pacific) and is managed in parallel with the NTS voice and CW nets. Traffic can flow between the three nets as required for effective delivery.

The NTSD mode of operation has evolved over the years in step with the advancements in the HF digital modes. References to AMTOR, APLink and Winlink 2.9, Winlink 3.0, and Winlink Classic will be found in a number of publications and articles. Today many NTSD stations function within the Winlink 2000 System described in the next sub-section.

The NTSD conforms to NTS standards and utilizes the ARRL Radiogram format. Traffic is directed by one NTSD station to the NTSD station closest to the message

17-2

addressee for final delivery, and can involve a hand-off to a local voice or CW traffic net. Perhaps the greatest strength of the NTS is that traffic is routed to an Amateur Radio Operator who takes responsibility for making contact with the intended recipient, an invaluable resource in time of emergency when the recipient may be displaced, perhaps located in a shelter or a location without public communications, and dispatch/ delivery has to be coordinated through the emergency response organization.

One of the better-detailed descriptions of the NTSD can be found at AE5V's NTS Digital web page.

WINLINK 2000

The Winlink System has been in existence for a number of years, and it has evolved to include both Amateur and commercial (Sailmail) components. As just discussed the NTSD has utilized the Winlink System through several iterative developments. Up to and including the Winlink Classic version the system was only capable of sending text messages to another Winlink operator. With the introduction of Winlink 2000, or WL2K, Winlink interfaced directly with the international e-mail system permitting the delivery of traffic to a non-Amateur recipient. Also, for the first time, WL2K could handle email attachments.

Using an email application called Airmail, the user made contact with a Participating Mail Box Operator (PMBO) station to transmit and receive their email. The PMBO forwards/receives its email traffic with one of several Central Message Servers (CMS) that in turn interface with the commercial email system. Data is exchanged between the PMBOs and CMSs over Internet Telnet links. The system is robust and redundant, with the CMSs located internationally within major computer centres with high levels of security and assured power. There are several presentations that can be downloaded from the Winlink website that describe in detail how WL2K system works, and how it has been implemented in a number of municipal emergency management organizations.

In 2003 the United States government recognized the importance of Amateur Radio to an effective national disaster response. It also recognized that there was a growing disparity between the communications needs of emergency management authorities and first responders, and the general capability of the Field Service. The ARRL Board of Directors conducted a comprehensive review that resulted in a call for a modernized digital messaging system. The Winlink Development Team initially responded in early 2004 with the Telpac (Telnet/Packet) module and a computer application that transformed a local packet radio station into an Internet gateway to one of the HF PMBOs. The result was that any Amateur equipped with a basic 2-metre packet radio station could have the same WL2K access as the HF operator.

17-3

Much has changed since. First, author KE6RK (Jim Corenman) modified the Airmail application to greatly expand its utility in the ECOM environment. Other developers created Airmail add-on or word processor templates that automate the process of formatting Radiogram and ICS-213 messages. Second, the Winlink Development Team (WDT) began a programme of updating all the WL2K software so that it would continue working efficiently as computer operating systems were updated. In particular the WDT developed the Paclink application which is tailored for use in an EOC or Support Agency environment. In part the WDT:

1   created an exclusive ARES ECOM subset within WL2K that is not "visible" to the general WL2K user, to provide dedicated support to the emergency management/ response communities;

2   began a process of updating the family of WL2K software modules to ensure compatibility and interoperability with the server and client computer operating systems found in the typical government or support agency office environment;

3   developed the concept of a local "hubbing" Remote Message Server, in effect a PMBO operating within a local 2-metre or 70 centimetre band packet radio network, capable of supporting full email exchange between elements of a municipal emergency response organization, despite a complete Internet failure;

4   developed a mail server application (Paclink Postoffice), meeting internationally accepted standards, designed to operate within an EOC or support agency office environment and to seamlessly interface with that organization's email system;

5   developed control software (Paclink AGW) that would work with the AGW Packet Engine and a wider range of (packet only) TNCs; and,

6   introduced a "tactical" address capability for use by EOC and support agency staff giving them automatic access to the Paclink Postoffice while at the same time keeping separate the Amateur Radio and client email functions as required by the Radio Regulations.

The result is a fundamental shift in both operating concept and capability that is challenging even for seasoned packet radio operators. On the other hand, properly exploited, the ECOM component of the WL2K System offers a highly sophisticated electronic mail capability that can be deployed rapidly and which utilizes off-the-shelf radio and computer equipment. Perhaps more important, the intended emergency management or first responder user can utilize the system with minimal training and modest Amateur Radio operator support.

17-4

Figure 1: Example of a local area WL2K VHF/UHF ECOM network

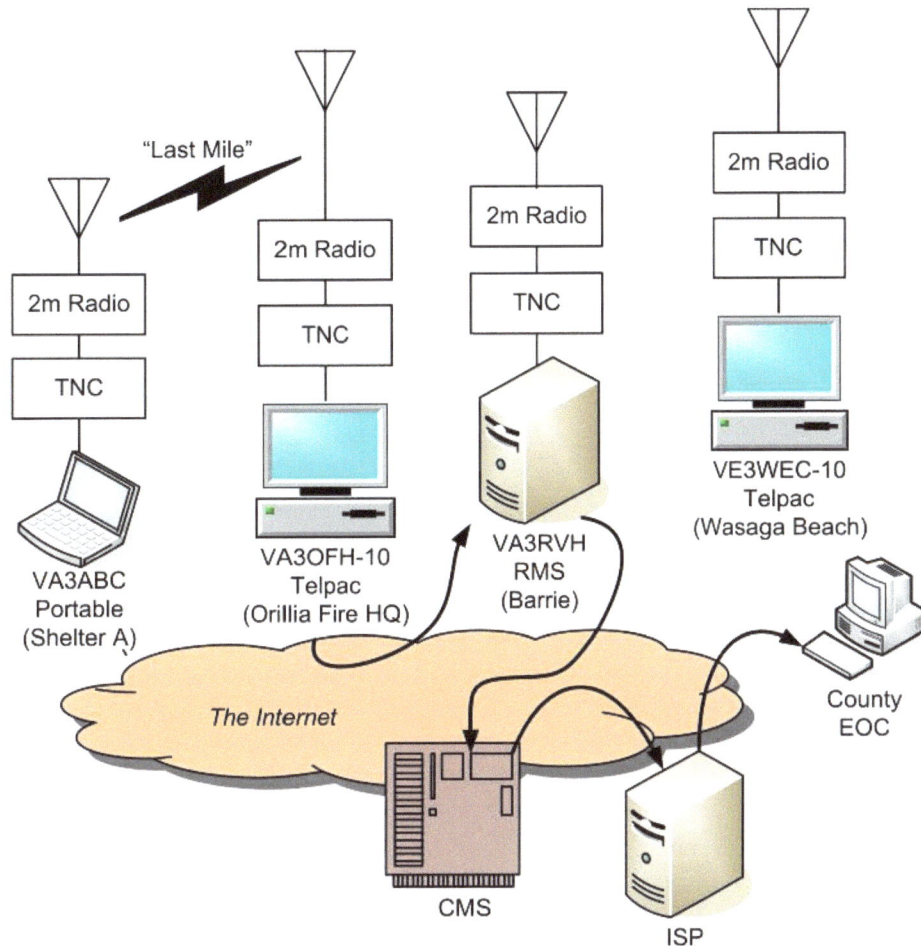

The diagram above shows an example of a local ECOM network that could be developed in a relatively urban environment. The scope of the network will be dependent on the size of the municipal unit (regional government, county, major urban area, etc.) and the size of the ARES/auxiliary communications organization available to support it. At the heart of the network is the "hubbing" RMS, with a collocated Telpac gateway. That gateway can be operated on the same server hosting the RMS or it can be in second location and connected via a Wifi or D-Star link. Additional Telpac gateways are placed at locations that offer good radio coverage, a connection to the Internet, and back-up power. Ideally two or more gateways would be within range of any location within the area of responsibility.

Depicted is a portable ARES WL2K station with VA3ABC deployed to a shelter that has limited fixed communications, a classic 'last mile' scenario. The Canadian Red Cross disaster response team operating the shelter utilize personal cell phones to communicate with their District headquarters and FRS radios between themselves. The majority of formal message traffic is logistical in nature. Approximately 80 persons are accommodated in the shelter, who send on average 25 personal welfare messages per day. In accordance with the Communications Annex of the Municipal Emergency Plan, every 15 minutes VA3ABC connects automatically to VA3OFH-10, a gateway located four blocks away at the city fire hall, to check for incoming email. The Telpac gateway automatically establishes a Telnet link to the hubbing RMS VA3RVH which downloads any waiting email traffic.

At 1430 hours the Shelter Manager dispatches a routine status report to the Social Welfare Coordinator at the County EOC. After completing the form the Manager attaches it to an email addressed to the Coordinator's EOC commercial email address, with an information copy to the Coordinator's Winlink 'tactical' address (for example, swcoord@winlink.org). When the Manager clicks on'send' the email is deposited in the Paclink mail server. VA3ABC automatically connects to VA3OFH-10 and, once the gateway has established the Telnet link to the RMS, uploads the email. The RMS saves the email to its database, establishes a Telnet link to a CMS, and the email is uploaded. The CMS in turn sends the email over the Internet to the recipient's Internet Service Provider mail server. From there it is forwarded to the EOC mail server, which delivers the email to the Coordinator's normal email account.

Figure 2: EOC WL2K LAN Network

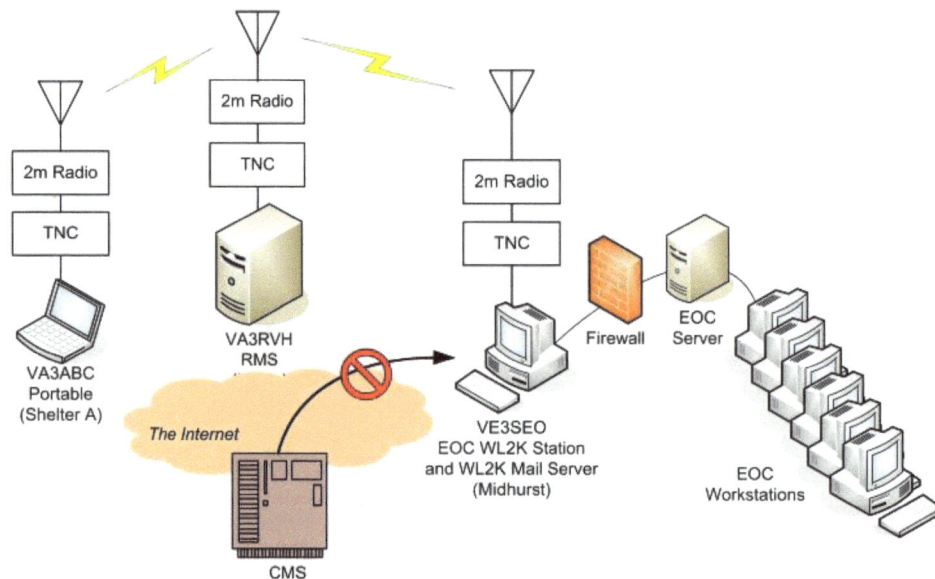

As useful as this "last mile" capability it in it's own right, the real power of the WL2K System comes into play when an Internet link is lost. Figure 2 depicts the situation where for some reason the EOC has lost its Internet connection to the service provider. Normally, to maximize efficiency, the EOC WL2K station (VE3SEO) would have its Paclink AGW module configured to poll the hubbing RMS via its telnet connection. For example, the information copy of the 1430 hours Shelter Report would have been downloaded via a Telnet link and routed from the Postoffice mail server through the EOC LAN to the Social Welfare Coordinator's secondary Winlink email account. The EOC staff would be conducting their business using their official email accounts and EOC mail server. The only WL2K traffic sent via the radio link would have been deliberate, perhaps test messages or internal ARES reports, sent by the ARES operator to verify system serviceability.

After the Internet failure occurs, the next time Paclink AGW initiates a poll to the RMS the Telnet link will fail and automatically it will initiate a connect to an external Telpac Gateway. The EOC staff simply change from their primary commercial email account to their Winlink tactical address account and traffic continues to be transmitted through the RMS.

As the scale of the Internet failure expands, and local Telpac gateways are affected, the Paclink AGW will receive a dirty disconnect. At that point it begins calling the RMS gateway. This configuration ensures that as a final resort all the WL2K stations in the network are communicating with the hubbing RMS over packet radio links and traffic continues to flow.

The likelihood of complete reliance on the packet radio network is low but it does happen. The impact, caused by the much lower data rate than Telnet links offer, is a reduction in the amount of message traffic that can be handled. In this eventuality message access priorities would be set by the EOC authorities.

LONG-RANGE WL2K COMMUNICATIONS

In areas of sparse populations the probability is that communications will be via HF WL2K. Operations would likely be through one of the public PMBOs. A monthly bulletin listing current PMBO callsigns, operating frequencies and Pactor modes is provided and this information is copied into the software set-up. Other add-ons such as propagation charts are also provided for. For transmission efficiency reasons serious consideration should be given to investing in a Pactor II/III mode modem.

DEVELOPING AN ECOM NETWORK

The very first step is for the ARES group members to become proficient with the Airmail and Paclink programmes. Bud Thompson, N0IA and an ECOM PMBO operator in Florida, has developed an excellent (self-guided) on-line "Winlink for Dummies" course that guides the student through the process of installing and configuring the software.

No TNC, data terminal, or radio is required at this point, just a computer and an Internet connection. In addition, the Airmail user group and the WL2K ECOM Reflector are invaluable sources for information and problem solving. The choice between using Airmail or Paclink depends on several variables.

At time of writing Airmail will only work with TNCs that have a Pactor capability. KE6RK has indicated that a wider choice of packet-only TNCs in a future update, as well as an AGWPE interface. Nor does Airmail have the same degree of automatic email handling as Paclink in a network environment.

On the other hand Paclink AGW is exclusively Packet although the forthcoming PaclinkMP version potentially has all the benefits of both.

Paclink is designed to operate with the AGW Packet Engine written by SV2AGW (George Rossopoulos). AGWPE contains a virtual TNC and can interface up to 100 applications with 100 "TNCs". The packet engine puts the TNC in KISS mode, and works with a wide range of legacy and modern TNCs. For Amateurs who do not currently have a TNC one of the several USB models in the $100 class are quite appropriate. Some Amateurs report success using AGWPE and a computer sound card, but for every positive report there are far more negative reports. The root cause seems to be timing issues between differing brands of computer and sound cards. It is established

17-7

wisdom within the ECOM community therefore that hardware TNCs should be relied on.

One benefit of using AGWPE/Paclink is that the Telpac module can be run concurrently on the same computer/TNC/radio. Thus each user can also be a WL2K access point for other mobile and portable stations.

With an understanding of the number of trained operators that will be available, the next step is for the Emergency Coordinator to establish with the municipal Emergency Planning Officer what role the group can perform. To be truly successful as an ECOM group there must be a partnership with the municipal authorities, with a formal understanding of the obligations and responsibilities undertaken by both sides. This will normally be in the form of a Memorandum of Understanding with operating details outlined in a confidential annex to the municipal Emergency Plan. In particular, for the WL2K System to operate effectively there should be municipally owned fixed Amateur Radio equipment installed at critical installations and serious consideration should be given to operating the radio links at 9600 baud. This requires more specialized (and costly) equipment and therefore is a client decision/responsibility

Establishing permanent 24/7 Telpac gateways with wide-area coverage and assured electrical power is the next goal. Dedicated digipeaters or integration into a regional packet radio network are effective methods for filling-in gaps in coverage. If a packet radio network exists one approach is to integrate a Telpac gateway with the packet radio node.

The final step is to establish an ECOM RMS. This step is not lightly taken as it requires a SYSOP dedicated to operating the RMS, and a partnership with an appropriate institution where the RMS can be hosted. Close liaison with the host institution's Information Technology staff is absolutely vital as there will be a number of policy and network security considerations to be addressed before the institution will be prepared to enter into a joint venture. Once the location has been identified the SYSOP should then make contact with the Winlink System Administrator who will provide the necessary guidance, RMS specifications, and required pre-installed support applications (e.g. anti-virus software). A WL2K SYSOP Yahoo User Group is available for managing the Winlink system and/or assistance.

MESSAGE FORMATS

In any emergency management operation record keeping is absolutely mandatory. It is required by law and/or regulation. All public service tactical radio circuits will be recorded (911 Call Centre, Dispatch Centres, etc.) Every EOC and incident site command centre will have a document control section where copies of all written directives, orders, and messages will be complied and filled. Amateur Radio operators supporting these activities will be expected to meet the same standards. There are three message formats that the ECOM operator must be familiar with: standard email, the ICS 213 form, and the traditional NTS Radiogram.

Standard email is rapidly becoming the norm for business communications. At this point there is no accepted national-level format standard for emergency management emails.

In efficiency terms, it is highly recommended that computer email programmes set up to send in Plain Text format. HTML looks pretty, but it adds a *significant* amount of

17-8

overhead in terms of the number of bytes of information that is transmitted. Where it would be inappropriate to configure the email application default setting to Plain Text, an alternative is to open up the address book, select and click open the applicable addressee, and check off the *Send E-mail using plain text only* box found at the bottom of the Name submenu (Outlook Express).

The Incident Command System has a number of pre-defined administrative forms. The ICS-213 Message Form is a widely recognized standard in the emergency management. This one-page document is in two parts; the top half comprising the outgoing message, the bottom half the response. It was clearly designed for use between offices within a single location or transmitted over facsimile to other locations. There is no single standard for ICS messages although *Firescope* is widely acknowledged. The Federal Emergency Management Agency (FEMA) has a standard as does the United States Coast Guard. How these ICS documents are to be used, and what format results in the most efficient use of transmission time, is a topic the Emergency Coordinator should have with the Emergency Planner as soon as possible.

A limitation of the ICS-213 is the lack of a unique identifier number in the format. If the emergency management officials do not have a local policy for applying one adding an NTS preamble in the covering email is worthy of consideration. When transmitting scanned ICS forms or other documents (i.e. in lieu of faxing) one successful approach to minimizing the amount of data is to scan it in black and white at the lowest possible resolution. If this is utilized, have the originator save the file, reopen it, and print it to ensure that it meets their approval for readability.

The Radiogram can be typed into an email, essentially just as a telex or telegram was sent by radio teletype in former times.

There are several applications and word-processor templates that will facilitate preparing an ICS-213 or Radiogram. One of the better ones for use with Airmail is QForms. The message is created in the QForm application and when saved the message is automatically sent to the Airmail SMTP mail server. A major feature is that only the text need be sent; the formatting instructions to display the ICS-213 or Radiogram for presentation/printing are pre-installed on the user's computer, avoiding the repetitive sending of the separate formatting file. Another feature of QForms is that it will automatically apply a sequential station control number to each message, making it unique document from the station operation point of view.

A last word of advice is to keep an open mind with respect to formats and "automatic" processing. First, the local Emergency Management authority will have defined a standard, whatever it is. It is their responsibility. As communicators we have no right or authority to change it, only to make recommendations during the routine planning process. In the heat of battle messages can arrive written on the lid of a box lunch, or worse. Our responsibility is to communicate that message as efficiently as possible. Ensure there is a date time group and a signature from the sender, then apply the appropriate format and get it underway.

17-9

SECTION 18: AFTER YOUR DEPLOYMENT IS OVER

This section provides important information about things you need to consider once an operation shuts down and your deployment is over.

Once you complete this section, you will be able to describe the tasks that need to be performed once an ARES deployment comes to an end.

TURN OVER LOGS

When your deployment ends (or when your shift ends, if practical), hand off your logs and operational notes to:

- your replacement

- your unit supervisor

- the communications supervisor

- the site manager, or

- another designated emergency management authority.

In ICS organizations, all documentation is sent to the documentation section usually on a daily basis. In fact, all documentation is the property of the served agency.

If you do not know who should receive the logs, contact the EC or communications supervisor and request clarification.

You must keep a written copy of all traffic for at least seven years following the operation.

DEBRIEFINGS

Once a deployment is over, it is important that everyone involved work together to assess the effectiveness of the response. This helps us improve our processes and practices for future deployments. It also ensures that significant contributions are recognized.

In addition, debriefings ensure that individuals who have suffered significant stress during the deployment are identified and assisted.

There are two key types of debriefing:

- Tactical debriefings (see page 18.2)

- Critical incident debriefings (see page 18.2)

These debriefings will normally be hosted by your EC, and typically take place one to four days after operations are complete.

18-1

You may be asked to participate in a series of debriefings, depending on the specific circumstances of the incident and your deployment.

Tactical debriefings

A tactical debriefing is a learning tool that will improve your effectiveness and your team's capabilities during future operations.

During the tactical debriefing, your group will address the following questions:

1   What was the mission or goal: exactly what were you there to accomplish?

2   Did you have a clear definition of who you were to communicate with and what the likely traffic would be?

3   Did you accomplish your mission or goal?

4   What did you do correctly and what went well?

5   In what ways did you exceed expectations? If nothing exceeded expectations, why not? Were the expectations unreasonably high?

6   What items did not meet expectations? How can you improve on those items?

7   What specific training do you now need?

8   Other than training, what else needs improvement?

9   Were there any surprises? Why?

It is very important that every ARES participant in the event be given the opportunity to contribute during the debriefing.

If you are unable to attend the formal debriefing, or if the incident continues for a number of days and you wish to capture your input before the debriefing, contact your EC to find out how to record your comments.

Critical incident debriefings

An 'emotional debriefing' may be needed after an ARES participant is involved in a critical incident. An emotional debriefing can minimize the effects of incident-related stress. The debriefing is an organized, open discussion. When appropriate, trained professionals may take part, and may be able to offer concrete suggestions for overcoming stress related to the incident.

A critical incident is one that is:

* Sudden and unexpected

* Perceived as life-threatening

* Disrupts one's sense of control

* Disrupts basic assumptions and beliefs

* Results in physical or emotional loss.

18-2

Physical reactions to critical incidents can include:

- Headaches

- Exhaustion

- Sleep disturbances

- Appetite disruptions

- A nervous stomach.

Behavioral and psychological reactions to critical incidents can include:

- Anger

- Self-blame

- Fear

- Anxiety

- Depression

- Hyperactivity

- A pronounced startle response

- A tendency to withdraw or isolate oneself

- Over-sensitivity

- Emotional numbness

- A heightened sense of danger

- Flashbacks

- A preoccupation with the incident.

If you have been involved in a critical incident, ensure that your EC is aware of the incident and is able to host a debriefing, if one is required.

DEALING WITH POST-INCIDENT STRESS

What can I do?

- Don't make any life altering changes.

- Get plenty of rest.

- Rather than jumping out of bed and rushing to start your day, plan to get up 15 minutes earlier each morning and take time to meditate.

- Structure your time - keep busy.

- Don't brood about past events or fret about future obligations.

- Do things that feel good to you.

- Talk to people.

- Help your co-workers as much as possible by sharing feelings and checking on how they are doing.

- Give yourself permission to feel bad, and share your feelings with others.

- Keep a journal.

- Realize that those around you are also under stress.

- Be aware of numbing the pain with overuse of drugs or alcohol; you don't need to complicate this with a substance abuse problem.

- Reach out - people do care.

- Maintain as normal a schedule as possible.

- Spend time with others.

- Eat well-balanced and regular meals (even if you don't feel like it).

- Change your eating environment. Get out of the office and enjoy your meal in the park. Occasionally eat by yourself in silence. Eat slowly, and enjoy yourself.

- Take a brisk walk.

18-4

Radio Amateurs of Canada

Amateur Radio
Emergency Service

Operations Training
Manual

Volume 2 - Support component

Document RAC-ARES-OPS

Release 2.0

September 2015

This training material has been prepared by volunteers on a not-for-profit basis in order to serve the public good. To the greatest degree practical, externally sourced information has been attributed and authorization sought for use, where required. Proprietary information and copyrighted material has not been intentionally included.

Contact:

Chief Field Services Officer, Radio Amateurs of Canada Inc., Suite 217, 720 Belfast Road, Ottawa, Ontario, Canada K1G 0Z5.

Radio Amateurs of Canada (RAC) and the authors of this document authorize the re-use and republication of content taken from this document only if ALL the following conditions are met:

1. Information is formally attributed to this document, as a RAC publication, or to the original copyright holder if applicable.

2. Information is used solely on a not-for-profit basis.

3. RAC is notified of the re-use in writing to the Chief Field Services Officer at: CFSO, Radio Amateurs of Canada, Suite 217, 720 Belfast Road, Ottawa, Ontario, Canada K1G 0Z5.

Contributors to this manual included the National Training Resource Group: Bob Boyd VE3SV, Bob Cooke VE3BDB, David Drinnan VE9FK, Don Mackinnon VE4DJ, Eric Jacksch VA3DSP, Forbes Purcell VE6FMP, Glenn Killam VE3GNA, Ian Snow VA3QT, John P. Cunningham W1AI, Jeff Dovyak VE4MBQ, Lance Peterson VA3LP, Monte L. Simpson K2MLS, Pierre Mainville VA3PM, and Tim Smith VE3HCB. Please see "Acknowledgements" on page 1-2.

This manual was created using Adobe FrameMakerTM.

Station management

Managing communications operations

Scheduling and selecting net controllers

SECTION 19: STATION MANAGEMENT

This section provides information needed by station managers responsible for setting up, provisioning and configuring an ARES emergency station.

Once you complete this section, you will be able to:

- Consider planning ARES stations

- Plan periodic station maintenance and validation

STATION PLANNING

When planning station requirements, consider the following questions:

- What equipment is needed in existing facilities?

- what buildings have antennas already erected?

- what locations have radios permanently installed?

- how do we get access to these locations?

- is there a cache of supplies available?

- where is it and how is it accessed?

- what is available?

- does someone periodically check it?

- do you have a personal "ready kit"?

- Does your ready kit enable you to establish an emergency station?

19-1

PERIODIC STATION MAINTENANCE AND VALIDATION

Periodic maintenance and testing of key stations is important. Key stations include:

Official emergency stations

Official emergency stations (OES) are:

- Personal stations used by designated ECs, AECs, net controllers, and relay operators

- Preinstalled, non-residential stations which will be used by ARES operators during exercises or emergencies.

Official Emergency Stations should be tested monthly if possible, and at least once every three months.

> *Note: Winlink 2000 tactical addresses must be used at least once every 90 days or they are automatically deleted from the WL2K database.*

19-2

Section 20: Managing communications operations

This section provides information that is useful to communications supervisors during an ARES operation.

Once you complete this section, you will be able to:

- Understand the duties of a communications supervisor

- Describe best practices for communications supervisors.

Duties of a communications supervisor

The communications supervisor performs ongoing management of ARES operations during a deployment. The communications supervisor performs tasks such as:

- selecting frequencies and defining nets

- assigning and scheduling net controllers

- deploying operators to sites and stations

- working with served agencies to identify and satisfy communications requirements

- managing communications and logistical problems as they arise.

Best practices for communications supervisors

The following best practices may make you a more effective communications supervisor:

- Start a log. Write down date, time and description of any significant activities, events, or observations. This helps you keep track of your responsibilities during your shift and may also help forensically after the operation.

- Do not wait to be called. Even if you are told not to respond, you can still prepare your group and monitor the situation. It is better to ramp up fast and then stand down rather than to wait until being called and working from a catch-up position.

- Use a formal and complete Incident Command approach, including organization, objectives, terminology and operational periods to manage your operations outside the ICS-defined incident area. (Within the incident area, ARES operators will fall under the existing Incident Command structure.)

- Send one person to the EOC or served agency to ensure that communications with the EOC or served agency is available to you. (Do this only if you have established relationships with the organization or served agency.)

- Avoid sending your personnel to useless locations. Use your expertise to make suggestions regarding where amateur communications can be of greatest use.

20-1

- During widespread disasters, consider the possibility that ARES operators will be unable to move easily due to blocked roads, traffic congestion or damaged bridges.

- Repeaters may be degraded or down. Be prepared to use both simplex and repeater frequencies, and train in the use of both.

- Once phone service is restored and reasonably reliable, consider standing down your operations as much as possible to ensure that your personnel are able to rest, in case they are needed again.

- Use your communications system to give constant and regular situation reports (sitreps). In the absence of official reports, talk only about your ARES response. Assign one person to read the latest sitreps on the air at least once an hour on operations frequencies and once every 15 minutes on check-in frequencies. Consider posting your sitreps on the Internet as well, if possible.

- Maintain communications with ARES ECs and partner organizations in adjacent areas (ARES groups and organizations with which you have mutual aid agreements) to ensure that they are ready to assist if needed. Update them periodically on your operational status.

- Use personnel who do not have amateur licenses to perform member callouts, logging of net traffic, sitreps, coordination, logistics support or other off-air tasks.

DURING ARES ACTIVATION PHASE

During the initial activation of ARES, you may be tasked by an EC or AEC to act as a Communications Supervisor.

ONGOING MANAGEMENT OF COMMUNICATIONS OPERATIONS

Locations

- Determine locations to be staffed.

Staffing

- Determine staffing requirements at each location.

- Determine appropriate shift lengths.

- Begin initial staffing work-sheet.

- State any special requirements operators may need, (mobiles, HTs, frequencies used, foul weather gear, and other equipment).

- Keep locations advised of staffing progress via appropriate tactical nets.

20-2

- Accept changes in staffing requirements and make adjustments to work-sheet and volunteer announcements.

- Ensure that there are extra operators available to cover off personnel attrition.

- When scheduling personnel to serve shifts at stations, provide a period of overlap to ensure that replacement operators are onsite before the current operators are due to go off-shift.

Using non-ARES trained volunteers

You may find that you have untrained amateurs willing to volunteer, or the situation may require that you solicit untrained or unregistered amateurs to augment your trained ARES operators.

If you have a need to solicit untrained or unregistered amateurs:

- Make frequent announcements on the net requesting volunteers for open staffing requirements.

When soliciting untrained or unregistered amateurs or accepting volunteers:

- Obtain call, first name and phone number for each volunteer.

- Consider retasking trained ARES operators to act as communications supervisors or site or station managers.

Nets

- Declare a directed net. Give and ask for major damage and injury reports unless otherwise requested. Set up a resource net if necessary.

SECTION 21: SCHEDULING AND SELECTING NET CONTROLLERS

This section provides information about selecting net controllers, and scheduling controllers during longer operations.

Once you complete this section, you will be able to:

- Describe criteria for selecting net controllers

- Schedule net controllers.

SELECTING NET CONTROLLERS

Choose net controllers based on availability, experience, and interest. When choosing a net controller from the available ARES operators, consider some of the qualities that often make for a good net controller:

- Good voice quality, with a friendly air of authority

- Sense of control and self-assuredness

- Decisiveness and the maturity to make good judgment calls

- Knowledge of band characteristics and area repeaters

- Good basic communications skills and fluent command of the language

- Physical condition that will tolerate high stress for extended periods of time

- A strong team player and organizer

- Good hearing

- Good listening

- Good ear-to-hand copying skills

- Decent (readable) penmanship

- Computer keyboard skills - touch typing

- Willingness to take and carry out direct orders

- Consistently demonstrates above-average operating techniques

- Good sense of humor

21-1

Remember the following important guidelines:

- The net controller must have good, reliable coverage of the net area (either on simplex, or through the repeater).

  Note: Net control should always be performed by a station that has a strong signal. Do not transfer net control duties to a weak or marginal station. If faced with a choice of a weak station manned by an experienced controller, or a strong station manned by an inexperienced controller, choose the strong station.

- An EC or AEC should not serve as a net controller unless absolutely necessary. (The EC or AECs may be required to coordinate with client management, or perform other mission-critical duties, and should not commit to running a net.)

- The net controller should be able to communicate with liaisons at served agencies, either by telephone, radio, liaison station, courier, or Internet.

- The net control station should have alternative, back-up power and a back-up transceiver.

SCHEDULING NET CONTROLLERS

When scheduling net controllers, remember the following guidelines:

- Provide an overlap of at least 15 minutes at shift changes. This allows the new net controller to get up to speed on net activities before the handoff.

- Schedule net control shifts to run 1-2 hours. Unlike operator shifts, net control shifts often involve almost constant, frenetic activity, and quickly result in exhaustion.

- When net controllers are few, try having net controllers switch off with their backup controllers regularly (for example, once an hour).

- When net controllers are few and you are running operational, tactical and support nets, try to rotate controllers at shift changes to different nets that offer different types and levels of activity.

- Accommodate individuals' natural schedules as much as possible. If you have some controllers who are more comfortable working overnight, be sure to schedule them to work overnight and not during the day.

Backup net controllers

For every net controller, also schedule a backup net controller that can take over in case of equipment failure or other situation at the primary net control station.

21-2

Radio Amateurs of Canada

Amateur Radio
Emergency Service

Operations Training
Manual

Volume 3 - Emergency
Coordinator component

Document RAC-ARES-OPS

Release 2.0

September 2015

Contact:

Chief Field Services Officer, Radio Amateurs of Canada Inc.,
Suite 217, 720 Belfast Road, Ottawa, Ontario, Canada K1G 0Z5.

Contributors to this manual included the National Training
Resource Group: Bob Boyd VE3SV, Bob Cooke VE3BDB, David
Drinnan VE9FK, Don Mackinnon VE4DJ, Eric Jacksch VA3DSP,
Forbes Purcell VE6FMP, Glenn Killam VE3GNA, Ian Snow VA3QT,
John P. Cunningham W1AI, Jeff Dovyak VE4MBQ, Lance Peterson
VA3LP, Monte L. Simpson K2MLS, Pierre Mainville VA3PM, and
Tim Smith VE3HCB. Please see "Acknowledgements" on page 1-2.

This manual was created using Adobe FrameMaker™.

ARES planning

Exercises

Creating standard operating procedures and documentation for your region

Administrative roles within ARES

SECTION 22: EMERGENCY COORDINATOR DUTIES

This section describes the duties of an emergency coordinator (EC). Primary responsibilities include planning, organizing, coordinating and communicating.

Once you complete this section, you will be able to:

- Outline the general duties of an emergency coordinator

- Discuss the planning and organization of an ARES group

- Coordinate with other ARES groups, served agencies, and stakeholders

- Perform EC duties before and during a disaster response. For more

  information about EC responsibilities, see the RAC EC webpage.

GENERAL DUTIES

- Establishing a viable working relationship with all the municipal Emergency Measures Coordinator and the various private agencies in the ARES jurisdictional area which might need the services of ARES in emergencies.

- Promoting and enhancing the activities of ARES for the benefit of the public as a voluntary, non-commercial communications service.

- Managing and coordinating the training, organization and emergency participation of interested amateurs working in support of the communities, agencies or functions designated by the Section Emergency Coordinator/Section Manager.

- Establishing an emergency communications plan for the communities and agencies that will effectively utilize ARES members to cover the needs for formal message traffic.

- Establishing local communication networks run on a regular basis and periodic testing of those networks by realistic drills.

- Establishing an emergency traffic plan, if possible utilizing the National Traffic System as one active component for traffic handling. Establishment of an operational liaison with Local and Section nets, particularly for handling traffic in an emergency situation.

- Doing all that is possible to further the favorable image of amateur radio by dedication to purpose and a thorough understanding of the mission of the Amateur Radio Service.

PLANNING

- Drafting brief, specific ARES plans to fulfill community needs for emergency communications.

22-1

- Developing training programs to fill special skill requirements of members as needed.

- Establishing a workable plan in coordination with other local two-way radio organizations for responding to non emergency communications requests; e.g., walkathons, parades, special events.

- Developing, implementing and maintaining a current "telephone tree" for use in alerting and activating ARES members in emergencies.

- Establishing regular, announced meetings of ARES members to plan programs and drills and to accomplish specific goals.

- Developing a local ARES operating manual to include all essential operating aids and reference information, with annual updates.

ORGANIZING LOCALLY

- Appointing Assistant Emergency Coordinators (AECs) and issuing AEC Certificates when needed. The AECs will be designated specific functions and/or agencies within the jurisdictional area.

- Maintaining a current roster information on all enrolled ARES members.

  - Recording special skills and equipment useful in emergencies.
  - Issuing ARES and/or municipal identification cards and cancellation when appropriate.

- Establishing and fostering radio nets as required to maintain an active ARES unit, develop capable net control stations, transact a full range of traffic, and disseminate news and bulletins of value to the amateur population in general, and to ARES in particular.

- Recommending OES candidates to the SM/SEC.

COORDINATING WITH ARES GROUPS, SERVED AGENCIES, AND STAKEHOLDERS

- Establishing effective liaison between ARES and emergency services' designees in local radio clubs and repeater associations.

- Coordinating and cooperating with ECs of adjacent areas and sections.

- Acting as principal area representative from ARES to area coordinating councils of volunteer emergency response teams.

- Through the SEC/STM, arranging for effective liaison and active cooperation with operators of the National Traffic System for both incoming and outgoing traffic during both normal and emergency conditions.

22-2

- Developing and organizing an emergency planning committee of all agencies that would be involved in a disaster in your jurisdiction with special emphasis on the agency with which RAC has an agreement – Canadian Red Cross.

COMMUNICATING

- Preparing EC bulletins and releases for periodic issuance over radio nets and at meetings of amateurs to keep ARES members (and local amateurs in general) informed of ARES matters.

- Conducting periodic meetings in person and on-the-air for the purpose of developing close coordination and a free exchange of information among ARES members.

- Using the municipal Emergency Measures Manager, where possible, to contact heads of agencies to be served to determine requirements and methods of introducing Amateur Radio into their operations. Communicate such plans to all ARES members

- Providing user-agencies with current contact information for alerting/activating ARES

- Submitting monthly reports to the SEC/DEC (as directed) covering ARES news, achievements, events, problems, contacts with user agencies, etc.

- Checking into local and section nets regularly--on all modes possible-- to be accessible to the membership and be aware of their participation, keep members informed and support their efforts, and provide special bulletins of interest and importance to members.

- Reporting regularly by radiogram, correspondence, or the official report form (FSD-211R) to the DEC/SEC on names, calls and telephone numbers of AECs and their areas of responsibility, public service events planned or impending, problems which should be of concern to the SEC/DEC, names and call signs of amateurs involved in communications, operations or exercises, and performance of individual members considered particularly noteworthy.

DURING AN EMERGENCY OR AN EXERCISE

- In times of disaster, evaluating the communication needs of the jurisdiction and responding quickly to those needs. The EC will assume authority and responsibility for emergency response and performance by ARES personnel under the EC's jurisdiction.

- After operations or exercises, providing prompt oral and written reports and critiques concerning served agencies and ARES operations to agencies and SEC/DEC.

22-3

Section 23: Emergency operations

Once you complete this section, you will be able to describe the tasks associated with ARES activation.

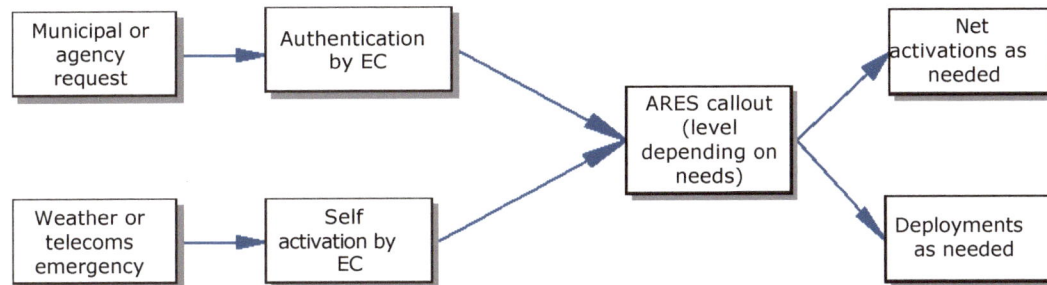

```
┌──────────┐    ┌──────────────┐                              ┌──────────────┐
│Municipal or│─▶│Authentication│                              │     Net      │
│  agency   │   │    by EC     │─┐                         ┌─▶│activations as│
│  request  │   └──────────────┘  ┐                       │   │   needed     │
└──────────┘                       ▶┌──────────────┐      │   └──────────────┘
                                    │ ARES callout │──────┤
┌──────────┐    ┌──────────────┐   │   (level     │      │   ┌──────────────┐
│Weather or│   │    Self       │ ▶│ depending on │      └─▶│ Deployments  │
│ telecoms │──▶│ activation by │─┘ │   needs)     │          │ as needed    │
│emergency │   │     EC        │   └──────────────┘          └──────────────┘
└──────────┘   └──────────────┘
```

ARES ACTIVATION

When you hear about a community emergency or telecommunications outage

When you hear about a community emergency or telecommunications outage, consider what level of activation is appropriate. Then perform the following steps:

1 Activate ARES to the lowest level that is appropriate. (See "Activation and mobilization" on page 8.1.)

2 If possible, contact your liaisons at appropriate served agencies (for example, the Canadian Red Cross) and ask them if assistance is required.

3 If you cannot contact your liaisons, consider visiting agency locations (for example, Red Cross headquarters or City Hall) to determine whether ARES support is needed.

4 If you receive or solicit a request for assistance, go to "When you receive a request from a municipality or served agency" on page 23.2.

5 Depending on the nature of the emergency, and what you find out in dialog with your liaisons, deactivate, maintain or escalate the ARES activation.

23-1

When you receive a request from a municipality or served agency

When you receive a request for support from a served agency, gather as much information as possible about the agency's communications needs, and about any aspects of the emergency situation that may affect ARES operations and operators. Then perform the following steps:

1   Authenticate the individual making the request. (See "Authentication" on page 37.1.)

2   Determine what level of ARES activation is required. (See "Activation and mobilization" on page 8.1.)

3   Activate ARES to the appropriate level. (See "Activation and mobilization" on page 8.1.)

4   Confirm with the requesting agency that activation has taken place.

5   Move ARES to an operational status:

    • Select or activate a Communications Supervisor (or take on those duties yourself, if no one else is available).

    • Dispatch ARES operators to designated duty locations.

    • Actively poll served agencies to ensure that changing communications requirements are captured.

    • Provide agency liaisons with contact information for the Communications Supervisor, as a backup in case you cannot be reached.

6   Confirm with the requesting agency that deployment is taking place, and ensure that the agency's site managers will be ready for the ARES operators that have been dispatched to them.

Activating ARES

To activate ARES, perform the following steps:

1   Notify the other ECs or AECs that an activation is taking place.

2   Initiate a limited or full callout of ARES operators.

3   Select a net control station to operate the initial ARES net.

4   Give the net controller a script to be read to ARES stations as they log into the net, outlining the scenario, whether it is an exercise or a real emergency, and any other pertinent information.

Callout procedures

At the beginning of an exercise, or when a need for ARES support is identified during an emergency, a callout is performed to activate the local ARES group.

During certain broad exercises, or during actual emergencies, the activation may be triggered by a request from an Emergency Management Organization (EMO), from the Canadian Red Cross, or from other provincial or municipal agencies. Managers at each agency should have a list of ARES ECs or AECs that they can contact to activate ARES. (This redundancy guarantees that at least one of the EC/AECs can be reached at any given time.)

In situations where telecommunications has failed, or where a community emergency has been declared but ARES has not been specifically activated, available ECs or AECs may decide to perform a limited (warm-up) or full activation in the expectation that a request may be received.

During a callout, any one of the ECs or AECs can trigger the callout (either autonomously, or in response to a request). The triggering EC/AEC first calls the next EC/AEC in the EC ring. Then the EC/AEC calls the operators for which they are responsible.

If an EC/AEC fails to reach the next EC/AEC in the EC ring, the EC/AEC takes on responsibility to call the second EC/AEC in the ring, and the operators assigned to the unavailable EC/AEC. If the second EC/AEC in the ring is also unavailable, the EC/AEC continues by calling the final EC/AEC in the ring, and then calls the additional operators belonging to the second missing EC/AEC. If the final EC/AEC is also unavailable, the EC/AEC personally calls all the operators directly.

This system ensures that all available operators are called, regardless of the availability of EC/AECs. So long as one EC/AEC out of the four are available, ARES can be triggered. This system also ensures a redundant, efficient callout that avoids multiple calls to operators.

MANAGING COMMUNICATIONS

For detailed information about managing ongoing communications operations, see "Managing communications operations" on page 20.1.

SECTION 24: MANAGING PERSONNEL AND VOLUNTEERS

This section provides guidelines to help you manage personnel and volunteers. Once you complete this section, you will be able to:

- Understand the personnel that may become involved in ARES operations

- Describe the mustering process

- Match capabilities to requirements

- Manage spontaneous volunteers.

AVAILABLE PERSONNEL

During exercises and planned operations, you are likely going to be working with an ARES group made up entirely of operators who have had some experience or have participated in at least some ARES training. However, during real disaster operations, you may also be compelled to deal with operators who are not ARES trained.

The following groups may either volunteer to participate, or actually self-deploy:

- Amateur radio club members, as a group

- Untrained, individual amateurs

- Amateurs with ARES training obtained in other regions, who are not currently registered with ARES locally

- ARES operators arriving from other areas under a mutual assistance request

- ARES operators who self-deploy from other regions

- Non-ARES trained amateurs who self-deploy from other regions

- Unlicensed amateurs in training who may already have equipment and familiarity

- Unlicensed radio owners who wish to self-deploy

Any 'walk on' volunteers that either represent themselves as amateurs or ARES operators potentially become a management problem that you will have to address. In some cases, such as radio club members or ARES operators arriving under a mutual assistance request, these will present valuable opportunities to increase your network capability and capacity. In other cases, such as unlicensed radio enthusiasts and even licensed amateurs with no ARES training, they will present a possible hazard to your operations. In any case, you cannot ignore these groups.

24-1

MUSTER

The process of mustering, or activating, your personnel will change depending on the type and severity of the emergency. Typically, the following methods are used:

- telephone callout

- on-air callout

- gathering at a single marshalling point

- gathering at multiple marshalling points

- direct-from-home dispatch (operators sent from their home locations directly to posts, without ever going to a marshalling area).

MATCHING CAPABILITIES TO REQUIREMENTS

Factors to consider

Training

Check the ARES membership database to see the training provided to each member. When possible, assign personnel based on training and experience. (For example, an operator who has been oriented on the PLEOC site is a better choice for PLEOC deployment than one who has not.)

Also consider other training the person may have had (for example, ground search and rescue, first aid, community aid, coast guard auxiliary, ATV use, etc.).

Fitness

Unfortunately, many amateur radio operators and some ARES personnel face fitness challenges that may limit how and when you should deploy them during actual emergencies. Consider not only known disabilities but also overall health when assigning personnel to posts. Also consider the schedule and likelihood of relief when making assignments. (Some posts may not expect relief for 24 hours or more, putting great stress on any operators assigned there.)

Language

If the disaster area includes regions or served agencies in which French is a common working language, does the person have enough fluency in French.

Mobility

Does the person have a vehicle that is capable and suitable for transport to and from the site or duty?

24-2

Is the person mobile enough to meet the onsite requirements? (For example, a person with a physical disability may not be suitable for duties shadowing a fire chief, or attached to a search and rescue team.)

Risk

Assess the risk associated with a posting and consider it in relation to the person's expressed preferences and the person's vulnerability. (For example, in a radiological environment, it is preferable to use operators who are no longer of childbearing age.)

MANAGING SPONTANEOUS VOLUNTEERS

You must be careful when dealing with the participation of spontaneous or unsuitable volunteers (for example, unlicensed radio enthusiasts). If these volunteers are perceived to be radio amateurs by served agencies, they become a management problem you must deal with even if it seems at first to have nothing to do with ARES.

Strategies you may wish to use:

- Assigning volunteers to assist with already staffed posts

- Asking volunteers to perform non-radio related duties elsewhere

- Asking volunteers to perform non-radio related communications duties (for example, handling telephone traffic).

SECTION 25: RECRUITING

This section provides guidelines to help you recruit participants into your ARES group.

Once you complete this section, you will be able to prepare and plan a recruitment campaign.

PREPARING FOR RECRUITMENT

Before you go out looking for new recruits, consider taking the following steps to ensure that your recruitment efforts are successful:

- Prepare training and documentation that is friendly and accessible.

- Put up a website or webpage that can be used during recruitment to deliver key information and drive interest.

- Create an invitation letter that you can send out to prospective participants.

- Identify amateur licensing and certification options in your area (to aid those who may be interested in participation but are not yet licensed).

- Define a 'vision' of participation that includes as many people as possible.

- Be clear about expectations and the 'ARES experience'.

- Map out a simple, clear process for interested parties to get more information and register.

- Identify any requirements for CPIC or background checks on the part of your served agencies.

- Design (in consultation with your served agencies) identification badges that will be issued to participants.

- Draft a training and meeting schedule that will provide a consistent level of activity during and after your recruitment campaign.

- Identify media points of contact for press releases and news story pitches.

PLAN YOUR RECRUITMENT CAMPAIGN

When planning your recruitment campaign:

- Review the database of licensed amateurs (available from the RAC website) to identify callsigns, names and addresses in your operational area.

- Create a schedule of hamfests in or near your operational area.

- Create a schedule of meetings for ham clubs in or near your operational area.

- Search for message boards and websites frequented by amateurs in your region.

- Consider recruiting from other volunteer organizations and clubs.

- Consider offering information briefings at workplaces, schools, colleges, community centres, and other venues.

- Create a membership database to track participant registration. Include categories for skills, availability (time of day, day of week, month of year), special restrictions, license class, etc.

- Identify key topics, events or persons who could be leveraged with the media to generate stories that will increase public awareness of amateur radio, ARES, or your specific group.

25-2

Section 26: ARES PLANNING

This section provides discussions about planning for your ARES group.

Once you complete this section, you will be able to:

- Design scenarios to assist in ARES planning

- Design operational configurations

- Describe best practices for emergency coordinators

- Make use of SET and other training opportunities.

The task of planning for ARES activities is a responsibility shared by all ARES participants. Planning begins with ARES emergency coordinators but also includes individual operators, station primes, technical support primes, and other participants. Ideally, planning also includes ARES clients who will make use of ARES capabilities during exercises and emergencies.

Designing scenarios

When designing scenarios, consider the following 'learned lessons' about disasters and disaster communications:

During a major disaster

- The extent of the disaster may be difficult to assess, though assessment will be needed to ensure the proper commitment of resources.

- Emergency equipment and field personnel may commit without being dispatched.

- There may be a greater demand for aid than can be met with the units available.

- Communications are likely to be inadequate.

- Trained personnel may become supervisors because they will be too valuable to perform hands-on tasks.

- Responding mutual aid units may become lost, and may require maps and guides.

- Citizens will volunteer, but their commitment will usually be short-term.

- HAZMAT situations may arise unexpectedly.

- The Command Post or EOC will become crowded with non-essential personnel.

- Staging will be essential; the flow of personnel, equipment and supplies may be overwhelming.

- Fuel may not be available if there is no electricity to run the pumps, or if fuel delivery is disrupted.

26-1

- The primary police department concern will be law enforcement; there may not be sufficient time or manpower to provide miscellaneous services.

- At night, there may not be enough generators or lights available.

- Many injured people may have to find their own way to medical treatment facilities.

- Volunteer and reserve personnel may be slow to respond; they will put their own families' safety first.

- On-duty public safety personnel will also be concerned about their own families, and some may leave their posts to check on them.

- Law enforcement and the media may clash; all media representatives should be referred to the Public Information Officer (PIO).

- Very few citizens will use evacuation and mass care centres; they will prefer to stay with friends and relatives, or to camp out in their own yards.

- The identification of workers and volunteers may be a problem; it will be difficult to determine who is working where and on what.

- There may not be enough handheld radios, and batteries will run short.

- Critical facilities will have to be self-sufficient, in case gas, lights, water or other essential services are disrupted for extended periods.

- Emergency responders will require rest and must be relieved.

- Equipment may be lost, damaged or stolen, and may never be accounted for.

- Someone will eventually get the bill; record-keeping and accounting procedures are important.

- If phones are working, the number of requests for service will be overwhelming. People will have to fend for themselves; it will be difficult for dispatchers to ignore these pleas for help.

- Some field units may "disappear"; you might not be able to reach them and will not know where they are or what they are doing.

- Security may have to be posted at hospitals, clinics, and first-aid stations to control hysterical citizens demanding immediate attention.

- Representatives from public agencies based outside the affected region may want to come and observe the operations or offer assistance.

- Department heads (EOC) staff may not have a working knowledge of their assigned areas of responsibility, and might tend to "play it by ear."

- Management may not be familiar with field response procedures, and may attempt to change standard operating procedures.

26-2

- Emergency responders (public safety and medical alike) may not be adequately trained to respond efficiently.

- Needed supplies, materials and equipment needed may not be readily available in the chaos of the initial response.

- There may be a general lack of necessary information; coordinators will want to wait for damage or casualty assessment information before establishing priorities.

- General information may be offered in response to specific questions when field units cannot verify the requested information.

- There may be an overcritical desire to "verify" all incoming information. If it is received from a field unit, it should be considered as verified.

- Some EOC and Command Post personnel may become overloaded; some will not be able to cope with the volume of activity and information they have to deal with, and some will not be able to cope with the noise and distractions.

In an earthquake

- Fires are likely to occur, caused by electrical shorts, natural gas, fireplaces, stoves, etc.

- Fires in collapsed buildings could be very difficult to control.

- Water could become contaminated and unsafe for drinking. Tankers may be needed for firefighting and for carrying drinking water.

- Electric power could be interrupted.

- It might be difficult to shut of the gas; valves that are seldom, if ever, used will be difficult to find, and may not work when they are found.

- There is likely to be an epidemic of flat tires; police, fire, and emergency medical vehicles will require repair in the field.

- Fires will need to be investigated; mutual aid will include arson investigators.

- Search dogs will be needed early in the operation.

- Riveted steel (oil and water storage) tanks may fail.

- Streets could become impassable in some areas; it will be necessary to clear streets of rubble in order to conduct emergency operations.

- There will be aftershocks; they will hamper emergency operations, create new fears among the citizenry and may cause more destruction than the original shock.

26-3

- Structural engineers will be needed to evaluate standing buildings for use as evacuation centres, command posts, information centres, first aid stations, etc.

- Many fire hydrants may become inaccessible (covered or destroyed by rubble) or inoperable.

OPERATIONAL CONFIGURATIONS

Frequency coordination

A key issue that needs to be addressed during planning is frequency coordination. This involves the selection of channels that will be used during exercises and emergencies. Channels will include repeater and simplex frequencies on 2m or 70cm, and HF frequencies.

Channels need to be prioritized in terms of reliability, availability, and coverage. It is particularly important that all operators know which channels to check during a callout. While individual channels can be allocated during an emergency by a net control station or EC, the need for task-specific channels needs to be mapped out ahead of time.

Determining repeater coverage

An important issue to deal with prior to exercises and emergency operations is coverage. Every repeater has a specific footprint, inside which you can reliably access the repeater. The footprint varies depending on the type of equipment (transmit power, receive sensitivity, and antenna characteristics), and operating conditions (outside, in-car, or inside buildings).

To determine repeater coverage for a given area, it is recommended that you use:

- a mobile transceiver with typical power output, high and low power settings, and a typical mobile antenna

- a handheld transceiver with high and low power settings, and a 'rubber duck' antenna

Arrange a period of time when a second station that has good coverage into the repeaters is available for comm checks. Drive around the area and at specific checkpoints, check communications on each repeater channel with each transceiver on high and low power settings. Mark the results on a roadmap for each checkpoint and each repeater.

Once the survey is complete, consider also the characteristics of each repeater. For example, find out which repeaters are equipped with emergency power, which may be affected by weather (such as high winds), and which can be considered 'highly reliable'.

Look at the footprint for each repeater and compare it to your operational scenarios. If you identify areas that will require communications but fall into different footprints (meaning that they will not be able to use the same repeater to communicate), consider assigning a relay station that can communicate reliably into both repeaters.

26-4

Determining simplex coverage

Identifying issues with point-to-point communications on simplex channels may be complex, particularly if you don't have direct access to some of the locations (for example, at an EOC).

You need to actually try communications between each high-value endpoint using the modes, frequencies and preferably the equipment that will actually be used during an exercise or emergency.

If you do not have direct access to a facility or location, attempt communications from near the location using equipment similar to the equipment that will actually be used.

Create a checklist of connections between endpoints, and check off each link with information about the quality of the link.

Addressing coverage and link issues

If you identify a dead spot (where no repeaters are available) in a critical area, or if you have a low-quality link, there are several steps you can take to rectify or work around the problem:

- Use higher-powered equipment or better antennas in that area.

- Inquire with repeater managers to see if there are any options for improving coverage.

- Use a mobile or portable repeater during the event.

- Establish a relay station that can take traffic from the affected area or can communicate with both ends of the bad link.

On specific point-to-point links, you may also consider using alternate bands or modes (such as packet, HF voice, 10 meter FM, or SSB on 2 or 6 meters), if equipment, antennas and qualified operators are available.

EC BEST PRACTICES

Address vulnerabilities

When planning your ARES response, remember that your team will suffer its own vulnerabilities. Consider the following guidelines:

- Running an ARES group should not be the responsibility of a chosen few. Get everyone involved as much as possible, and delegate.

- Do not hamstring participants unnecessarily with titles. It is the responsibility of everyone in your group to ensure that your system functions properly.

26-5

- Focus on doing a proper job. Spend the time needed to do it right.

- Look for single points of failure or weak links in your organization or practices, to ensure that you are able to provide services reliably during a crisis.

Keep an open mind

As an emergency coordinator, your role is to listen to all the members of the group and then make educated decisions based on those inputs.

Remember the following guidelines:

- Every one of us is a volunteer. We spend our own time and use our own equipment and money preparing for emergency communications duties.

- Make everyone feel that their voices have been heard. Remember: you need them, not the other way around.

- Always open your meetings to anyone who is interested in attending, including the public. Nothing should be closed, by invitation only, or secret.

- If your meeting location or operations centre cannot hold the anticipated number of people in your group, then find another place to hold your meetings. Most public libraries or schools have rooms that you can use at little or no cost.

- Work to develop as large a membership as possible. A larger pool of operators will make your communications group more effective. Even operators who wouldn't be suitable as net control operators or shelter station operators could be useful as an at-home loggers or runners.

- If you cannot maintain a high profile with your membership and within your community, then try to find someone else who can take over the role. All ECs and AECs need to be both active within the community. This means attending local non-emergency events and all training and general meetings. You also need to attend all the local area amateur radio club meetings, even if you aren't a member. The face you show will dictate how many people will turn out for an event.

- Do not assume that people will automatically show up to do your bidding during an emergency.

- Listen, take notes and get back to anyone who may have a question.

- Publish an email address and encourage people to contact you regarding problems, questions or suggestions.

Even though ARES is a volunteer group, in an emergency the members will have to quickly follow the directions of the EC. In an emergency there will likely be no time for discussion or for personal likes or dislikes.

26-6

Take identification seriously

Make sure that each and every participant in your group has a photo ID that verifies their membership in your organization. On the ID, include an expiration date and fields for your signature and the holder's signature.

Ensure that the photo ID cards are as professional looking as possible, and comparable to any official government or served agency ID. There are many places that offer "passport" size photos.

Make it the responsibility of each member to supply you with

two photos. One is for the ID, the other is for your records.

Getting in during a drill and getting in during an emergency are two different things. Many officials may be unaware of our existence. A professional-looking ID will help cement your legitimacy. Proper IDs also make your members feel that they belong to an official, professional group, instilling them with a sense of professionalism that will help them fulfill their duties.

If possible, provide served agencies with sample of your ID card so they can include it in their directives.

Train your volunteers using different resources

There are never enough resources at your disposal when you hold training classes. Make sure that the information you provide is current and comprehensive.

Remember the following guidelines:

- Take the time to investigate what materials would best suit the training needs of your group, based upon locale and known weaknesses in your area. For instance, do not stress earthquake rescue if your area never has earthquakes.

- When you train, make sure you supply your members with plenty of handouts they can refer to after the training sessions.

- Host question and answer sessions.

- Never assume that everyone understands everything you might have presented. When you do train using drills, vary the drills and break down the drills so that each phase of your group's communications duties can be tested and reviewed.

- When each drill is complete, host a review. During the review, ask your team members what they think could be done better.

Reliable communications requires reliable equipment

It is unlikely that all your members will have the same equipment, and you will probably face some challenges related to that equipment. Equipment failure is one of the greatest vulnerabilities in any communications system. Frayed cables, a failure to pre-program operating frequencies, and antenna shortcomings can all present serious challenges during operations.

Remember the following guidelines:

- Assess each member's equipment for suitability and susceptibility. Each rig, cable, mic, antenna and power system should be inspected at least once a year. Look for patched-up cables, frayed power cords, questionable connectors or beat-up looking radios.

- ECs should offer to take an inventory of each member's equipment to facilitate deployment planning based on equipment capabilities.

- If you have prearranged locations, consider preinstalling antennas and coax cables to reduce setup times.

Consider setting up an SOP for each site you may be manning with all the details need for the site. ARES operators should not be dispatched to hospitals or other critical sites with makeshift equipment and antennas that may or may not work. Your partners and served agencies will notice. If a member goes into a duty site and their equipment looks professional, and they are able to become operational without visible issues, this too will be noticed. Every station must work right the first time.

26-8

Use what works

Amateur radio is a hobby of experimentation, and new modes are constantly being developed and promoted by various individuals, clubs and organizations. Some new modes and technologies might seem well suited for emergency communications work. However, you should remember that an emergency deployment is not an opportunity to test new modes, methods or technologies.

The main mode of communications used during almost every emergency is voice communications. Anyone can be properly trained to use a microphone. It takes much more knowledge, training and equipment to use a laptop, modem and software.

Another issue is the availability and reliability of equipment. Will all your members be equipped to service a laptop that stops functioning?

Test your sites

Visit every site that your group could possibly be assigned to and create a master book listing each site, the probable location within each building where the station setup will be, how easy it is to reach any repeaters you have at your disposal, and the simplex range from each location.

Share information

If you expect adjacent ARES groups to support you, send them copies of all information and updates so they can be assigned locations on initial callouts.

Stay up to date

Your operational plans should be reviewed annually to correct any shortfalls detected during the past year. Every five years the operational plan should be fully reviewed and, if necessary, rewritten completely.

Mutual aid

There may be times when your group's resources will be stretched beyond its capabilities. When the severity of a situation reaches a point that you can no longer offer the complete services or manpower needed, you will need to request mutual aid response from either another emergency communications group located within your service area or a group further away. It is imperative that your group develop mutual aid agreements with adjacent communications groups. Simple cross training would also be very beneficial. Develop a good working relationship with other groups, and remember that the National Emergency Coordinator (NEC) is available to help you develop these relationships. (The NEC must also be called in whenever you activate a mutual aid agreement during a disaster response.)

Once a year, practice a "mock drill" together. This is a good way to learn from each other. Also note that when a mutual aid request comes from another group and you are the one supplying the additional service, you will be doing so under their umbrella and are responsible to their EC. Do not take over. Just assist as requested.

26-9

Sell your group

To make your ARES group an effective tool for served agencies, you need to do a "selling job". Not everyone is aware of ARES, its capabilities, or its role during disaster responses. You can change that by interacting professionally with your served agencies and other responder groups. It is very important to avoid being overly zealous.

Document what you do and how you can help. Take photos and write a short account of how your emergency communications group has played a role during past events.

When dealing with the media, only one person should serve as spokesperson for your group. This will avoid mis-quotes and mis-information. **Delegate and build teams**

Where possible delegate responsibility to others in your group. Do not try to do everything yourself. Delegating responsibility not only makes your job easier and allows you to do more, it also helps to engage your members and promotes participation and skills building.

If possible, create RED teams or jump teams within your group. A core of committed and readily available members allows you to plan with greater certainty and demonstrate a reliable minimum capability to served agencies.

Get organized

To be effective, you need to be organized. You should:

- Keep a list or database of members, tracking licensing status, current address and contact information, and availability

- Keep a description of equipment and SOPs for each official emergency station (for example, at an EOC).

You may also wish to offer members the option of including their equipment in a common ARES equipment database. By recording serial numbers, you can help facilitate the return of equipment in situations where an owner's label is defaced or lost during a deployment. An equipment database can also help you demonstrate functional capabilities and plan your responses (for example, by knowing in advance which operators have cross-band repeat capable transceivers, or packet-capable stations).

26-10

MAKING USE OF SET AND OTHER EXERCISE OPPORTUNITIES

A simulated emergency test (SET) is a training exercise used to test plans, procedures, policy and equipment under simulated disaster conditions. SETs can also serve to demonstrate the value that ARES provides in times of need to served agencies such as the Canadian Red Cross, Emergency Preparedness organizations, and to the public.

The annual ARES SET is a North America wide exercise administered by the ARRL in the United States and RAC in Canada. Both ARES and the National Traffic System (NTS) components are involved. The SET gives communicators the opportunity to focus on the emergency-communications capability within their communities, while interacting with NTS nets.

SETs may range from simple table-top exercises involving ARES members to full-scale exercises involving a number of emergency service organizations.

SETs provide learning experiences for operators and emergency coordinators, allowing them to gain experience in communications using standard procedures and a variety of modes under simulated emergency conditions. Lessons learned during SETs help you maximize your readiness and address any issues before you face a true disaster response.

To be effective, SETs should be well-planned and should use scenarios that are relevant to the community or region served by your group. You need to get as many people involved as possible, especially newly licensed amateurs. Promote your SET on nets and repeaters.

TIPS FOR EMERGENCY COORDINATORS

The following best practices may make you a more effective emergency coordinator:

- Compile a list of phone numbers (home, office, cellular) for all key personnel associated with your served agencies and partner organizations.

- Get into digital communications. The more you can do with digital, the more useful you will be in a disaster.

- Provide SOPS to help operators perform each role with which they might be tasked.

26-11

SECTION 27: EXERCISES

Once you complete this section, you will be able to:

- Discuss emergency exercises and training

- List the types of exercises

- Describe the tasks involved in the design and implementation of an ARES exercise

- Explain what to do after an exercise

- Describe ways to use public service events as ARES exercises.

EMERGENCY EXERCISES, DRILLS, AND COMMUNICATIONS PRACTICE SESSIONS

Part of staying prepared is periodic training and practice. We hope to take advantage of the following opportunities for exercising our preparedness and communications skills:

- Formal emergency exercises held by regional emergency and safety organizations.

- Less formal emergency exercises for radio amateurs, conducted by ARES groups.

- Facility-specific exercises (for example, Field Day operations at an Emergency Operations Centre).

- Regional not-for-profit events and operations requiring communications support.

- Informal drills between ARES members (for example, message handling during weekend sessions).

- Net operations (for example, a once-monthly ARES net hosted on one of the local repeaters).

- News bulletins, Q&A quizzes, allegories and other useful aids provided in a printed bulletin or over the web.

Exercises serve a number of functions:

- Ensuring that ARES practices, processes and personnel are able to meet the needs of served agencies

- Identifying opportunities to improve practices and processes

- Identifying the need to improve operator performance through further training or practice

- Demonstrating capability and best practices to served agencies and partner organizations

27-1

TYPES OF EXERCISE

The following types of exercise may be used individually or combined to form more involved exercises:

1   Repeater coverage test

2   Simplex coverage test

3   Activation

4   Informal 'tactical' message handling

5   Formal message handling

6   NTS interzone exercise

7   Multinet exercise

8   Rapid community assessment

9   Road rally exercise

10 Packet communications

11 Combined 'served agency' exercise

12 Mobile repeater test

13 SAR exercise

14 Site test

15 Capabilities demonstration

DURING AN EXERCISE

1   Announce the emergency situation. Activate the emergency net. Dispatch mobiles to served agencies.

2   Have designated stations originate messages on behalf of served agencies. Test messages may be sent simulating requests for supplies. Simulated emergency messages (just like real emergency messages) should be signed by an authorized official.

3   Emphasize tactical communications for served agencies.

4   As warranted by traffic loads, have liaison stations on hand to receive traffic on the local net and relay to your section net. You should also be sure that there is a representative on each session of the section net to receive traffic going to the local area.

5   Operate at least one session (or substantial segment of a session) of the local net on emergency-only basis. Or, if a repeater is on emergency power, allow only emergency-powered stations to operate through the repeater for a certain time period.

AFTER THE EXERCISE

An important post-SET activity is a critique session to discuss the test results. All ARES members should be invited to the meeting to review good points and weaknesses apparent in the drill. Emphasize ways to improve procedures, techniques, and coordination with all groups involved. Report your group's effort using the appropriate forms (available at http://www.rac.ca/fieldorg/setform.htm) and include any photos, clippings and other items of interest.

USING PUBLIC SERVICE EVENTS AS EXERCISES

Using ARES participants and practices to provide communications support during public service events gives ARES participants an opportunity to test their equipment, deployment methods, and communications practices in real-life situations that may not be very similar to an emergency, but are more realistic than table-top or simple message handling exercises. Public service events might include marathons, parades, or community events like festivals that require traffic control or service coordination.

SECTION 28: CREATING STANDARD OPERATING PROCEDURES AND
DOCUMENTATION FOR YOUR REGION

This course provides a range of information resources and best practices for ARES operation. However, you will also need standard operating procedures (SOP) specific to your region and your scenarios.

Once you complete this section, you will be able to:

- Explain the importance of SOPs

- Describe the contents of an SOP

- Write an SOP.

A good SOP is essential when bringing in trained operators from other areas or groups.

Operational experience: *In Alberta, labour laws mandate that any task that has a potential for hazard or injury must have a hazard assessment and a written SOP. This can be as simple as a tripping hazard due to an open filing cabinet drawer when carrying a large object or box.*

If someone is injured or killed and there is no SOP, all supervisory personnel involved directly or indirectly are liable. This can even include a town council and a mayor. This even affects nonprofit groups and registered clubs. An SOP is a standard guide to assist trained staff in assessing and responding to a situation.

If an amateur radio group is going out to install a tower or antenna, it needs a hazard assessment, a written safety plan and an SOP for that activity. This is also true if ARES responds to an emergency or provides services at an event.

Operational experience: *In fire departments, the rule of thumb is, "If it is a re-occurring situation, write an SOP. If it happens for the first time, then wing it. If it happens again, write an SOP!"*

You may choose to establish a steering committee within your ARES group to make decisions and create appropriate SOPs.

This section provides information that you will need when preparing your SOPs.

28-1

CONTENTS OF AN SOP

A standard outline for SOPs is outlined below:

COVER PAGE
- NAME OF GROUP
- NAME OF DOCUMENT
- GROUP CREST (if available)
- FULL ADDRESS OF GROUP
- DATE OF DOCUMENT

LETTER OF PROMULGATION OR PURPOSE OF DOCUMENT
- INCLUDE AUTHORITY FOR DOCUMENT AND
- SIGNATURE OF AUTHORIZING AGENT OR DIRECTOR

EXECUTIVE SUMMARY OF DOCUMENT IF REQUIRED

DISCLAIMER

DISTRIBUTION LIST

RECORD OF CHANGES OR CORRECTIONS
- IDENTIFICATION OF CHANGE OR CORRECTION; REFERENCES TO MESSAGE DATE-TIME-GROUP; ETC.
- DATE, CHANGE/CORRECTION ENTERED
- CORRECTION/CORRECTION ENTERED BY (SIGNATURE)

TABLE OF CONTENTS
(CAN HAVE BOTH A BRIEF AND DETAILED INDEX)

BODY OF THE DOCUMENT
- CHAPTER 1 - MISSION AND POLICY
- CHAPTER 2 – ORGANIZATION
  - DUTIES OF EMERGENCY COORDINATOR (COML)
  - DUTIES OF ASSISTANT EMERGENCY COORDINATOR (ICCM)
  - DUTIES OF THE NET CONTROL STATION (NCS)
  - DUTIES OF THE STATION SUPERVISOR
  - DUTIES OF THE RADIO OPERATOR
  - DUTIES OF THE MESSAGE LOGGER
  - DUTIES OF THE COUNTER PERSON
  - DUTIES OF THE RUNNER/COURIERS

- CHAPTER 3 – ADMINISTRATION
  - ACTIVATING THE PLAN
  - MOBILIZING PROCEDURES
  - DUTIES OF THE NCS
  - OPERATIONS
  - DRILLS TESTS AND ALERTS
  - STANDING ORDERS
- CHAPTER 4 – TRAINING AND QUALIFICATIONS
- CHAPTER 5 – OPERATIONAL CONCEPT
  - STANDARD PROCEDURES
  - INTRODUCTION
  - PURPOSE
  - BEGINNING OPERATIONS
  - STATION LOGS
  - RADIO ROOM SECURITY
  - THIRD PARTY CONTACTS
  - CHANGING NEEDS
  - CHANGING SHIFTS
  - THE STANDARD MESSAGE FORM
  - RADIO TRAFFIC
  - RECEPTION OF MESSAGES
  - INFORMAL TRAFFIC
  - STANDARD ORDERS FORMAT
  - SITUATION
  - MISSION
  - EXECUTION
  - GENERAL OUTLINE
  - TASKS
  - COORDINATION INSTRUCTIONS
  - TIMINGS
  - ATTACHMENTS AND DETACHMENTS
  - SERVICE/SUPPORT
  - COMMAND AND SIGNALS
  - TIME CHECK
  - WARNING ORDERS
  - DEPLOYMENT/MOVE ORDERS
  - SAFETY BRIEFING
  - PRE-SHIFT BRIEFING

28-3

- CHAPTER 6 - GENERAL COMMUNICATION OPERATING
  - SIGNALS OPERATING INSTRUCTIONS
  - OPEN NETS
  - CONTROLLED NETS
  - NET CONTROL STATION ACTIVITIES
  - JOINING NET
  - LEAVING NET
  - CLOSING DOWN
  - TEMPORARY SHUT DOWN
  - RELAYING TRAFFIC
  - CLOSING NET
  - STATION AUTHENTICATION PROCEDURES
  - CHANGING FREQUENCIES
- CHAPTER 7 - RADIOTELEPHONE PROCEDURE
  - CALLSIGNS
  - TACTICAL CALLSIGNS
  - VOICE PROCEDURES
  - PROWORDS AND PHONETICS
- CHAPTER 8 - DIGITAL COMMUNICATIONS PROCEDURES
- CHAPTER 9 - DIGITAL MODES
- CHAPTER 10 - SAFETY

(Each paragraph in a chapter should be numbered in sequence with the chapter and paragraph number. IE 4.12 - chapter 4 paragraph 12)

ANNEXES

- ANNEX A – NET ORGANIZATION
  - CALL OUT PHONE TREE
  - ARES CONTACT LIST

  - CONTACT LISTS FOR
    - SERVED AGENCIES
    - REGIONAL AMATEURS
  - MASTER ASSEMBLY LIST
  - STAND-BY ROOSTER
  - NET CONTROL DIAGRAMS
- ANNEX B – PRINCIPALS OF FREQUENCY ASSIGNMENT
  - ARES FREQUENCY PLAN
  - CANADIAN BAND PLANS
  - PROVINCIAL REPEATER LIST
  - PROVINCIAL IRLP LIST
  - SIMPLEX CHANNEL LIST
  - IRLP LIST
  - SERVED AGENCY FREQUENCY LIST
- ANNEX C - OPERATING SIGNALS, PROSIGNS AND PROWORDS

- ANNEX D- EMERGENCY COMMUNICATIONS (ECOM) PLANNING
  - MEDIVAC
  - AIRCRAFT DOWN
  - LOST PERSON
- ANNEX E – DATA SYSTEM
- ANNEX F - VHF REPEATER SYSTEM
- ANNEX G- SPECIALTY NETWORKS
  - TACTICAL
  - COMMAND AND CONTROL
  - LOGISTICS
  - REAR LINK
  - ICP TO EOC
  - EOC TO ADJACENT EOCs SERVED AGENCY FREQUENCY LIST
  - INTER-AGENCY
- ANNEX H - GLOSSARY OF ABBREVIATIONS, SHORT TITLES, AND COMMUNICATION TERMS
- ANNEX I – EQUIPMENT PLANNING
  - RADIO EQUIPMENT LISTS
  - PERSONAL "GO BAG" LIST
  - TOOL LIST
  - EMERGENCY COORDINATORS EQUIPMENT LIST (COMML)
  - AEC/COMM CENTRE EQUIPMENT LIST (INCM)
- ANNEX J - JOINT SERVICE INTEROPERABILITY PLANS
- ANNEX K - CALL SIGNS, SPECIAL CALL SIGNS AND COLLECTIVE CALL SIGNS
- ANNEX L - ABBREVIATED TEXTS
  - RAC NUMBERED RADIOGRAMS
  - RAC RADIOGRAM
  - INCOMING/OUTGOING MESSAGE LISTS
  - RADIO LOGS
  - ICS FORMS LIST AND FORMS CATALOG
  - ARES REGISTRATION FORMS
  - MESSAGE NUMBER CARDS
  - COMM CENTRE SIGNAGE
- ANNEX M - TELECOMUNICATIONS
  - TELEPHONE
  - FAX
  - INTERNET
  - E-MAIL
  - WORLD WIDE WEB
  - NATIONAL WEB SITE
  - AREA, REGION AND PROVINCIAL WEB SITES
- ANNEX N – SERVED AGENCY RESPONSE PLANS AND INSTRUCTIONS

28-5

- ANNEX O – SAFETY
  - RADIO FREQUENCY HAZARDS
  - UNKNOWN HAZARDS
  - STAFF ACCOMMODATIONS
- ANNEX P – RADIO REGULATIONS AND RADIO INFORMATION CIRCULARS

LIST OF ILLUSTRATIONS

TIPS FOR WRITING A GOOD SOP

If your SOP is going to be effective, it needs to be well written and appropriate for your audience. Consider the following tips when writing your SOP:

- Familiarize yourself with modern writing standards. A good reference is *Strunk and White, Elements of Style.*

- Query your team to see if there is anyone with professional technical writing or editing experience who can assist in the effort.

- Keep in mind that the SOP is not in and of itself your training document. The SOP is meant to be used *in the field,* during actual exercises and operations. Write it with that in mind, focusing on important information and leaving out anything that operators do not need *while performing their work.*

- Write in the **active voice.**

- Include flowcharts and diagrams whenever practical.

- Keep the language as simple as possible, without distorting its meaning.

- Use short sentences with specific messages and meanings. Do not be ambiguous.

- Make any imperatives (actions) very easy to find on the page.

- Use lots of white space on each page.

- Provide a detailed table of contents and index.

- Number each chapter and paragraph (for example, 4-14).

CREATING CALLOUT TREES

If your ARES group has a large number of participants, or covers a large area, organize the callout list geographically.

Remember to update your callout tree regularly.

If you have participants who you do not expect would be routinely available for callouts, include them on an extended callout list, or ensure that those participants are at the bottom of your callout list.

28-6

If you have formalized mutual aid agreements with ARES groups in other regions, gather key names and contact information from those ARES groups and include them in at the bottom of your callout tree.

CHECKLISTS

Prepare customized checklists for your ARES team members:

- Equipment

- Personal articles

- Site-specific checklists

SECTION 29: ADMINISTRATIVE ROLES WITHIN ARES

This section provides additional information about administrative roles (roles that do not normally. interact at the operational level) within ARES.

Once you complete this section, you will be able to describe key ARES roles within RAC.

SECTION EMERGENCY COORDINATOR (SEC)

The SEC is the assistant to the SM for emergency preparedness. The SEC is appointed by the SM to take care of all matters pertaining to emergency communications and the Amateur Radio Emergency Service (ARES) on a section-wide basis. The SEC post is one of top importance in the section and the individual appointed to it should devote all possible energy and effort to this one challenging organizational program for Amateur Radio. There is only one SEC appointed in each section of the RAC Field Organization.

SEC qualifications and functions:

- The encouragement of all groups of community amateurs to establish a local emergency organization.

- Recommendation to the SM on all section emergency policy and planning, including the development of a section emergency communications plan.

- Cooperation and coordination with the Section Traffic Manager so that emergency nets and traffic nets in the section present a united public service front, particularly in the proper routing of Welfare traffic in emergency situations. Cooperation and coordination should also be maintained with other section leadership officials as appropriate.

- Recommendation of candidates for Emergency Coordinator and District Emergency Coordinator appointments (and cancellations) to the Section Manager and determine areas of jurisdiction of each amateur so appointed. At the SM's discretion, the SEC may be directly in charge of making (and canceling) such appointments. In the same way, the SEC can handle the Official Emergency Station program.

- Promotion of ARES membership drives, meetings, activities, tests, procedures, etc., at the section level.

- Collection and consolidation of Emergency Coordinator (or District Emergency Coordinator) monthly reports and submission of monthly progress summaries to the SM and RAC Headquarters. This includes the timely reporting of emergency and public safety communications rendered in the section for inclusion in TCA.

- Maintenance of contact with other communication services and serve as liaison at the section level with all agencies served in the public interest, particularly in connection with the federal, provincial and local government, civil preparedness, the Canadian Red Cross, etc.

29-1

Your position description includes assisting your successor as much as possible to ensure a smooth transition in your position. This involves promptly updating and turning over the position records and supplies to your successor so that there is a little loss of continuity as possible. A business-like transition reflects well on your professionalism, responsibility and consideration as well as on RAC.

Recruitment of new hams and RAC members is an integral part of the job of every appointee. Appointees should take advantage of every opportunity to recruit a new ham or member to foster growth of Field Organization programs, and our abilities to serve the public.

Requirement: The Section Emergency Coordinator is required to be a Full RAC member and hold an Amateur Operator's Certificate (or equivalent, as stipulated by the Radiocommunication Regulations) and should always operate radio equipment only within the limits and privileges of the certificate and qualification held.

SECTION MANAGER

The Section Manager is the senior elected RAC official in a section. The Section Manager:

- Recruits and appoints Section-level assistants to serve under his/her general supervision and to administer the following RAC programs in the Section: emergency communications, message traffic, and on-the-air bulletins.

- Supervises the activities of these assistants to ensure continuing progress in accordance with overall RAC policies and objectives.

- Appoints qualified RAC members in the Section to volunteer positions of responsibility in support of Section programs, or authorizes the respective Section-level assistants to make such appointments.

- Maintains liaison with the the VP of Field Services (VPFS) and makes monthly reports to the VPFS regarding the status of Section activities; receives from the VPFS information and guidance pertaining to matters of mutual concern and interest; keeps informed on matters of policy which affect Section-level programs.

- Conducts correspondence or other communications, including personal visits to clubs, hamfests and conventions, with RAC members and affiliated clubs in the Section; either responds to their questions or concerns or refers them to the appropriate person or office in the organization; maintains liaison with representative repeater-frequency coordinating councils having jurisdiction in the Section.

- Writes, or supervises preparation of, a monthly "Section News" column in TCA to encourage member participation in the RAC programs in the Section.

Your position description includes assisting your successor as much as possible to ensure a smooth transition in your position. This involves promptly updating and turning over the position records and supplies to your successor so that there is a little loss of continuity as possible. A business-like transition reflects well on your professionalism, responsibility and consideration as well as on RAC.

Recruitment of new hams and RAC members is an integral part of the job of every appointee. Appointees should take advantage of every opportunity to recruit a new ham or member to foster growth of Field Organization programs, and our abilities to serve the public.

Requirement: The Section Manager is required to be a Full RAC member and hold an Amateur Operator's Certificate (or equivalent, as stipulated by the Radiocommunication Regulations) and should always operate radio equipment only within the limits and privileges of the certificate and qualification held.

ASSISTANT SECTION MANAGER

The ASM may serve as a general assistant to the Section Manager or as a specialist. That is, the ASM may assist the Section Manager with general leadership matters as the Section Manager's understudy, or the ASM may be assigned to handle a specific important function that does not fail within the scope of the duties of the Section Manager's other assistants.

At the Section Manager's discretion, the ASM may be designated as the recommended successor to the incumbent Section Manager, in case the Section Manager resigns or is otherwise unable to finish the term of office.

The ASM should be familiar with the "Guidelines for the RAC Section Manager," which contains the fundamentals of general section management.

Your position description includes assisting your successor as much as possible to ensure a smooth transition in your position. This involves promptly updating and turning over the position records and supplies to your successor so that there is a little loss of continuity as possible. A business -like transition reflects well on your professionalism, responsibility and consideration as well as on RAC.

Recruitment of new hams and RAC members is an integral part of the job of every appointee. Appointees should take advantage of every opportunity to recruit a new ham or member to foster growth of Field Organization programs, and our abilities to serve the public.

Requirement: The Assistant Section Manager is required to be a Full RAC member and hold an Amateur Operator's Certificate (or equivalent, as stipulated by the Radiocommunication Regulations) and should always operate radio equipment only within the limits and privileges of the certificate and qualification held.

DISTRICT EMERGENCY COORDINATOR (DEC)

The RAC District Emergency Coordinator is appointed by the SEC to supervise the efforts of local Emergency Coordinators in the defined district. The DEC's duties involve the following:

- Coordinate the training, organization and emergency participation of Emergency Coordinators in your district of jurisdiction.

29-3

- Make local decisions in the absence of the SEC or through coordination with the SEC, concerning the allotment of available amateurs and equipment during an emergency.

- Coordinate the interrelationship between local emergency plans and between communications networks within your District of jurisdiction.

- Act as backup for local areas without an Emergency Coordinator and assist in maintaining contact with governmental and other agencies within your District of jurisdiction.

- Provide direction in the routing and handling of emergency communications of either a formal or tactical nature, with specific emphasis being placed on Welfare traffic.

- Recommend EC appointments to the SEC.

- Coordinate the reporting and documenting of ARES activities in your District of jurisdiction.

- Act as a model emergency communicator as evidenced by dedication to purpose, reliability and understanding of emergency communications.

- Be fully conversant in National Traffic System routing and procedures as well as have a thorough understanding of the locale and role of all vital governmental and volunteer agencies that could be involved in an emergency.

Your position description includes assisting your successor as much as possible to ensure a smooth transition in your position. This involves promptly updating and turning over the position records and supplies to your successor so that there is a little loss of continuity as possible. A business-like transition reflects well on your professionalism, responsibility and consideration as well as on RAC.

Recruitment of new hams and RAC members is an integral part of the job of every appointee. Appointees should take advantage of every opportunity to recruit a new ham or member to foster growth of Field Organization programs, and our abilities to serve the public.

Requirement: The District Emergency Coordinator is required to be a Full RAC member and hold an Amateur Operator's Certificate (or equivalent, as stipulated by the Radiocommunication Regulations) and should always operate radio equipment only within the limits and privileges of the certificate and qualification held.

EMERGENCY COORDINATOR

The RAC Emergency Coordinator is a key team player in ARES on the local emergency scene. Working with the Section Emergency Coordinator, the DEC and Official Emergency Stations, the EC prepares for, and engages in management of communications needs in disasters. EC duties include:

- Promote and enhance the activities of the Amateur Radio Emergency Service (ARES) for the benefit of the public as a voluntary, non-commercial communications service.

- Manage and coordinate the training, organization and emergency participation of interested amateurs working in support of the communities, agencies or functions designated by the Section Emergency Coordinator/Section Manager.

- Establish viable working relationships with federal, provincial, municipal government and private agencies in the ARES jurisdictional area which need the services of ARES in emergencies. Determine what agencies are active in your area, evaluate each of their needs, and which ones you are capable of meeting, and then prioritize these agencies and needs. Discuss your planning with your Section Emergency Coordinator and then with your counterparts in each of the agencies. Ensure they are all aware of your ARES group's capabilities, and perhaps more importantly, your limitations.

- Develop detailed local operational plans with "served" agency officials in your jurisdiction that set forth precisely what each of your expectations are during a disaster operation. Work jointly to establish protocols for mutual trust and respect. All matters involving recruitment and utilization of ARES volunteers are directed by you, in response to the needs assessed by the agency officials. Technical issues involving message format, security of message transmission, Disaster Welfare Inquiry policies, and others, should be reviewed and expounded upon in your detailed local operations plans.

- Establish local communications networks run on a regular basis and periodically test those networks by conducting realistic drills.

- Establish an emergency traffic plan, with Welfare traffic inclusive, utilizing the National Traffic System as one active component for traffic handling. Establish an operational liaison with local and section nets, particularly for handling Welfare traffic in an emergency situation.

- In times of disaster, evaluate the communications needs of the jurisdiction and respond quickly to those needs. The EC will assume authority and responsibility for emergency response and performance by ARES personnel under his jurisdiction.

- Work with other non-ARES amateur provider-groups to establish mutual respect and understanding, and a coordination mechanism for the good of the public and Amateur Radio. The goal is to foster an efficient and effective Amateur Radio response overall.

- Work for growth in your ARES program, making it a stronger, more valuable resource and hence able to meet more of the agencies' local needs. There are thousands of new peoples coming into the Amateur Radio Service that would

29-5

make ideal additions to your ARES roster. A stronger ARES means a better ability to serve your communities in times of need and a greater sense of pride for Amateur Radio by both amateurs and the public.

- Report regularly to the SEC, as required.

Your position description includes assisting your successor as much as possible to ensure a smooth transition in your position. This involves promptly updating and turning over the position records and supplies to your successor so that there is a little loss of continuity as possible. A business-like transition reflects well on your professionalism, responsibility and consideration as well as on RAC.

Recruitment of new hams and RAC members is an integral part of the job of every appointee. Appointees should take advantage of every opportunity to recruit a new ham or member to foster growth of Field Organization programs, and our abilities to serve the public.

Requirement: The Emergency Coordinator is required to be a Full RAC member and hold an Amateur Operator's Certificate (or equivalent, as stipulated by the Radiocommunication Regulations) and should always operate radio equipment only within the limits and privileges of the certificate and qualification held.

Radio Amateurs of Canada

Amateur Radio
Emergency Service

Operations Training
Manual

Volume 4 - Reference information

Document RAC-ARES-OPS

Release 2.0

September 2015

This training material has been prepared by volunteers on a not-
for-profit basis in order to serve the public good. To the greatest
degree practical, externally sourced information has been attributed and authorization sought for use, where required. Proprietary
information and copyrighted material has not been intentionally
included.

Any and all use of the RAC AMATEUR EMERGENCY SERVICE
AND DESIGN trade-mark requires licence or permission from Radio
Amateurs of Canada Incorporated.

Contact:

Chief Field Services Officer, Radio Amateurs of Canada Inc.,
Suite 217, 720 Belfast Road, Ottawa, Ontario, Canada K1G 0Z5.

Radio Amateurs of Canada (RAC) and the authors of this document
authorize the re-use and republication of content taken from this
document only if ALL the following conditions are met:

1. Information is formally attributed to this document, as a RAC
   publication, or to the original copyright holder if applicable.

2. Information is used solely on a not-for-profit basis.

3. RAC is notified of the re-use in writing to the Chief Field
   Services Officer at: CFSO, Radio Amateurs of Canada, Suite
   217, 720 Belfast Road, Ottawa, Ontario, Canada K1G 0Z5.

Contributors to this manual included the National Training
Resource Group: Bob Boyd VE3SV, Bob Cooke VE3BDB, David
Drinnan VE9FK, Don Mackinnon VE4DJ, Eric Jacksch VA3DSP,
Forbes Purcell VE6FMP, Glenn Killam VE3GNA, Ian Snow VA3QT,
John P. Cunningham W1AI, Jeff Dovyak VE4MBQ, Lance Peterson
VA3LP, Monte L. Simpson K2MLS, Pierre Mainville VA3PM, and
Tim Smith VE3HCB. Please see "Acknowledgements" on page 1-2.

This manual was created using Adobe FrameMaker(TM).

Glossary

Software selection and configuration

Pro words and phrases

ARES forms and stationery

Anderson Powerpole connectors

Safety issues for ARES personnel

First aid techniques

Using this manual in your training

Section 30: Glossary

This section lists terms that are used in ARES activities or may arise during discussions of ECOM issues.

> *Note: This glossary section is shared across all ARES guides and documents, including those provided to served agencies and clients. You may see very basic terms explained in very simplistic ways in this glossary, for the benefit of agency personnel and others. In addition, you may see terms defined here even though those terms do not appear in this training manual.*

2-point safe

A measure of the redundancy of a process or system. Two-point safe means that the process or system can tolerate a single critical 'failure' and still achieve its purpose. For example, a callout procedure is 2-point safe if it will succeed even if one of the designated ECs is unavailable.

3-point safe

A measure of the redundancy of a process or system. Three-point safe means that the process or system can tolerate double critical 'failures' and still achieve its purpose. For example, a callout procedure is 3-point safe if it will succeed even if two of the designated ECs are unavailable.

AEC

See "assistant emergency coordinator" on page 30.2.

amateur radio operator

A person who has been certified and licensed by the Government of Canada (Industry Canada) to install and operate non-commercial radio systems on allocated frequencies. As part of their certification, amateur radio operators are tested on operating procedures, systems design, radio theory, interference prevention, and other key subjects. Operators are legally allowed to build and implement systems without the need for type acceptance, and are permitted to use a wide range of frequencies suitable for local, point-to-point, long distance, and even satellite communications. The term 'amateur' refers to the provision that these operators must not accept any financial compensation for their services, and cannot transmit commercial communications (communications as part of 'for profit' enterprises).

APCO

The Association of Public Safety Communications Officials, International, is made up of law enforcement, fire and public safety communications personnel.

APRS

See "automatic position reporting system" on page 30.2.

30-1

ARES operator

A licensed amateur radio operator who is trained and qualified to participate in an ARES operation.

assistant emergency coordinator

AEC. An ARES volunteer who shares some or all of the emergency coordinator's responsibilities and duties. See "emergency coordinator" on page 30.5.

automatic position reporting system

APRS. A system that broadcasts a station's position by radio, allowing automated tracking and plotting. In most cases, position data is generated by a GPS unit attached to the broadcasting station.

authentication

The process used to ensure that a party is actually who they say they are, and that they are authorized to send or receive specific types of information.

availability net

See "standby net" on page 30.15.

AX25

A data transmission protocol used on amateur packet connections. AX25 is very similar to the X25 protocol commonly used on commercial data circuits.

automated traffic

Automated traffic is any form of communications that does not involve operators at both ends of the connection (for example, a semi-permanent amateur television transmission, or a packet relay of Internet weather information).

Blackberry

A digital messaging device used by many businesses and by some officials at the municipal, provincial and federal level. Blackberry units are specialized digital assistants (PDA) that operate on an Aliant wireless data network. Blackberry PDAs and Blackberry cellphones allow the efficient exchange of emails and text messages.

client

A client is a specific organization (a municipality, aid agency, or government entity) whose emergency communications needs are met using ARES resources. See also "served agency" on page 30.14.

challenge-response authentication

Challenge-response is a form of authentication that uses secret code tables issued only to authorized communications stations. A station receiving critical messages, information or instructions challenges the sender to authenticate by reading out a reference code. The challenged station reads back the alphanumeric response code corresponding to the challenge code in their code table. (In certain situations, a sending station may choose to challenge a receiving station, in order to ensure that a message or instruction has been received by the intended station.)

command net

A form of task-specific net used to support senior executives and primary stakeholders.

COMMS

An acronym for communications. ARES operators are encouraged to use the term COMMS on all station identification signs at emergency response sites, and to wear COMMS-labelled identification vests or caps.

communications officer

An official responsible for communications for a served agency, government department, or other entity. The role of communications officer is not used in ARES, but ARES operators may have to interact with communications officers working for the provincial government, municipalities, or served agencies during emergency operations.

communications supervisor

An ARES role responsible for managing the overall health and functioning of ARES operations on an hour-by-hour basis. A communications supervisor ensures that client needs are met, troubleshoots logistics and communications problems by assigning operators to locations and nets, and escalates issues to the EC when required. (The role of communications supervisor is often filled by the EC or AEC, particularly during the beginning phases of an ARES operation.)

CW

A mode of communications where text is sent using a series of tones. Long tones are called dashes, and short tones are called dots. CW is slower than other modes, but is useful in situations where low-power HF stations must communicate, or in cases of poor propagation. CW can be sent and received manually by skilled operators, or can be send and received using a CW console (often a PC equipped with appropriate software).

DCO

District Communications Officer

DEC

See "district emergency coordinator" on page 30.4.

30-3

deputy incident commander

DIC. An officer who is assisting an incident commander or has been delegated incident commander duties. See "incident commander" on page 30.9.

DIC

See "deputy incident commander" on page 30.4.

digital data messaging

Digital communications is used in situations where messages need to reach their destinations without any errors, and need to be logged and recorded. Digital messaging is particularly well suited to formal traffic that is lengthy in nature.

directed net

A formal net with a net controller, who directs all communications on the net. Stations request permission from net control before calling other stations or passing traffic.

disaster welfare inquiry

DWI. A Red Cross term for welfare traffic. Most disaster welfare inquiries are carried over telephone networks. DWI traffic is not normally carried over ARES channels, except in situations where a 'local hop' is required to reach a telephone network. (Red Cross welfare traffic is not normally carried on the NTS.)

district emergency coordinator

The RAC District Emergency Coordinator (DEC) is appointed by the SEC to supervise the efforts of local Emergency Coordinators in the defined district.

duplex

Communications using more than one frequency. Typically, duplex communications take place over a repeater. All stations transmit on one frequency, and listen on a second frequency. A repeater rebroadcasts the transmissions from the first frequency onto the second frequency, at greater power and range.

DWI

See "disaster welfare inquiry" on page 30.4.

EC

See "emergency coordinator" on page 30.5.

ECOM

Emergency communications.

EMC

Emergency Measures Coordinator. This is an Emergency Management Organization officer responsible for disaster planning and response in a specific region.

EMCG

Emergency Management Communications Group. This is a volunteer group of amateur radio operators attached to the New Brunswick provincial Emergency Management Organization. Similar groups are attached to provincial EMO groups elsewhere in the Maritimes.

ECOM

Emergency communications.

emergency coordinator

EC. An ARES emergency coordinator has a number of responsibilities before, during and after ARES operations. In summary, an EC manages ARES exercises and operations, training of ARES personnel, maintenance of relationships with ARES served agencies and clients, management of ARES infrastructure, public communications, and RAC reporting.

Emergency Management Organization

The Emergency Management Organization (EMO) is an organization that operates at the federal, provincial or municipal level to provide disaster planning, logistics and response coordination during national, provincial, regional or municipal emergencies.

emergency operating procedure

A procedure used in unusual, emergency conditions to perform a task.

emergency operations centre

An emergency operations centre (EOC) is a location that has been set up to support disaster response officials performing planning, coordination, communications and other control processes during an emergency. Pre-configured, designated EOCs exist in many locations.

emergency pack

See "ready pack" on page 30.13.

emergency response vehicle

A vehicle configured to provide an emergency service (for example, an ambulance) or serve a specific function during an emergency (for example, a command trailer).

EMO

See "Emergency Management Organization" on page 30.5.

EOC

See "emergency operations centre" on page 30.5.

EOP

See "emergency operating procedure" on page 30.5.

ERV

See "emergency response vehicle" on page 30.5.

extended ready pack

A pack or kit that contains everything an ARES operator will need to operate comfortably for several days. Ready packs may be prepared by individual operators to meet their specific needs, or may be prepared by jump team leaders to support a group of operators. See also ready pack.

FEMA

The Federal Emergency Management Agency – a federal organization in the United States that supports state and local civil-preparedness and emergency management agencies.

formal voice communications

Formal voice communications is used in situations where messages need to reach their destinations without any errors, need to be logged and recorded, or are being relayed by intermediate stations.

free net

An EMCG term for an open net.

FRS

Family Radio Service (FRS) radios are simple, low-powered two-way radios that can be operated by anyone without the need for a license. FRS radios are cheap and readily available, making them ideal for situations where communications needs to be extended over a local site by giving two-way handheld radios to unlicensed runners, officials, and volunteers. FRS radios have 14 channels and a range in a typical site environment of about 1.5 km. (Longer range, unlicensed GMRS radios are now also available in Canada.) Although many FRS radios offer 'privacy codes' (CTCSS tone squelch), FRS communications are inherently insecure and can be easily monitored by anyone with a scanner or FRS/GMRS radio. FRS radios cannot communicate with radio systems used

30-6

by amateurs, emergency services, or businesses, although they can communicate with GMRS radios on FRS channels.

GMRS

General Mobile Radio Service (GMRS) radios are simple two-way UHF radios that can be operated by anyone without the need for a license. GMRS radios are more expensive than FRS radios, but are still reasonably affordable. They are ideal for situations where communications needs to be extended over a local site, or between adjacent sites, by giving two-way handheld radios to unlicensed runners, officials, and volunteers. GMRS radios have 22 channels (14 of which will interoperate with FRS radios) and a range in a typical site environment of about 5 km (1.5 km when communicating with FRS radios). Some GMRS radios are repeater-compatible, but most are simplex only. GMRS radios cannot communicate with radio systems used by amateurs, emergency services, or businesses.

GMT

Another term for universal coordinated time.

ground truth reports

Reports provided by trained or untrained observers located in (or resident in) an affected area.

ham

An archaic term for amateur radio operator. This term is less formal and its use is no longer encouraged. Similarly, the term 'ham radio' is now less commonly used than 'amateur radio'.

hardship conditions

Hardship conditions may be encountered when operating in the field, or at shelter locations after a major disaster. If you are operating under hardship conditions, assume that you will have to be completely self-sufficient, and operating without any support or infrastructure. This means bringing your own power (for example, generator and fuel), camping gear, station setup gear, and even several days worth of food and water.

health and welfare traffic

See "welfare traffic" on page 30.17.

HF

See "high frequency" on page 30.8.

high frequency

HF. A range of frequencies that typically allow simplex communications over extended ranges (from tens of km to worldwide coverage). HF radio systems (mobile or base) typically use more complex antennas than VHF or UHF radio systems, and may be equipped to use both voice communications and CW.

IC

See "incident commander" on page 30.9.

ICS

See "incident command system" on page 30.8.

identification vest

An identification vest uses ICS colour-coding and labels to identify the wearer's function, making it easier to coordinate resources onsite. Identification vests worn by communications personnel are typically yellow or lime coloured, and have a label that reads EMERGENCY COMMUNICATIONS, ECOM, ECOMM or COMM. See "Tactical and identification vests" on page 14.18.

incident command system

ICS. A formal system used for managing emergencies. ICS is a standardized on-scene incident management concept designed specifically to allow responders to adopt an integrated organizational structure that can meet the needs at hand without being hindered by jurisdictional boundaries. ICS was developed to address the following problems:

- Too many people reporting to one supervisor

- Different emergency response organizational structures

- Lack of reliable incident information

- Inadequate and incompatible communications

- Lack of structure for coordinated planning among agencies

- Unclear lines of authority

- Terminology differences among agencies

CS enables integrated communication and planning by establishing a manageable span of control. ICS divides an emergency response into five manageable functions essential for emergency response operations: Command, Operations, Planning, Logistics, and Finance and Administration.

In the ICS, the incident commander wears a green vest. Other command staff wear red vests. Operations personnel wear orange. Logistics personnel (including communications personnel) wear yellow or lime vests. Planning officers wear blue. And finance and administration personnel wear grey.

incident commander

IC. The public safety or law enforcement officer responsible for an operation (for example, a police operation, search and rescue operation, or evacuation). The IC is responsible for all aspects of the response, including developing incident objectives and managing all incident operations.

JEOC

Joint Emergency Operations Centre

jump kit

See "ready pack" on page 30.13.

jump team

A group of operators that are completely self-contained and able to transport themselves to required locations, establish communications, and function without external support for extended periods. See jump team operator. **ump team operator** An operator that is completely self-contained and able to transport mself to a required location, establish communications, and function without external support for extended periods.

30-9

liaison station

A liaison station acts as an answering service and filter between the primary net and a served agency. It can also monitor activity on a sub-net that is serving a particular agency using a secondary channel.

In some cases, a liaison station acts as an informal net control station for those ARES operators assigned to support a specific agency. (This is done only on open nets. See "open net" on page 30.12.)

Liaison stations are very important in many nets, especially large-scale nets or those spread over a wide area. They are invaluable in a net that is serving several different agencies. The net controller can create liaison stations "on the fly" as requirements arise.

MDOC

See "multidisciplinary operational team" on page 30.10.

MGRS

A form of universal transverse mercator, a mapping coordinate system. MGRS can be selected as a display option on most modern GPS units, and is used primarily in search and rescue and land tracking situations.

Morse

A 'language' used to exchange text using CW mode. Morse uses an alphabet consisting of 'dits' and 'dashes', combined to form individual characters, digits and symbols. See "CW" on page 30.3.

MP3

A very efficient digital file format used to record and archive audio recordings. In ARES, MP3 format is often used to record on-air traffic for later review, either for training or forensic purposes.

multidisciplinary operational team

MDOC. This is a Red Cross term for a group that performs assessments of need in specific areas.

National Interagency Incident Management System

An American emergency management system that is based on the incident command system.

NCS

See "net control station" on page 30.11.

near vertical incidence skywave

Near Vertical Incidence Skywave (NVIS) HF communications uses high-angle skywave paths between stations instead of ground-wave or surface-wave propagation. Mobile stations using whip antennas bent parallel to the ground can communicate more reliably over ranges of several hundred miles. Signal strengths with high-angle skywave are weaker, but communications is more reliable, less subject to fading, and more consistent between stations. Intervening terrain and obstructions between stations such as hills, mountainous areas, and built-up areas with tall buildings do not interfere with NVIS communications.

net, command

See "command net" on page 30.3.

net, directed

See "directed net" on page 30.4.

net, open

See "open net" on page 30.12.

net, tactical

See "tactical net" on page 30.16.

net control station

A station designated to control or manage traffic on a radio net. A net control station may be located at an EOC or other central location, or it may be located offsite at a fixed, home station. In some situations, even a mobile or handheld station may used for net control (though this is not recommended).

net controller

See "net control station" on page 30.11.

NIIMS

See "National Interagency Incident Management System" on page 30.10.

NVIS

See "near vertical incidence skywave" on page 30.11.

OEC

Offsite Emergency Centre. This term has been replaced by emergency operations centre (EOC).

OES
See "Official Emergency Station" on page 30.12.

Official Emergency Station
OES. A Canadian licensed radio amateur may be appointed as an OES by RAC if they are a RAC member and are interested in setting high standards of emergency preparedness and operation. An OES must meet the following requirements:

- Regular participation in the local ARES, if any, including all drills and tests, emergency nets and emergency situations.

- Ability to operate without commercial power.

- Ability to operate on at least one emergency-useful band while mobile.

- Must be fully acquainted with standard NTS and local municipal message forms and capable of using them to handle third-party messages.

- Reports monthly to RAC.

one-time pad
A list or table of codes that are used in ARES operations for challenge-response authentication.

open net
A net that allows informal communications, with or without a net controller. If there is a net controller, the controller acts to provide coordination, record keeping, and other support. On an open net, stations do not need to get net control permission before calling or passing traffic.

PCO
EMO/EMCG Provincial Communications Officer.

point safe
A measure of redundancy in a process or system. See "2-point safe" on page 30.1 and "3-point safe" on page 30.1.

RAC
See "Radio Amateurs of Canada" on page 30.12.

Radio Amateurs of Canada

RAC. The organization that represents radio amateur operators in Canada, and provides a single interface between the Government of Canada and the radio amateur community.

rapid emergency deployment

A highly urgent deployment of a small number of operators and stations, following a simple, streamlined plan to meet short-term needs. See "RED team" on page 30.13.

ready pack

A pack or kit that contains everything an ARES operator will need to operate comfortably for up to 12 hours. Ready packs are prepared by individual operators to meet their specific needs. It is recommended that ready packs be prepared in advance so that they contain most or all of the items needed, and can be grabbed in a hurry when needed. (Also called an emergency pack or jump kit.) See also extended ready pack.

RED team

A rapid emergency deployment (RED) team is made up of operators who commit to being available anytime, day or night, weekday or weekend, on call to quickly respond to communications callouts. RED team members keep ready packs on hand and ensure that they are able to respond to requests for assistance. The purpose of the RED team is to provide core communications in the short term, allowing a more controlled, planned activation of other operators to meet sustained needs.

relay stations

Situations are encountered where the distance from one area to another is too great for effective direct communications and repeater linking is either not available or is at capacity.

A relay station may be used to relay specific information between two sites. The relay station may also monitor repeater activity and report appropriate information to a second site by way of telephone or Internet communications.

repeater

A radio system that receives weak signals from mobile or handheld transceivers on one frequency, and instantaneously rebroadcasts the signals at higher power on a second frequency. Repeaters give low-power transceivers extended range and reliability, allowing convenient communications over a wide area.

SATERN

The Salvation Army's emergency radio network, used to coordinate aid during recovery operations. SATERN is activated to support shelters and aid stations in affected regions after disasters, but use affiliated stations far outside the affected region to serve as net control stations, and to originate traffic to and receive traffic from the affected region. SATERN uses ARES-compatible message protocols and forms, and is interoperable with ARES, but SATERN registered operators receive specific guidelines and job aids from their SATERN coordinator.

sartech

Search and rescue technician.

SARTEX

Search and rescue technician.

search and rescue

SAR. An operation to locate a missing person, vessel, or object. SAR operations in our area are typically conducted by the police and by the River Valley Ground Search and Rescue (RVGSAR) group. ARES may be involved in larger SAR operations that exceed existing capacity, or require specialized communications support.

self-deployment

Self-deployment occurs when radio operators mobilize to a post without receiving a request or instruction to do so. Self-deployment may be appropriate depending on the situation, but is not recommended if communications is available between the operator and the 'chain of command' (either municipal officials, the ARES EC, the EMO communications officer, or direct contacts at served agencies).

served agency

A served agency is an agency or entity (such as the Canadian Red Cross) who are 'clients' of ARES. ARES provides services to these served agencies as required, under its mandate to provide emergency communications services.

shelter in place

Shelter in place is an approach to sheltering individuals during emergencies that involves keeping individuals in safety areas and relying on safety supplies and practices to provide protection.

shoutcast

An Internet protocol and application used to broadcast audio over the Internet. In the context of ARES and emergency communications, shoutcast can be used to let stakeholders, and even the general public, listen in on emergency traffic over the Internet (if Internet connectivity is available). A receiver is connected to a shoutcast-configured computer, which in turn transmits the received audio to any user that connects to it. Shoutcast can be scaled up to serve large audiences, if needed, and can also provide secure access. Shoutcast may serve as an alternative to IRLP and Echolink in some situations.

simplex

Communications on a single frequency, with all stations transmitting and receiving on that one frequency.

30-14

simplex repeater

A transceiver that has been configured with a specialized audio module to retransmit any received signals. The simplex repeater records the audio from a received signal on a digital recording chip, and when the signal stops, immediately begins retransmitting that recorded audio on the same frequency (simplex). This provides a 'dirty', simple way of extending communications range. The disadvantages of simplex repeating include the following:

- Audio is broadcast twice in a row (once during the initial transmission, and once during the retransmission), which can be time consuming and confusing.

- Each station using a simplex repeater must be aware of the likelihood of 'doubling', where two stations that cannot hear each other on simplex are transmitting at the same time.

- Simplex repeaters cannot be used in tandem to further extend range.

SOP

Either a standard operating procedure or, less commonly, a station operating procedure.

standard operating procedure

SOP. A procedure used under normal conditions to perform a task.

standby net

A standby (availability) net is used as an on-air rallying point for off-duty or unassigned operators, or for operators just joining the operation. The standby net is used to deploy operators to specific duty stations and to perform other ARES-specific coordination.

station operating procedure

SOP. A procedure that apply to a specific communications station.

TAC

A channel designation (for example, TAC-2, for Tactical Channel 2).

tactical vest

A tactical vest is a vest that includes features to support the tasks performed by the wearer. For example, a tactical communications vest includes pockets for radios and battery packs, pass-throughs and hoops for cords, and velcro strips and clips for microphones. See "Tactical and identification vests" on page 14.18.

tactical voice communications

Tactical voice communications is used in situations where messages need to pass back and forth between stations without delays, and do not need to take the form of formal voice communications.

30-15

tactical net

A form of task-specific net used to support specific operations or projects.

terminal node controller

TNC. A modem that interfaces with a two-way radio to allow the exchange of text and data files.

TNC

See "terminal node controller" on page 30.16.

UHF

See "ultra high frequency" on page 30.16.

ultra high frequency

UHF. A range of frequencies suited to local communications in urban areas. UHF radio equipment may be handheld, mobile or fixed (base). Unit-to-unit range is typically 1 to 30 km, but is often extended through the use of a repeater.

unified command

Unified command was created in recognition that most incidents (spills, forest fires, floods) have impacts that cross jurisdictional boundaries such as local, federal, provincial, international, and First Nations.

universal coordinated time

UTC. A time standard used in operations and communications that extend outside a single timezone. UTC does not change with daylight savings time.

universal transverse mercator

UTM. A mapping coordinate system used instead of latitude and longitude for land tracking and land-based military operations.

UTC

See "universal coordinated time" on page 30.16.

UTM

See "universal transverse mercator" on page 30.16.

very high frequency

VHF. A range of frequencies suited to local communications in urban areas outside buildings, and in rural or forested areas. VHF radio equipment may be handheld, mobile or fixed (base). Unit-to-unit range is typically 2 to 40 km, but is often extended through the use of a repeater.

vest

A vest is worn over other clothing to provide identification or carry gear. See "identification vest" on page 30.8 and "tactical vest" on page 30.15.

VHF

See "very high frequency" on page 30.17.

welfare traffic

Message traffic that is intended to provide 'comfort'. Welfare traffic includes family inquiries and responses, and other personal communications that do not relate to emergency operations or safety. During ARES operations, welfare traffic is assigned the lowest precedence (priority).

Zulu

Another term for universal coordinated time.

SECTION 31: SOFTWARE SELECTION AND CONFIGURATION

This section will provide information about choosing and configuring the software you will use during ARES operations. See:

- "Packet radio"

- "APRS" on page 31.2

- "Logging" on page 31.2

- "Data conversion" on page 31.2

- "Data compression" on page 31.3

- "GPS tracking and mapping" on page 31.3

- "Networking" on page 31.3

PACKET RADIO

Packet radio software can be as basic as a terminal emulation program that lets you 'talk' to your TNC from your computer's keyboard, or it can be a full-featured text and file transfer program, ARES communications program, or even 'packet node' software.

HyperTerminal

HyperTerminal is a very basic TTY program that is built into most versions of Windows. To access HyperTerminal, go into your Start menu, drag through Programs to Accessories to Communications, and then click on HyperTerminal.

ARESPACK

ARESPACK runs on a basic IBM-PC and allows you to send and receive emergency communications messages very efficiently.

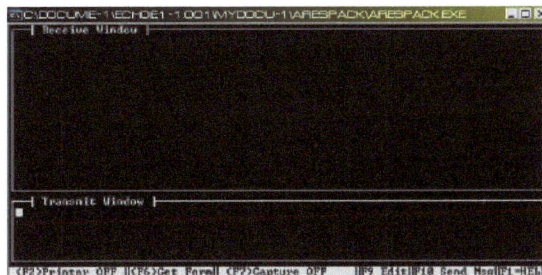

ARESPACK provides online message forms that guide you through the creation of a formal message. ARESPACK also provides automatic printing, so any traffic received by your station is immediately printed on your printer without your intervention, automating incoming messaging handling.

> *Note: ARESPACK does not 'work and play' well with other applications that may call the serial port, and does not work at all on many newer Windows operating systems. If you are going to use ARESPACK, it is recommended that you install it on an older, surplus PC that runs Windows 95 or 98, and is not needed for other uses that will require the installation of additional software.*

APRS

Automatic Position Reporting System (APRS) software is a specific type of packet software that is used for reporting the location of a station, based on GPS coordinates. APRS may be considered for applications where vehicles or even individuals need to be tracked on an ongoing basis (for example, for tracking the locations of evacuation buses, or for mapping positions during ARES-support search and rescue operations).

LOGGING

Logging software can make it easy to enter and track traffic and communications. This has value both during and after an event.

During an event, you may be asked to confirm the transmission, receipt or status of important traffic. After an event, forensic or postmortem examination of communications logs may be very important to any investigation related to an emergency.

DATA CONVERSION

If you are given message traffic in a digital format for transmission over packet, you may need to convert that data into a format that can be used at the receiving end. (For example, you may receive a list of evacuees in an Excel spreadsheet format, but the receiving station may only be equipped to print out text files.) You may also be required under the operating rules to examine any traffic prior to transmission, to ensure that it does not contain prohibited traffic (for example, commercial traffic).

31-2

In order to convert or examine traffic that arrives at your station in the form of digital files (either from other stations or from end users at your own location), try to ensure that you have the ability to open, print and save common file formats. Common applications include MS Word, Excel, Access, and even PowerPoint.

DATA COMPRESSION

WinZip (or a compatible program) can be used to compress data files before sending them over the packet link. Since packet itself does not include any compression schemes, WinZip will be very effective in reducing the filesize and transmission time of any file. You may even choose to compress lengthy text transmissions by placing them into a text file locally, then compressing that file, and then sending the compressed file. The station at the far end must have WinZip (or a compatible program) to decompress the received file.

GPS TRACKING AND MAPPING

If you plan to use a GPS unit and laptop during emergency operations (for example, if you have a GPS/laptop kit assembled for your car), you should preconfigure your laptop with software that will allow you to capture and communicate your location, track history, waypoints, or even maps.

EasyGPS and ExpertGPS

EasyGPS is a simple but versatile application that lets your PC communicate with most common GPS receivers using a serial data port and cable. EasyGPS lets you download waypoints and routes from your GPS unit into a file that you can store or send to others. You can also use EasyGPS to receive data from others and upload it to your own GPS unit. EasyGPS is freeware, and can be downloaded from the Internet at no cost.

ExpertGPS is an enhanced version of EasyGPS that also allows you to download track data from your GPS, and overlay data on top of maps (for example, topographical or road maps) or aerial photographs. ExpertGPS is currently available online at a cost of USD $60.

NETWORKING

Networking software allows you to plug your laptop computer into an Ethernet or wireless (Wifi) LAN at an operation site. All Windows PCs include networking software as part of Microsoft Windows.

Configuring Wifi

If you have a Wifi-equipped laptop, familiarize yourself with your Windows software and Wifi operation before you need to use it during an exercise or an emergency.

To set up your Wifi configuration under Windows 2000 and earlier versions of Windows, refer to the documentation provided with your laptop or your Wifi network card.

31-3

To set your Wifi configuration under Windows XP, go into Network Connections in the control panel and open the interface associated with your Wifi card or connection. Click View Wireless Networks. If you are in a location where Wifi is available, the wireless network will appear in the network list.

To connect to a wireless network, click on it and then click Connect. If the network is secured (for emergency sites, it should be), enter the access key in the dialog that appears. (To get the access key, check with the Site Manager.)

In most cases, your computer's TCP/IP settings will be auto-configured when you connect to the network. If you have connected to a wireless network but cannot 'see' other computers (or the Internet, if the site's wireless network is Internet-enabled), see "Configuring network settings" on page 31.4.

Configuring Ethernet

If you have an Ethernet-equipped laptop, familiarize yourself with your Windows software and network configuration before you need to use it during an exercise or an emergency.

To connect to an Ethernet network, connect an RJ45 cable between the nearest Ethernet jack and the Ethernet port on your laptop. In most cases, your computer's TCP/IP settings will be auto-configured when you connect to the network. If you have connected to an Ethernet network but cannot 'see' other computers (or the Internet, if the site's network is Internet-enabled), see "Configuring network settings" on page 31.4.

Configuring network settings

See:

- "Autoconfiguration" on page 31.4

- "Manual configuration" on page 31.6

Autoconfiguration. If the site's network is set up to autoconfigure your laptop's network settings using DCHP, but your laptop does not automatically connect to the network, perform the following steps:

1   Open your Network control panel, or under Windows XP go to Network Connections in your control panel and open the connection associated with the Ethernet or Wifi network adapter you are trying to use.

2   If you see a General tab, click it.

31-4

3   If you see a list of connection items (as shown below), go to Step 5.

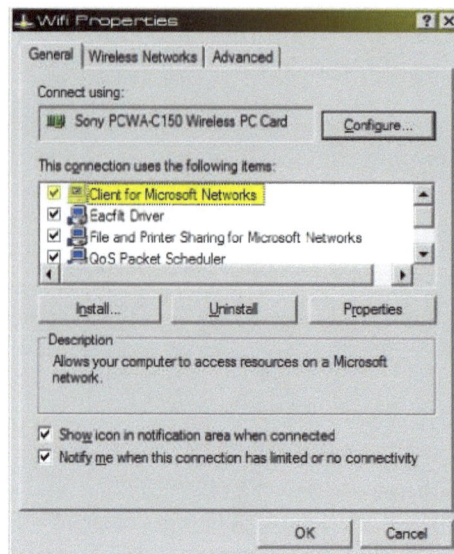

4   If you see a Properties button, click it.

5   Scroll down to Internet Protocol (TCP/IP) and select it.

6   Click Properties.

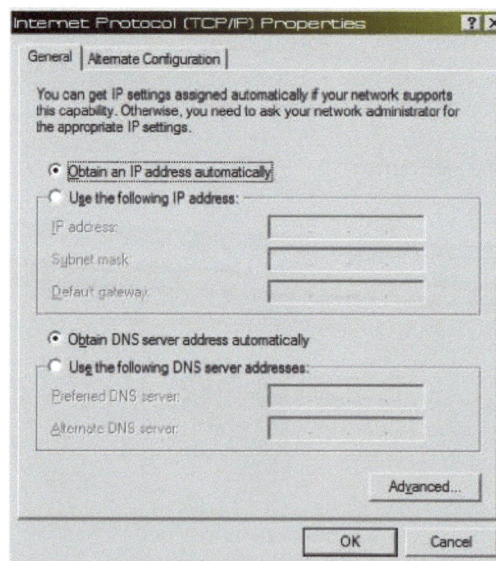

7   If the Obtain An IP Address Automatically radio button is NOT selected, select it.

8   If the Obtain DNS Server Address Automatically radio button is NOT selected, select it.

9   Click OK.

10   Click OK again.

11   If you are prompted to restart the computer, do so.

Manual configuration. If the site's network is not set up to autoconfigure your laptop's network settings (if DCHP is not running), perform the following steps to connect to the network:

1   Get network settings from the Site Manager. You need the following information:

   •   IP address that you can use on the network

   •   Subnet mask

   •   Gateway (router) IP address

   •   DNS server addresses. (If there are no DNS server addresses available, use 207.181.101.4, and 207.181.101.5.)

2   Open your Network control panel, or under Windows XP go to Network Connections in your control panel and open the connection associated with the Ethernet or Wifi network adapter you are trying to use.

3   If you see a General tab, click it.

4   If you see a list of connection items (as shown below), go to Step 5.

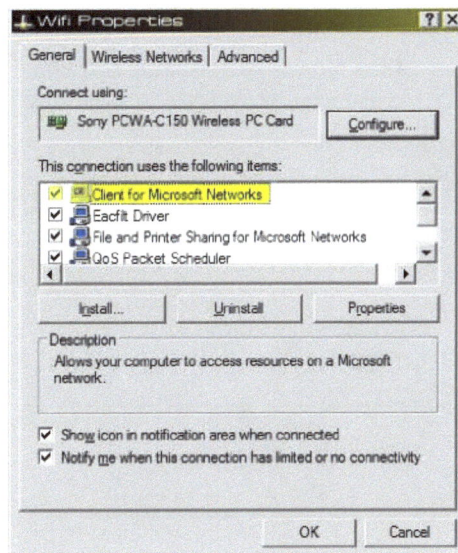

5   If you see a Properties button, click it.

6   Scroll down to Internet Protocol (TCP/IP) and select it.

7   Click Properties.

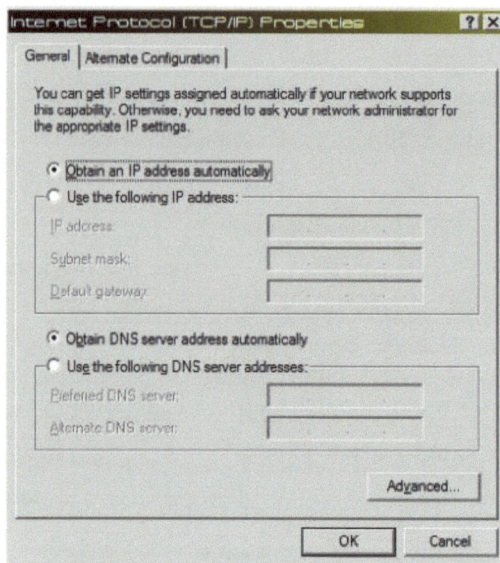

8   Select the Use The Following IP Address radio button, then enter the IP address, subnet mask and gateway into the appropriate fields.

9   Select the Use The Following DNS Server Addresses radio button, then enter the DNS settings into the appropriate fields.

10   Click OK.

11   Click OK again.

12   If you are prompted to restart the computer, do so.

Section 32: Prowords and phrases

ACKNOWLEDGE - Let me know you have received and understood this

message AFFIRMATIVE - Yes, or permission granted, or I agree

ALL STATIONS - This message is for all stations

BREAK - I hereby indicate the separation between portions of the message

CONFIRM - My version is ... is that correct?

CORRECTION or WRONG - An error has been made in this transmission (message indicated). The correct version is...

DISREGARD - Consider this transmission as not sent

FIGURES - The following characters are non-numeric characters (letters)

GO AHEAD - Proceed with your message

GROUP - The following characters are a mix of numbers and letters

HOW DO YOU READ? - How do you hear me?

I SAY AGAIN - USE "I SAY AGAIN", NOT REPEAT

I SPELL - I am going to spell a word/name

LETTERS - The following characters are non-numeric characters (letters)

MAYDAY - spoken word, repeated three times, for distress communications (LIFE IS IN IMMEDIATE DANGER!)

MAYDAY RELAY - The relaying of a distress call

MIXED GROUP - The following characters are a mix of numbers and letters

MONITOR - Listen on channel/frequency....

NEGATIVE - No or Permission not granted or I do not agree

OUT - I am finished and do not expect a reply

OUT TO YOU - I am finished talking to you and wish to talk to another station

OVER - I am finished and require an answer

PAN PAN - The spoken word, repeated three times, for an urgency communication (WE HAVE A POSSIBLE EMERGENCY!)

RADIO CHECK - I am testing my radio

32-1

READ BACK - Read back the entire message as received

ROGER - I have received your last transmission

SAY AGAIN - Send your last transmission. DO NOT USE "REPEAT"!!!

SAY AGAIN ALL AFTER/BEFORE - Re-send part of message after or before

SECURITY - Spoken word, repeated three times, for safety communications
(WARNING OF A POSSIBLE DANGER! IE: WIND DIRECTION CHANGE)

RADIO SILENCE - The spoken words to impose radio silence to keep frequency clear
for emergency traffic or emergency communications

SIGNAL CHECK - How do you read me

STAND BY - I must pause for a few seconds (maximum of 15 sec.)

THAT IS CORRECT - Self explanatory.

VERIFY - Check coding, check text with originator and re-send

WAIT OUT - I can not receive your message at this time the net may continue (more
than 15 sec. delay)

WILCO - Instructions received, understood and will be complied with

WORDS TWICE - Communications are difficult, I am sending or send each word
twice

SECTION 33: ARES FORMS AND STATIONERY

This section provides printable forms and stationery for ARES operations:

Forms and aids in this section are printed on one side of the page, even if printing double-sided, to allow easy photocopying and duplication.

ARES MESSAGE FORM (RADIOGRAM)

SBA(				RADIO			SRAc		

NUMBER	PRECEDENCE	H X	STATION OF ORIGIN	CHECK	PLACE OF ORIGIN	THE FILED	UT C	DAIE	UTC

TO:

TELEPHONE NUMBER (i

SIGN

FROM REC'D		DATE	TIME	TO SENT		DATE	TIME

Precedences - Abbreviate by using first letter   Handling

(E) = EMERGENCY

Any message having life and death urgency to any person or group of persons,   which is transmitted by Amateur Radio in the absence of regular commercial facilities.   This includes official messages of welfare agencies during   emergencies   requesting supplies,   materials   of instructions vital to relief of stricken populace in emergency areas. When in doubt, do not use it

(p) = PRIORITY

This classification is for a) important message having specific time limit

b) official messages not covered in the emergency category c) press dispatches and emergency related traffic not of the utmost urgency d) notice of death or injury in disaster area, personal or official

(W) = WELFARE
HXE

This classification refers to either an inquiry as to the health and welfare of an individual in the disaster area or an advisory from the disaster area that indicates all is well   Welfare traffic is handled only after all emergency and priority traffic is cleared. The Red Cross   equivalent to date)
an incoming Welfare message is DWI (Disaster Welfare Inquiry)
HXG
(R) =ROUTINE

Most traffic in normal times   will bear this designation   In disaster situations, traffic labeled Routine, should be handled last, or not at all when circuits are busy with higher precedence traffic.

HXA   (Followed by number.)   Collect landline delivery authorized by addressee within ___ miles   (If no number, authorization is unlimited.)

HXB   (Followed by number) Cancel message if not delivered within   _ _ hours of filing time,   service originating station

HXC   Repo rt date   and time   of delivery (TOD) to origination station

HXD   Report to originating station   the identity of station from which received, plus date, time and method of delivery.

Delivering   station get   reply   from addressee, originate message back

HXF   (Followed by number.) Hold delivery until (

Delivery by mail or landline toll call not required   If toll or other expenses involved, cancel message and service originating station

PUBLIC SERVICE ACTIVITY REPORT

Available from http://www.rac.ca/downloads/fsd.pdf.

Radio Amateurs af.%du C:aoada
Memo=-: Scoot,. of 1´, e Imeniatioual Anlztens Radio Union

Public Service Activity Report

.iboar This Forms

Ewa yen .into nur Pradio donotes7bou.nds of personhovre of supplementary public unite soirennoisanons isling real eraioges_os.   siraitiosedemergency EPSE and 3r moon sorb as parades sad marathons.
Pa,cpasoc :Li 7·1E..   of   ihows Amateur Radio at its 11.t k chi:Lally unpcstant Mar RAC bring
iCC   of Lit }n:-1:c sere :e work ID the anaphors of Inclusu:₄ Canada and odor public officials. the
        the fonn below nit] be an imporram ad:Lk:ice to she records. Please complem author= frann :o RAC
        112L-SiZairrP, 720 Belfass Rd, Suite 217, Dann, ON MC. 025. Mark it to the attention of VP Fold Sersteo
        b.d a copy to your RAC Section Manager as well.

1 Nature of the acliway (Check one)

   Comonouranons Enosagowcy. Amateurs supplied common...Ions required to replace or
   supplement normal oomonmications means.

        Amarairs were deployed for emergen7 comonmicarions, buremergency sioncion did nor devotop.

        Spacio1mant Amateurs supplied commimicadven for a parade, race, mararhoa etc.

   Too or drill A naming arshity m which AlnitellTS parlicipared_

2 Brief dmmiptiosi of eclis ay._____

3 Places or areas involved, _____

4 Number of Amareurs par dilating: _____

5 Emit stars dasolime: _____ 6 .

7 Duration of swain (hours):_____ a .

P Numbs of repeaters used: _____

---

111 Estimated person-power co	S_____ (person-hours tin. $10 00.doom)
11. Esdaufrad cosy of equipment used: _____ S	Shand-heists, repeaters, el,)
12. royal enamored NE of sena.: _____ S	Ladd amounts fromlinm10 and 11)

13. Nets and:or frequencimused(indndng repeater call rigs):
_____
_____
_____

14. Number Of messages handled: _____

15. Names of spend. receiving communicanons support
_____
_____
_____
_____

16 Please list call signs of Amertmirs who snore maim partici:p.m
_____
_____
_____

17. Oboes continent:
_____
_____
_____
_____

   Please attach Amos of Ansafenrs is ream, newspaper skrrprnss or other supparforg data.

Lacarion of orgamoariora City or Town: _____ Province: _____

Your name: _____ Cali sign, _____

Address:
_____

PAC appointment, if any: _____ evaail address: _____

Telephone: Rm. L__) _____Boo. (__) _____

I anal Not the iitrarnlanan pnwided adove n ¢amplerç and eras to the best of my knowledge.

Sionacure: _____ DEW: _____
ESD-157-8.

Page intentionally blank.

ACTIVATION AND DEPLOYMENT MISSION STATEMENT AND BAND PLAN

Date:

1. Served Agency:

a . Address of Served Agency:

b . Name of Served Agency Point of Contact:

c . _____   POC Phone Numbers: Office: _____
   Cell: _____   Home: _____

d . _____ Check if additional Served Agencies are listed on the back of this page.

2. Describe the mission:

_____

_____

3. Address/location for deployed stations:

a. Station Alpha: _____

b. Station Bravo: _____

c. Station Charlie: _____

d. Station Delta: _____

e. _____ Check if additional deployed station addresses/locations are on the back of this page.

4. What is the expected duration of deployments? _____

5. Radio equipment requirements

a. HF stations: Mobile _____ Portable _____ Fixed Base _____

b. VHF stations: Mobile _____ Portable _____ Fixed Base _____ Handheld _____

c. UHF stations: Mobile _____ Portable _____ Fixed Base _____ Handheld _____

6. Band Plan

a. Network Requirements: (Describe from/to communications requirements.)

(1) Net One:

(2) Net Two:

(3) Net Three:

(4) _____ Check if additional nets are provided on the back of this page.

b. Frequencies, offsets, and tone requirements:

(1) Net One:

(a) _____ Simplex _____ Duplex _____ Split _____ Other

(b) Frequencies _____

(c) _____ Offset _____ Tone

(2) Net Two:

(a) _____ Simplex _____ Duplex _____ Split _____ Other

(b) Frequencies _____

(c) _____ Offset _____ Tone

(3) Net Three:

(a) _____ Simplex _____ Duplex _____ Split _____ Other

(b) Frequencies _____

(c) _____ Offset _____ Tone

(4) _____ Check if additional frequencies, offsets, and tones are listed on the back.

LOG OF OPERATIONS

PROJECT NAME _____ DATE _____ NET LOCATION _____

PROJECT LOCATION _____ NET CONTROL OPERATOR _____

MESSAGE NUMBER	TIME LOCAL	ORIGINATING CALLSIGN	TRAFFIC TYPE	TRAFFIC FOR	TRAFFIC FROM	TIME DELIVERED	DELIVERED TO REMARKS

FILE:NET-LOG.GIF_0997_VE3XE

Page intentionally blank.

BEFORE EMERGENCY

Prepare yourself by providing radio equipment together with an emergency power source upon which you can depend.

Test both the dependability of your emergency equipment and your own operating ability in the annual Simulated Emergency Test and the several annual on the air contests especially Field Day.

Register your facilities and your availability with your local Emergency Coordinator.

IN EMERGENCY

Listen before you transmit. Never violate this principle.

Report at once to your Emergency Coordinator so that the EC will have up-to-minute data on the facilities available. Work with the local civic and relief agencies as the EC suggests.

Operate on the air in accordance with regulations.

SOS and "Mayday" are the International distress calls for emergency only. They are for use only by stations seeking emergency assistance.

Respect the fact that the success of the amateur effort in emergency depends largely on circuit discipline. The established Net Control Station should be the supreme authority for traffic routing.

Cooperate with those we serve. Be ready to help, but stay off the air unless there is a specific job to be done that you can handle more efficiently than any other station.

AFTER EMERGENCY

Participate in debriefings with your EC.

Page intentionally blank.

EMERGENCY REFERENCE INFORMATION FOR AMATEUR RADIO STATION

	Frequency	Time	Days
ARES Net			
SKYWARN Net			
Section/Local Net			
Packet BBS			

33-11

EXAMPLE QUICK-REFERENCE CARD

EXAMPLE ARES BROCHURE

ARES
Amateur Radio Emergency Service

ARES is a volunteer organization that delivers communications services during emergencies. ARES (pronounced AIR-EEZ) provides qualified communications personnel who establish ad-hoc communications links where and when they are needed. ARES augments the community's existing communications infrastructure, providing the additional capacity that is often needed during emergencies.

> **ARES is a volunteer organization that costs you nothing, and provides emergency radio communications where and when it is needed.**

ARES relies on the services of amateur radio operators who volunteer their time, equipment and expertise for the benefit of the community and the public good.

Taking advantage of ARES services during exercises and emergencies

If you are responsible for managing communications for your municipality, the Red Cross or another aid agency, you should consider how useful ARES may be during exercises or during an actual time of need.

What ARES is and is not

ARES does not replace the communications infrastructure used by police or other emergency responders, by the municipalities, or by individual agencies. Instead, ARES augments existing communications solutions, letting you scale up your communications capacity in times of need. ARES gives you additional communications capacity at emergency operations centres (EOC), community shelters, hospitals, evacuation points, and other facilities.

Which agencies and organizations can use ARES?

ARES is available in times of emergency to provide communications support on behalf of government and aid agencies, including municipal governments, the Emergency Management Organization, the Red Cross, and the Salvation Army. ARES may also be available during non-emergencies to assist with certain qualified public service events, run by government or not-for-profit entities, where those events offer an opportunity to provide operator training. ARES cannot be used to carry commercial communications (for-profit activity) of any kind.

How qualified are ARES personnel?

All ARES communications operators are government-certified radio operators. (They are called 'amateur radio operators' because they do not accept money for their communications services, and are not licensed to support business activities.) ARES personnel conduct themselves with professionalism and competence. Most operators have many years of experience with radio communications. Many are current or retired technical specialists or military or commercial telecommunications specialists.

In addition, specific ARES training is given to ARES operators to ensure that they are well versed in procedures related to public safety communications and emergency support. ARES conducts periodic exercises and drills to maintain standards, refine processes and optimize services.

ARES is an organization that exists throughout Canada and the United States, and is not limited to this region. Lessons learned during Ontario blackouts, California brushfires, and prairie tornadoes are applied here too, taking advantage of a large pool of emergency communications experience. Today's emergency communications practices are the result of many decades of refinement, technological advancement, and real-life experience. ARES and other amateur radio organizations have proven their worth by providing high-quality communications support during thousands of disasters and emergencies, often in situations where no other communications options were available.

> **Use ARES to provide communications at field sites, evacuation points, community centres, seniors facilities, hospitals, schools, arenas, EOCs, and other key locations during exercises and emergencies.**

33-13

ARES services

A number of specific services are available, letting you tailor ARES communications support to fit your needs. *Emergency communications stations*

Emergency communications stations provide voice and even data communications between specific locations (for example, emergency operations centres, aid stations, shelters, hospitals, and other key locations). These stations augment your existing communications, adding capacity and flexibility.

Shadowing

Shadow communications operators accompany 'high-value' personnel in your organization. This ensures that key personnel are kept in touch, regardless of location, communications overloads or failures, or other factors. Operator training ensures that the personnel being shadowed benefit from the communications assistance without any additional overheads.

Mobile communications

ARES mobile communications service attaches communications operators to mobile units (such as evacuation buses, assessment units, search and rescue teams, or other mobile concerns requiring communications support). Communications operators ensure connectivity between the mobile units and EOCs or coordination points, taking advantage of ARES network capacity and broad areas of coverage.

Data messaging

In situations where you need to move files or formal data from one site to another and the Internet is not available, ARES packet stations can use data radio channels to send text or files (such as lists of names). Packet can be invaluable during emergency situations. Data can be sent to the next floor, the next building, the next city or even across the country, regardless of telecommunications or Internet failures.

Rapid community assessment

During many types of emergency, getting information about conditions in the community at large can be crucial to planning your response. ARES provides an easy way to get basic information very quickly. During community emergencies (for example, severe weather events or power outages), ARES can provide rapid assessment of conditions at a large number of locations throughout the region. The types of information that could be requested include status of electrical and telephone service, wind and weather conditions, road conditions, or even reporting of physical damage (for example, flood damage). This service augments your existing procedures for community assessment, providing rapid feedback of basic data from a large number of points.

Before an emergency

Incorporate ARES into your own training scenarios, drills, exercises, processes and practices. ARES is available for most exercises, regardless of scope. You may also wish to perform pre-clearance of ARES operators, or issue or validate operator identification.

Backup communications

The ARES backup communications service places ARES emergency communications stations at or near your existing high-value communications stations (such as those at City Hall, EOCs, hospitals, etc.) to provide backup service in case of problems or overload in your key communications links. This is useful in situations where your primary communications systems are working and meeting your needs, but where you cannot afford to run without a backup.

National communications relays

ARES provides communications outside the local area when required. Formal message traffic is carried over data circuits and high-frequency voice channels to other ARES stations throughout Canada and even the US, and from there to recipients via telephone or email. This service is similar to HF capabilities used by FEMA, and is useful during emergencies that disrupt telephone and Internet communications over a wide area.

Contact us

For more information about including ARES in your upcoming exercises and drills, or for training materials that you can use in your own training, contact Saint John Regional ARES at info@emergencyplanning.ca, or phone us at 506-643-8490.

This brochure was produced by Nocturne Communications Inc., a full-service corporate communications service provider. Visit www.nocturne.ca

33-14

SECTION 34: ANDERSON POWER POLE CONNECTORS

ABOUT POWERPOLES

PowerPole connectors let you create 12v connections between power supplies and equipment. They assemble like building blocks, allowing for a variety of configurations. They've been adopted as the standard power connector by ARES. They've also become popular because of their simplicity and flexibility. They're cheap, reliable and easy to use in the shack or the field.

These connectors are also becoming more popular with amateurs in general because of their convenience, flexibility and simplicity.

PowerPole connectors are cheap, reliable and easy to implement and modify in the field. They allow amateurs and ARES operators to 'mix and match' 12V equipment and power supplies without having to worry about adapting a number of different connection types.

Why use special connectors?

If you're using another connector system now, you may be wondering why you should bother with PowerPole connectors. The larger advantage is compatibility with other operators and with equipment you may be loaned during ARES operations, but ignoring ARES for a moment there are also benefits to you in your own shack or mobile.

These connectors are very easy to assemble and use. They make switching and moving equipment around much easier, since all your 12v interconnects will be compatible. If assembled properly they provide polarity protection (meaning that you can't accidentally cross positive and negative, something that can happen for example with a 'trailer connector' system if you accidentally connected two power supplies). They provide exceptionally low contact resistance, which means less voltage drop and better equipment performance. They're very resistant to overheating, melting and fire. At about a dollar for an assembled connector, they're very cheap when compared with other types of connectors. And connector blocks and commercial power panels are available to give your shack a clean look, giving you the 12v equivalent of a 120v power bar.

But a key reason for using PowerPoles is to standardize with other amateurs.

Standardization provides huge benefits during disaster operations. It means that operators and their equipment can be integrated together at emergency operations centres, in mobiles and in the field. It means that you'll be able to power and charge your equipment when you arrive at an EOC, or when you're operating in someone else's vehicle, or when you're borrowing a portable power source or other equipment. With a PowerPole system in your car, you'll be able to operate equipment loaned to you by an EOC or another operator. PowerPole connectors are being set up in the Point Lepreau EOC and the KV EMO EOC to allow quick equipment swapouts and the charging of operator equipment. The expectation is that all ARES operators will be compatible with this power system.

What are they?

Let's talk about what a PowerPole connector actually looks like. Basically, there are two modular plastic blocks, one red and one black, that snap together side by side to make up a connector. ARES has a standardized way of putting the red and the black together, but we'll talk about that a little later.

When you're connecting gear to a power supply, both of the connections (power side and radio side) actually look exactly the same, unlike a Molex or other specialized connector. This is called a 'genderless' connection. (There isn't a male and a female PowerPole connector.) You flip one of the connectors upside down to allow it to mate with the other connector. By flipping the connector over, you're lining up the red on one with the red on the other.

This lack of gender might seem a bit odd, since it allows you to connect two pieces of gear together by accident (or even two power supplies). But the flexibility is actually an advantage. For example, in the field, you may decide to connect two battery supplies in parallel.

34-2

Looking more closely at the plastic shells, you'll see a tongue-in-groove fitting on the sides of each shell. This allows you to lock the shells together. When you buy the connectors, they come as a collection of empty shells and matching contacts. You assemble the connectors yourself, first by connecting the contacts to wires, then by inserting the contacts into shells, then by locking shells together to complete the connector.

The contact sits locked in place inside its shell. When the connector is mated, the two contacts are 'spring loaded' to provide a good surface area for current. (These pictures show cutaway images, obviously. In real life the contacts are hidden from view and protected inside the shell.)

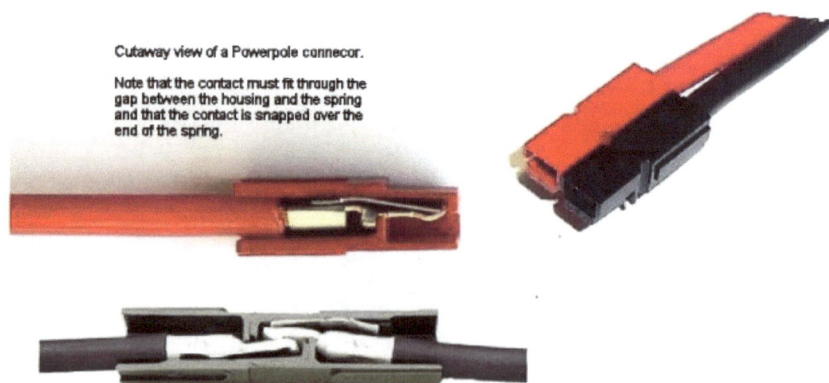

Cutaway view of a Powerpole connecor.

Note that the contact must fit through the gap between the housing and the spring and that the contact is snapped over the end of the spring.

The contacts are available in a range of sizes with different current ratings. The standard is a 15 or 30 amp contact.

TYPICAL INSTALLATIONS

How you use PowerPoles depends on your station. If you have a home station, you probably want to use PowerPoles for connecting portable equipment like handhelds to

34-3

your station power, or for connecting equipment that you might want to move during an emergency. If you expect to have other guest operators at your station, you should consider providing spare PowerPole connections to your power supply so their equipment can be jacked into the station power.

If you have a mobile station, you'll probably want to use PowerPoles on any equipment that you might remove from the vehicle occasionally. You'll also want to provide spare connections to power equipment you borrow during an emergency, or equipment you own but do not normally bring with you. PowerPoles are compact, so you'll be able to provide a number of extra power connections without creating a mess or taking up space.

You can even use PowerPoles in man-portable packs. By running wiring and PowerPoles through the pack you're planning on using for deployments, you'll be able to quickly and neatly assemble a portable station when the time comes.

You'll find a use for PowerPoles any time you need to distribute 12v power. From an ARES point of view, PowerPoles are especially useful because they make it easy to assemble safe, neat, compatible power distribution setups in the field.

Implementing a PowerPole system

When you want to start using PowerPoles, it's a good idea to sit down with a piece of paper and plan out how you're going to distribute power and interconnect your equipment. You need to figure out how many connectors you need, and whether you want any other PowerPole components.

Once you've mapped out your plan and you know how many connectors you'll need, it's time to find a vendor. You can buy PowerPole supplies from a radio dealer or from an electronic parts distributor.

Planning power distribution

When you map out your station power, consider the different 12v supplies you have, the various 12v devices (not just your radios), and where these supplies and devices are going to be used. The point is to figure out where you need to distribute power, and where you need to connect and disconnect devices.

Once you have a rough map, start identifying changes in configuration (for example, moving a radio between your shack and car) that will require connectors. Think about equipment that you might want to move in the case of an emergency, like a portable HF radio. Think about supporting other operators or borrowed equipment.

Think about where you're going to place connectors for power distribution. In your car, you might decide to put the power connections under the passenger seat, or you might mount a power distribution block under the dash where it's more accessible.

On your map, figure out where you need to provide fusing. If you have a connector that might serve a handheld or a small HF rig, fusing isn't a simple issue. Do you fuse it for 5A or for 35A? Make sure that fuses will be easy to access. (Label them too, when the time comes.)

If you already have a connector system (for example, a set of cigarette lighter plugs, trailer connectors, Molex or other specialized connectors), you need to decide whether you want to keep them in addition to your PowerPoles. The simplest thing to do is to replace your current connectors entirely with PowerPole. But if you want to keep your current system, you can use PowerPole connectors in parallel or in series to allow the use of both connection systems. This means you do not have to change what you do now, but you'd also be compatible with PowerPole systems.

Components and quantity

A simple rule of thumb is to buy two connector contacts and shells for each power supply (making one connector), and four for each radio or 12v device (making one connector for the radio and one for its power supply).

34-5

Operation

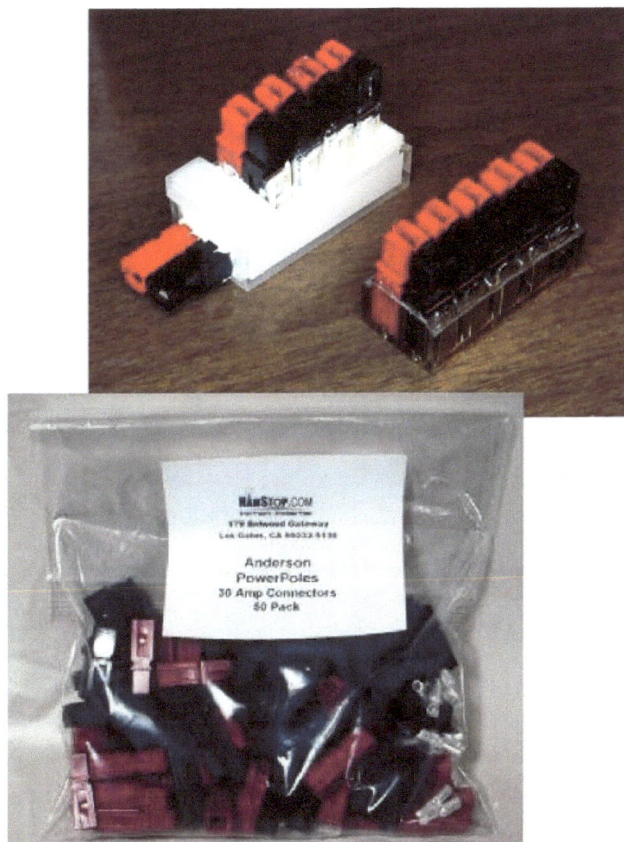

An even simpler thing to do is simply buy a bag of connectors. Buy too many. And when you run out, buy more. Connectors are available in bags of 10 or 20, and are cheap. It's easier to have a bag or two in your shack or ready kit and assemble connections where and when required.

More complicated power plans may involve power distribution panels or blocks, which are the PowerPole equivalent of a 120v power bar. You can build these yourself very quickly by simply sliding connectors together using their tongue-in-groove shells. Or you can buy more professional looking distribution panels from manufacturers like Saratoga and MFJ.

When you order PowerPole components, the simplest thing to do is to order a bag of connector parts from an electronics or amateur radio vendor. You'll get an equal number of red and black shells, and a matching number of contacts (typically half 15A and half 30A rated).

If you order from a distributor, you'll need to specify exactly how many shells of each colour and how many contacts of each rating you'll want.

If you want to avoid the homebrew look and use pre-manufactured power panels, Canadian amateur radio vendors sell a number of different models. These can be expensive, running from $70 to $200 for various sizes and features. You can also find pre-manufactured PowerPole gear on eBay.

Some PowerPole users swear by the Anderson crimping tool, which is specifically designed for marrying PowerPole contact tabs to wires. However, other users make do with ordinary crimping tools without problems. You can also use a solder gun or torch to make these connections, however, so think twice before spending money on specialized tools.

Tools

Anderson sells a specialized crimping tool that can be used with PowerPole connectors. However, this crimping tool is expensive and unnecessary.

34-7

Operation

You can crimp the connection using any standard connector crimping tool.

You can also easily solder the connection using an electric or butane soldering gun.

Try your existing methods and tools. If they do not work, think about spending the money on a crimping tool.

If your club is considering promoting PowerPole as a standard, an Anderson crimping tool might be something the club could purchase and loan out to members as needed.

Building connectors

Building PowerPole connectors is very simple. You choose an appropriate tab size. Solder or crimp the contact tab to the wire, then insert the tab into the shell. Slide the two shells together, and you're done.

You can crimp connectors using the specialized (but expensive) Anderson crimping tool, or crimp using a standard wire crimper.

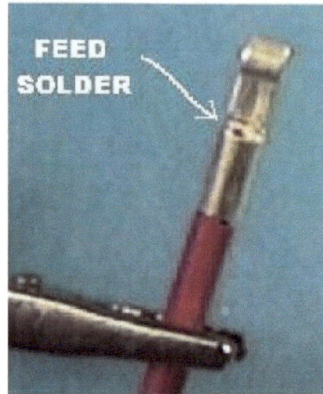

FEED SOLDER

You can also solder wires to contact tabs very easily, since the tab is not inserted into the housing until after soldering

Also be careful when inserting the contact tabs into the housings.

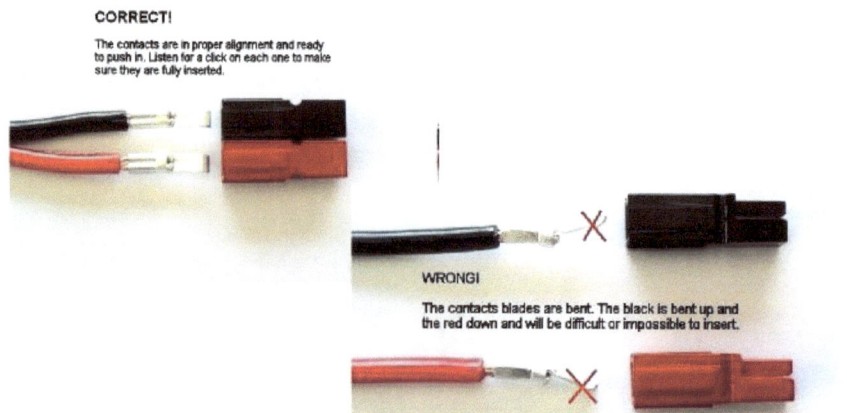

CORRECT!

The contacts are in proper alignment and ready to push in. Listen for a click on each one to make sure they are fully inserted.

WRONG!

The contacts blades are bent. The black is bent up and the red down and will be difficult or impossible to insert.

You need to be careful to ensure that the two shells are oriented properly. Looking into the connector from the front, with the metal contact tabs at the bottom, the red shell must be on the left. This is very important. If you get this wrong, you're going to blow something up.

How you lock the two shells together is a matter of personal preference and the application. In most cases, simply using the tongue-and-groove fittings in each shell provides a good lock, and it is unlikely that the two shells will accidentally separate. However, some people prefer to make the joint permanent. There are several ways to do this. The simplest is to apply a little crazy glue AFTER joining the two shells.

You can also join multiple connectors together to make a block to allow you to power more than one device. You can daisychain the wire from one contact to the next, and use the tongue-in-groove fittings provided on the top and bottoms of the shells to 'stack' them.

When you assemble connectors, you can use them at the end of equipment power cables or power supply feeds, or use them in combination with other connectors (such as cigarette lighter plugs) to make PowerPole adapters.

Locking connectors

Anderson 'Block Lock' – expensive but effective

Electrical tape

Wire tie

Velcro wire harness

Glue

Operations Training Manual RAC-ARES-OPS

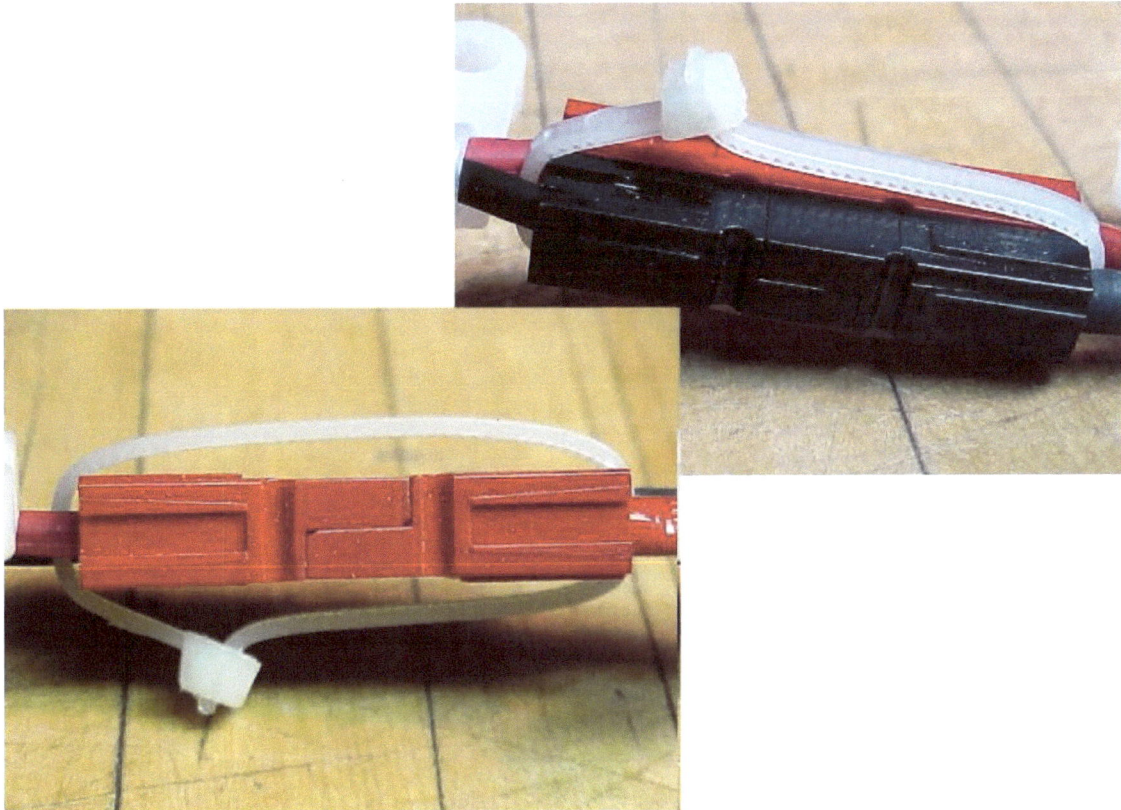

Taking connectors apart

You might want to take a connector apart to clean or replace a contact, increase wire size, or fix a bad joint or loose crimp

To take a connector apart:

Pry up the bottom part of the contact tab with a small flathead screwdriver or

penknife Pull the contact out of the housing by the wire

Slide the two housings apart (unless they are glued)

POWERPOLE PROJECTS

Adapter cords

Power distribution block

PowerPoling your car

PowerPoling your shack

Building PowerPole connectors into equipment

34-12

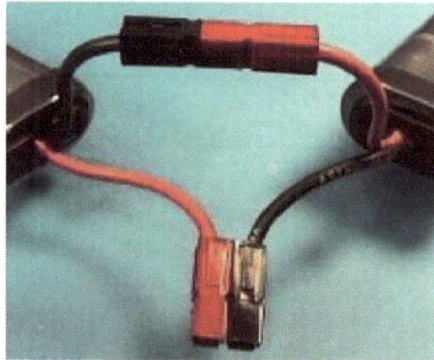

W1CAR

IMPORTANT CAUTIONS

Never connect to equip using another colour (not red and black) – this might mean different voltages or AC is being used!

Always check polarity when using a new site or system

Ensure that fusing is appropriate

Connector integrity - shorts are possible if tabs pull out of shells

Don't connect two power supplies unless they can be safely used together!

You may want to connect a power supply and a battery for charging purposes, or connect two batteries for load-sharing.

OTHER TYPES OF CONNECTORS

Molex

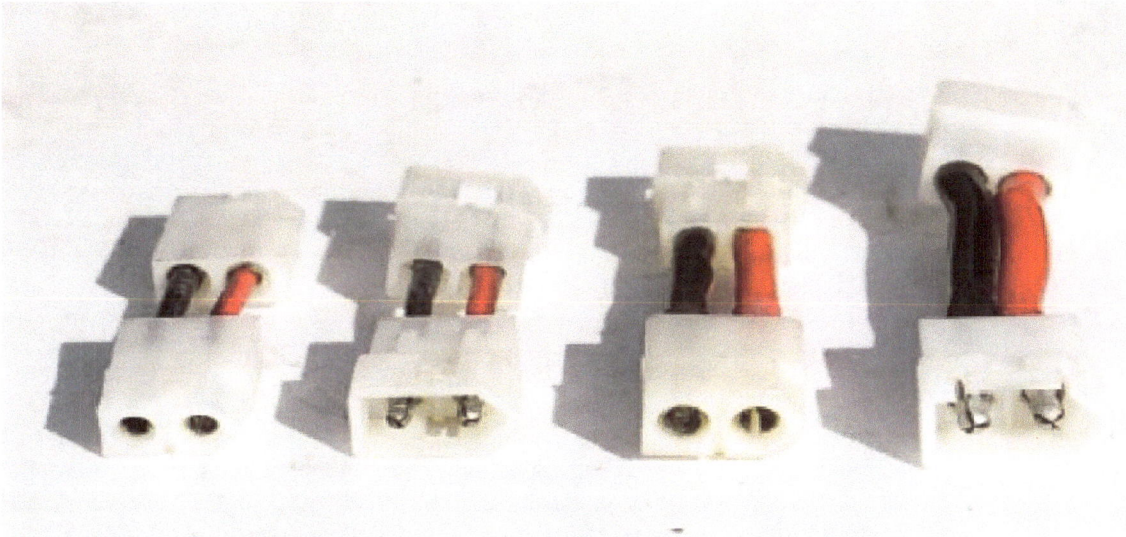

SECTION 35: SAFETY ISSUES FOR ARES PERSONNEL

Many emergency response volunteers have never been exposed to the safety training that is provided by large companies. In fact, many people go through their entire lifetime without ever taking a safety course! This document will not make you a safety expert. It is intended to fill a void for people who have had no safety raining and to demonstrate to them that they need to participate in health and safety training that may be available through their employer or other safety-training providers.

BASICS

You are entitled to a safe place to work. As an employee, you have the right to know about a hazardous situation. You also have the right to refuse to work in dangerous surroundings or to perform a job that you aren't capable of doing safely. Employers provide each employee with the information, instruction, and supervision necessary to ensure their safety. They make each employee aware of known hazards. They respond as soon as possible to reports of hazards, report all incidents, and maintain records. In other words, you are entitled to a safe place to work.

EMERGENCY CONDITIONS

This is all very good in theory but as an emergency response volunteer, you may find yourself in the middle of a hazardous situation with no time for training! You may wind up in a situation that was never anticipated or experienced by you or anyone else in the area! To determine whether you can perform the required tasks safely, you may have to rely on your senses and judgment and on fellow workers whom you've never seen before. Each situation is different and therefore these steps need to be adjusted to suit the situation. However, your safety and that of your co-workers is always, always, always, your number one priority! Remember, rarely is there ever just one person killed in a confined space. It is always two, the victim and the first rescuer!

PRIORITY ONE

Your personal safety is your number one priority.

The health and safety of the emergency response volunteers is of paramount importance! You are there to help and you must ensure that you don't become another victim who has to be rescued!

PRIORITY TWO

Secure the site!

The site must be secured so that no one else gets hurt, victims are safe, and evidence is preserved. This means blocking access to the site to keep others out.

35-1

LAST PRIORITY

Only after ensuring the safety of the rescuers, other people, and the securing the site, can you do what you came to do!

QUALIFICATIONS

If, when you arrive at the site of an incident, you see someone working there; don't assume that it is safe for you to be there too. That person may have special

training or safety equipment and be using procedures that allow them to work safely in an environment that would be hazardous to others. On the other hand, they may simply have bad judgment and no safety training! Play it safe! Utilize the expertise of trusted individuals and site supervisors.

HAZARDS

A hazard is a condition or changing set of circumstances that has the potential to cause injury or illness or damage to equipment or property. To properly assess a hazard, you need to know the work area, processes, activities, equipment, tools, and supplies that are present or used in the immediate area. You may even need the expertise of a structural engineer and special machinery before proceeding. As an emergency volunteer who has just arrived on site, some of this may be impossible. If you're lucky, you may be able to acquire some of this information from people who live or work in the immediate area or from other emergency workers who arrived before you. Use your senses but don't rely solely on them. There may be hidden hazards such as odorless chemicals or gasses. A puddle of liquid that looks like water may be a corrosive, explosive, or poisonous chemical. Major hazards may distract you long enough to walk into a less obvious but just as deadly situation! Be alert for commonplace items that may be overlooked. For example, guards or shields may be missing from tools or equipment and with the many distractions around you they just might "jump up and bite you"!

SUMMARY

- Protect others.

- Secure the site.

- Identify and assess the hazards.

- Determine the risk level for each hazard.

- What is the probability of something going wrong?

- What are the consequences if something goes wrong?

- Prioritize the work at hand.

- Determine how to achieve your goal safely.

35-2

SECTION 36: FIRST AID TECHNIQUES

Note: The material presented here does not replace First Aid and CPR training presented by the Canadian Red Cross or the St. John Ambulance.

First aid and CPR for Amateur Radio Emergency Service (ARES) emergency communications providers is important for us, fellow team members and our stakeholders. ARES or other EMCOMM providers are encouraged to participate in first aid and CPR training provided in our communities. Sources for training include:

- Canadian Red Cross (http://www.redcross.ca)

- St. John Ambulance (http://www.sja.ca).

There may be other course providers in your community.

First aid is emergency help given to an injured or suddenly ill person using readily available materials. We may be called on to provide first aid to a family member on the playground, a fellow ARES member in the local Emergency Operations Centre (EOC) or to a motorist hurt in a motor vehicle collision. We need to be prepared for an injury or a person succumbing to illness at any time.

Many would be first aiders have become discouraged for fear of being sued for stopping to give first aid. To allay this apprehension Good Samaritan Laws have been enacted throughout Canada and the United States. What is the Good Samaritan Law? The principle protects people who act in good faith, without compensation and who do not exceed the scope of their training. This law does not mean you can't be sued, but it provides protection for those volunteers who meet the criteria.

Once we make the decision to give first aid we must not forget our primary responsibility is keep others, including ourselves, from becoming victims or casualties as identified in First Aid First on the Scene published by St. John Ambulance. It is imperative we observe the Universal Precautions that have been taught in First Aid and CPR courses. Two important items needed by first aiders:

- Rubber/vinyl/latex gloves

- Disposable rescue mask or a mask with a disposable one-way valve

Always remember the best insurance we have is to continually wash our hands when dealing with the injured or ill. For those instances where hot water and soap are not available we should carry hand sanitizer.

How much should you use?

Place a small amount on the palm of your hand and rub it over your entire hand. If the gel evaporates in less than 15 seconds, you have not used enough.

36-1

There is no substitute for First Aid and CPR training. The following is a recap of some of the common first aid emergencies you may encounter while performing EMCOMM duties:

Remember the ABCs:

- Airway

- Breathing

- Circulation

Shock: There are many types of shock and medical emergencies that cause it. The basic cause of shock is insufficient circulation of the blood in the body. Severe shock can also result from medical emergencies such as diabetes, epilepsy, infection, poisoning or a drug overdose.

Signs and symptoms of shock

Signs	Symptoms
pale skin at first, turns bluish-grey	restless
bluish-purple lips, tongue, earlobes, fingernails	anxious
	disoriented
	confused
cold and clammy skin	afraid
breathing shallow & irregular, fast or gasping for air	dizzy
changes in level of consciousness	thirsty, maybe **very** thirsty
weak, rapid pulse— radial pulse may be absent	

It is not shock if. . .

. . .the casualty is warm, the skin is dry with full colour and the person is fully conscious.

Before trying to give first aid for shock we must first find what caused the condition. Caution must be exercised so we do not aggravate an already serious situation. If there have been no head or spinal injuries elevate their feet and maintain the body temperature. If the person is not fully conscious, but breathing satisfactorily they must be placed in a position so they do not drown in bodily fluids. Casualties with injuries should be left in the position found so we do not further aggravate injuries.

Choking: This is a blockage of the airway. The blockage can be something as simple as a piece of candy, dinner steak or medication. The best indicator the person is choking is their grabbing their throat. It is important for us to find if the person who is choking has good air or exchange, poor air exchange or no air exchange and this fact will guide us in providing first aid. If the person choking and has good air exchange encourage them to cough to expel the object. The type of first aid we provide to the person depends on their physical size either by age or weight. If the person is pregnant or in a wheel chair our first aid procedures will have to take this into consideration. Be prepared to administer the Heimlich maneuver if the person needs first aid intervention.

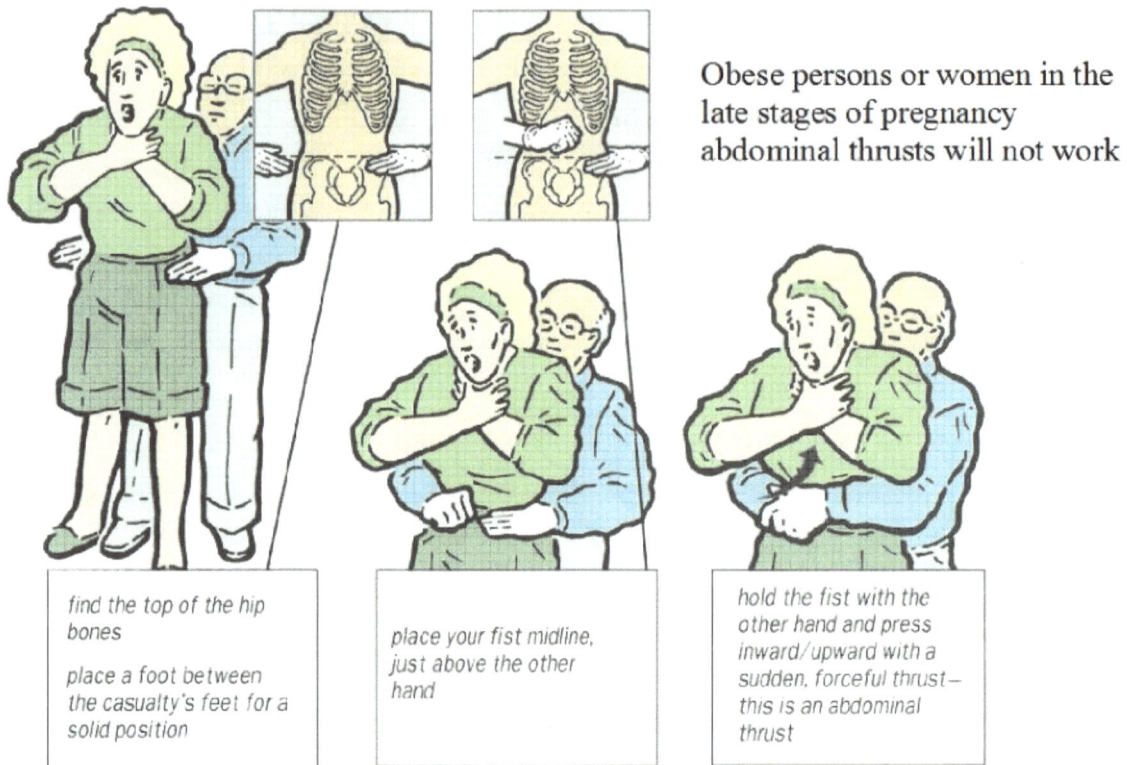

Obese persons or women in the late stages of pregnancy abdominal thrusts will not work

find the top of the hip bones

place a foot between the casualty's feet for a solid position

place your fist midline, just above the other hand

hold the fist with the other hand and press inward/upward with a sudden, forceful thrust—this is an abdominal thrust

Keep giving the Heimlich maneuver until either the object is removed or the casualty becomes unconscious. If the person becomes unconscious you will need to help the person to the floor or ground insuring they do not injure themselves.

If the foreign object does not dislodge or the patient loses consciousness we must activate the Emergency Medical System (EMS) by calling 9-1-1 or other telephone number for your community. Even if the object is expelled the casualty should be observed for other injuries.

Many of our EMCOMM assignments require that we work by ourselves, sometimes in remote places. What if we are the victim of a choking mishap? First you should try to cough the object up. If coughing fails follow the guidelines below from St. John Ambulance.

36-3

put a fist, thumb-side in, midline on your abdomen just above your hips

hold the fist with your other hand and pull inward/upward forcefully

give yourself abdominal thrusts until you can cough forcefully, breathe or speak

a second method is to use a solid object like the back of a chair, a table or the edge of a counter

position yourself so the object is just above your hips. Press forcefully to produce an abdominal thrust—keep giving yourself thrusts until you can cough forcefully, breathe or speak

If you are very large or in the late stages of pregnancy, give yourself chest thrusts instead. Place a fist, thumb-side down, in the middle of your chest. With your head turned to the side, fall against a wall hard enough to produce a chest thrust.

The information on choking in this chapter is a small part of the complete training on managing airway emergencies. Be sure to follow the complete instructions provided by your first aid/CPR instructor.

Prevention should be our goal and exercising care and caution while eating will help us meet the goal.

Breathing Emergencies: As EMCOMM workers we may encounter breathing emergencies following an injury or electrical shock. Our first job is to determine if the casualty is breathing. We can use the steps we learned in CPR to see if they are breathing:

First we need to determine if the person is conscious so we need to tap their shoulders and ask "are you ok?"

LOOK to see of the person's chest is rising and falling or are the casualty's lips blue?

LISTEN for the movement of air through the mouth or nose

FEEL, can you feel their breath on your cheek or ear as they breathe out or feel the chest rising and falling

Many times all a first aider has to do is open the airway and the casualty will start breathing. If they do not start breathing you must begin artificial respiration. The best way to open the airway is to use the head tilt neck lift method. If there are signs of head

36-4

or neck injury you will need to use another method to open the airway so you do not cause further injury. The jaw thrust maneuver is an effective way to open the airway with minimal movement of the head and neck.

Hint: Do you have a CPR mask or face shield in your first aid kit? This is an excellent investment and they can be found inexpensively on the internet.

Place the casualty face up, protecting the head and neck during any movement. Open the airway by tilting the head.

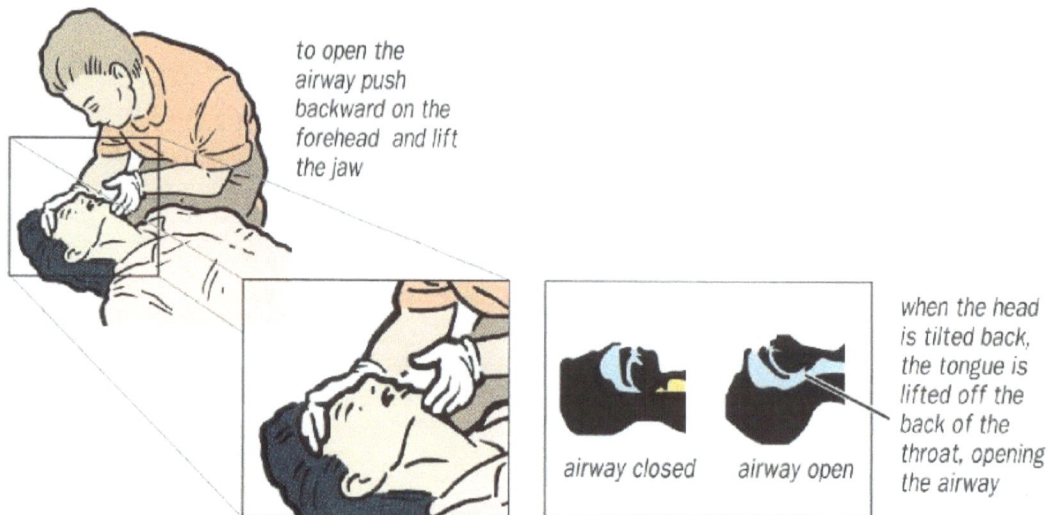

to open the airway push backward on the forehead and lift the jaw

airway closed   airway open

when the head is tilted back, the tongue is lifted off the back of the throat, opening the airway

If the casualty starts breathing on their own after you have opened the airway all you may have to do until help arrives is to maintain the airway. If they do not start breathing you will need to start rescue breathing or artificial respiration.

Breathe into the casualty twice. For an adult casualty, blow for 1 second. Use enough air to make the chest rise.

take a normal breath and seal your mouth around the casualty's mouth

pinch the nostrils

blow in and watch for the chest to rise

move your mouth away and release the nostrils to allow the air to escape

look for the chest to fall, listen for air sounds and feel for air being exhaled against your cheek

give another breath

If the chest doesn't rise when you blow:

♦ reopen the airway by tilting the head

♦ pinch the nose again

♦ make a better seal around the mouth

♦ try blowing again

If the chest still doesn't rise, give first aid for choking

36-5

Note: It is important to insure that the airway has been opened properly. While performing Rescue Breathing/Artificial respiration watch for the chest to rise and fall, if it doesn't try opening the airway once again. An incorrectly opened airway may cause air to get into the stomach or stomach distension and a first aider must be prepared to deal with this condition.

The next step is to check the carotid artery. If there is a pulse, but the casualty is not breathing on their own continue artificial respiration breathing for them 10 - 12 times per minute about once every five to six seconds. Remember to check the pulse every two minutes.

Children and infants breathe faster than adults and to follow your first aid training/CPR training when dealing with them:

CPR: The information on CPR will build on the information provided in the rescue breathing section. It is important to remember to determine if the casualty is conscience, breathing, if not and the casualty is an adult call for help, 9-1-1. Remembering A-B-C, next start rescue breathing and then check for a pulse at the carotid artery. If a pulse is felt continue with rescue breathing. If no pulse if felt start CPR following the instructions you received in your CPR class. When starting CPR loudly announce, "starting CPR call 9-1-1!" if you haven't been able to call yourself. The graphic below will provide a quick reminder on where and how to give compressions. The compression rate published in November 2005 provides for 30 compressions to two breaths. Compression depth for an adult will be 3.8 cm to 5 cm.

Make sure the casualty is on a firm, flat
surface and position your hands on the chest for chest
compressions.

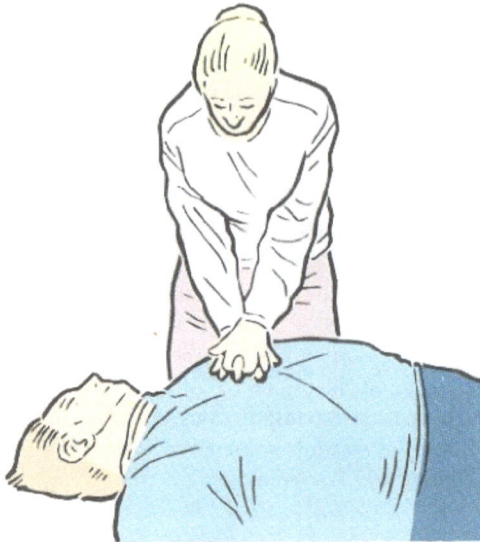

kneel so your hands can be
placed mid-chest

place 2 hands in the centre of
the upper chest and give 30
compressions

With your hands in place,
position your
shoulders directly
over your hands and
keep your elbows
locked.

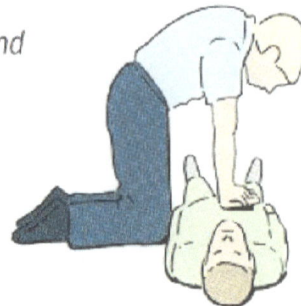

Hand positioning is important to avoid further injury to the casualty. By making sure your compressions are straight up and down, avoiding a rocking motion, you will minimize the chances of further injury. While properly performing CPR, especially on the elderly, there is a chance ribs will be broken. If you hear popping sounds and feel broken ribs continue with CPR after making sure your hands are in the correct position when performing compressions.

Once the first aider has started CPR they should not stop until properly relieved by another first aider, an EMT/Paramedic or physician. There is one other situation where the rescuer may stop performing CPR and that is if they are too exhausted to continue. This should be the exception as you should be loudly announcing "Starting CPR call 9-1-1" and making a loud announcement periodically for someone to call 9-1-1 and to assist you.

Stroke: The medical conditions that cause a heart attack may also cause a stroke when blood to the brain is reduced or cut off. The acronym F.A.S.T. is an easy way to help check for signs of a stroke and to get help:

- Facial droop - one side of the face doesn't move as well as the other side

- Arm drift - have casualty hold both arms out - one arm may not move or drifts down

- compared to the other.

- Speech - Casualty slurs words, uses incorrect words or is not able to speak.

- Time - Get immediate medical help - the earlier stroke is treated the better the outcome.

Other symptoms may include weakness, numbness or tingling, vision problems, headache and dizziness.

Working in the EMCOMM world can be stressful and we need to think about the risk factors for heart illnesses and stroke. The Canadian Heart and Stroke Foundation has defined risk factors as:

"Risk factors are items which raise the chances of getting certain diseases. Some risk factors for heart disease and stroke, such as family history and gender, can't be altered.

Other risk factors can be modified by lifestyle changes. The Heart and Stroke Foundation encourages taking control of the factors that can be changed. The following five strategies are recommended to control modifiable risk factors: Be smoke-free; eat a healthy diet; know your blood pressure; be physically active on a regular basis; and take time to relax.

Even during disasters or emergencies we need to heed the advice of "take time to relax."

Wounds and bleeding: There are numerous types of wounds that cause light to serious bleeding. Bleeding may also be from three sources: capillaries, veins and arteries. Normally bleeding from capillaries and veins is dark red slow or oozing. Blood from

36-8

arteries is bright red and flows freely. Regardless of the type of wound or where the blood is coming from there are four ways for a first aider to stop the bleeding:

- Direct pressure

- Elevation

- Pressure points

- Tourniquet. (This is always the last resort. The first aider may be risking the limb to save the casualty's life.)

Time is of essence and while a sterile dressing and bandage is preferable it may be that the first aider will need to improvise and use the cleanest material available to control the bleeding. Make sure your first aid kit is well supplied with a selection of dressings and bandages.

Hint: Do you remember what the major cause of shock is? Be prepared to not only deal with the injury, but shock as well.

Obviously it would be best if we can avoid injuries and stress safety at all times at home, work and play. Does your EMCOMM group have a safety officer?

Injuries to Bones, Joints and Muscles: The first aider should be looking for open wounds and treating them with a method that does not further aggravate injuries already received by the casualty. The best advice is to splint the injury as it lies. Most injuries to bones, joints and muscles benefit from RICE, which stands for:

- Rest

- Immobilize

- Cold

- Elevation

If you must move the casualty because of a life threatening hazard move them as a single unit and minimize movement of the body.

Burns: There are four levels or degrees of burns with a first degree burn being the least damaging and fourth degree being most damaging. With all burns we will face the potential for wounds that should be covered by a dry sterile dressing. For minor burns we can use cold water to help reduce the discomfort. Sprays and ointments are not recommended as they may further complicate the injury. The following points also need to be considered when dealing with burns:

- Shock

- Infection

Operations Training Manual RAC-ARES-OPS

- Breathing complications

- Swelling

EMCOMM workers may see electrical or RF burns. First and foremost for the rescuer is personal safety. Eliminate the source of power before attempting to move the casualty. Keep an insulated device such as a cane, handy near high powered communications equipment or generators.

Work safely around radio equipment and electrical sources to prevent mishaps and injuries.

Diabetic Emergencies: There are two types of diabetes, type 1 or hypoglycemia and type 2 or hyperglycemia. The Canadian Diabetes Association reports that 10% of those with diabetes have type 1 and the incidents of Type 2 diabetes are increasing dramatically. There is a possibility that as EMCOMM workers we may encounter someone who is having a diabetic emergency. Communicating with the casualty is very important. A person with type 1 diabetes may need help finding something to eat, especially something that contains sugar. A person with Type 2 diabetes may need help taking their insulin or other medications. Look to see if the casualty has a medical alert device. The device may contain information helpful to aiding the person. If you cannot determine what the casualty needs provide them with food or drink containing sugar. Be prepared to treat the casualty for shock. Call 9-1-1 so the casualty can be treated by a medical professional as soon as possible.

Bronchial Asthma: Asthma is a condition that causes an airway constriction and reduces the amount of air the casualty gets to their lungs. The Canadian Lung Associations has provided the following information about asthma:

People with asthma often have one or more these symptoms:

- Wheezing

- Chest tightness

- Coughing

- Feeling short of breath

Casualties experiencing an asthma attack need prompt assistance in using their inhaled medication. Call 9-1-1 promptly and then take time to deal with the casualty. They may be excited and disturbed and the first aider's job is to keep them calm as possible until medical help arrives.

Ben Franklin once said "an ounce of prevention is worth a pound of cure." As you plan and prepare for your next EMCOMM mission include safety as an item in your plan. Consider having a safety officer to monitor the setting up, the operation of and the taking down of the equipment. Remember to take care of yourself during the disaster/ emergency. Take breaks periodically. Eat regular meals and take medications as your

36-10

doctor has prescribed. Most importantly if you have special needs communicate them to your EC so they can assist you in taking care of your health.

All content in this section is from The Complete Guide to First Aid and CPR First on the Scene, Fourth Edition, 2006, St. John Ambulance. With thanks for permission to reprint to St. John Ambulance.

SECTION 37: USING THIS MANUAL IN YOUR TRAINING

This section provides important guidelines and recommendations for trainers and ARES ECs who are implementing an ARES training program using this training manual.

REMOVING CONTENT THAT YOU DO NOT NEED

This training manual contains a great deal of information. When preparing for your training session, you may decide to remove content because:

- You need to shorten the material to fit the time available

- Content does not apply in your area, or is not correct in your area

- Your participants are already familiar with key concepts

- You have more appropriate, localized training manuals and resources.

This manual is set up to make it easy to remove entire sections.

ADDING YOUR OWN CONTENT

Case studies

Choose an example of an emergency (real or exercise) which can be used to illustrate lessons to be learned by ARES groups. These can be:

- Local exercises carried out by the group

- Personal experiences

- ARES columns in magazines

- Feature articles in magazines, such as TCA, CQ or QST

Review the article and make a summary of the event, including:

- The scenario and conditions preceding the emergency

- The course of events

- What ARES actions and responsibilities were

- How the event concluded

37-1

Try to avoid just reading the article from the source.

Highlight points to be learned from the event, both good and bad.

These may be detailed in the article or can be your own conclusions.

Draw parallels to your local situation, including actions, preparations and facilities.

Ask the students for their views on what happened and what they feel could have been done to improve the amateur's response.

Ask the students what they would do in their own group to deal with a similar situation locally.

PREPARING TO BE AN EFFECTIVE TRAINER

Preparing a lesson plan

- The Tie Back - "In your last class You learned--------. In this class we will expand on what you have learned by learning ------"

-

---T

he Introduction

- The What
- What you are going to learn
- The time allotted
- The Where
- Where you will use this knowledge and skill
- The Why
- Why you need this knowledge and skill
- The How
- How you will apply this knowledge or skill
- The Test
- Where and how you will be tested
- By formal exam or
- On exercise or both
- Or demonstration
- Approach
- How this lesson will be taught
- Usually in a number of stages, blocks or modules
- Control statement

- How the class will be conducted
- For question, raise your hand
- There will be no class answers

- Safety

  - If there is any hazards that will be encountered during the lesson
  - The instructor will give a safety briefing at this time

- The Lesson

  - The lesson is usually conducted in several stages
  - Each stage has an introduction
  - The introduction of the stage
  - The teaching of the stage
  - Confirmation of the stage
  - Usually by questions to the class or
  - By demonstration of a skill
  - A review of the stage just covered

- Confirmation

  - At this time the instructor will confirm all the stages of the instruction by
  - Asking questions to the class
  - Confirming skills by
  - Demonstration of the full activity or
  - By conducting an exercise

- A Review

  - At this time the instructor will review the main points of the lesson and
  - Stress any safety or
  - Possible hazards at this time

- Final Confirmation. The instructor will at this time take any "last minute" questions from the class.

- Conclusion

  - At this time the instructor should review what the students have learned
  - Why they have been taught the lesson and
  - Where and when it will be required

- A Motivation

    - At this time the instructor should motivate the class by stating "You have learned -------which is a necessary part of--------and will be necessary for --!"

- A Tie to the Next Class

    - " Your next class is ----.
    - It is at (location) at (time).
    - It will be ----.
    - Your instructor will be-------."

In class

- Ensure that you feel well-prepared.

- Hold your head up and make eye contact.

- Be familiar with the content so you do not need to read from a screen or page.

- Be prepared to answer questions about the content.

PROVIDE FEEDBACK

Use the form provided below to make recommendations regarding the content of this manual.

Send your feedback to us at rachq@rac.ca in PDF format, by fax at 613-244-4369, or by mail at:

Chief Field Services Officer
Radio Amateurs of Canada, Suite 217, 720 Belfast Road, Ottawa, Ontario, Canada K1G 0Z5.

RAC TRAINING MANUAL FEEDBACK

Name: Callsign: Date:

Phone: Email:

Address: _____

Priority (circle):   URGENT / ROUTINE / LOW

Type of change (circle): EDITORIAL CHANGE / INFO CORRECTION / INFO ADDITION

                          LOCAL INFO / ATTRIBUTION / OTHER

Affected sections: _____ Affected pages:

Change or addition (give as much detail as possible):

_____

_____

_____

_____

_____

_____

Attach additional pages, if needed.

September 2015
Issue 2.0

RAC-ARES-OPS

Operations Training Manual

First update September 2015 by:

CFSO Advisory Board

Doug Mercer VO1DM, Allan Boyd
VE3AJB, Garry Jacobs VE6CIA

www.ingramcontent.com/pod-product-compliance
Lightning Source LLC
Chambersburg PA
CBHW061134030426

42334CB00003B/35

9780978086954